A Spiritual Audit of
Corporate America

Ian I. Mitroff and
Elizabeth A. Denton
Foreword by Warren Bennis

A Spiritual Audit of Corporate America

A Hard Look at Spirituality, Religion, and Values in the Workplace

Jossey-Bass Publishers • San Francisco

The authors gratefully acknowledge permission to use the following sources:

p. xxv: Moore, T., *The Education of the Heart* (New York: HarperCollins, 1996), pp. 214–215.

p. xxv: from *Sources of the Self* by Charles Taylor. Copyright © 1989 by the President and Fellows of Harvard College. Reprinted by permission of Harvard University Press.

Chapter One, epigraph: Moore, T., *Care of the Soul: A Guide for Cultivating Depth and Sacredness in Everyday Life* (New York: HarperPerennial, 1994), pp. xi.

p. 18: From *Fire in the Soul* by Joan Borysenko. Copyright © 1993 by Joan Borysenko. By permission of Warner Books.

Chapter Three, epigraph: Copyright © 1998 by the New York Times Co. Reprinted by permission.

Chapter Four, epigraph: Copyright © 1997 by Time Inc. Reprinted by permission.

p. 62: William Nix, *Transforming Your Workplace for Christ* (Nashville: Broadman and Holman Publishers, 1997), p. 13. All rights reserved. Used by permission.

p. 63: Nix, p. 63.

p. 64: Nix, p. 74.

Page 261 constitutes a continuation of the copyright page.

Jossey-Bass books and products are available through most bookstores. To contact Jossey-Bass directly, call (888) 378-2537, fax to (800) 605-2665, or visit our website at www.josseybass.com.

Substantial discounts on bulk quantities of Jossey-Bass books are available to corporations, professional associations, and other organizations. For details and discount information, contact the special sales department at Jossey-Bass.

 Manufactured in the United States of America on Lyons Falls Turin Book. This paper is acid-free and 100 percent totally chlorine-free.

Library of Congress Cataloging-in-Publication Data

Mitroff, Ian I.
    A spiritual audit of corporate America : a hard look at spirituality, religion, and values in the workplace / Ian I. Mitroff and Elizabeth A. Denton; foreword by Warren Bennis. — 1st ed.
      p. cm. — (The Warren Bennis signature series)
  Includes bibliographical references and index.
  ISBN 0-7879-4666-4 (hard : alk. paper)
    1. Work—Moral and ethical aspects.   2. Business—Religious aspects.
3. Quality of work life.   4. Spiritual life.   5. Corporations—Religious
aspects.   6. Employees—Conduct of life.   7. Management—Religious
aspects.   I. Denton, Elizabeth A., 1947–   II. Title.   III. Series.
  HD4905.M53   1999
  261.8'5—dc21

                                          99-6693
                                           CIP

FIRST EDITION
HB Printing 10 9 8 7 6 5 4 3 2 1

Warren Bennis

A Warren Bennis Book

This collection of books is devoted exclusively to new and exemplary contributions to management thought and practice. The books in this series are addressed to thoughtful leaders, executives, and managers of all organizations who are struggling with and committed to responsible change. My hope and goal is to spark new intellectual capital by sharing ideas positioned at an angle to conventional thought—in short, to publish books that disturb the present in the service of a better future.

Other Books in the Warren Bennis Signature Series

Self-Esteem at Work by Nathaniel Branden
The Corporate Culture Survival Guide by Edgar H. Schein

Contents

Foreword   xi
       Warren Bennis

Preface   xiii

Part One: Acknowledging Soul and Spirit

1. Park It at the Office Door: The Unacknowledged
   Soul of Corporate America   3

2. A Strange but Formidable Alliance: Barriers to
   Studying and Defining Spirituality   15

Part Two: Auditing Soul and Spirit

3. The Divided Soul of Corporate America   31

Part Three: Models for Fostering Spirituality

4. Taking Over Your Company for Christ:
   The Religion-Based Organization   57

5. Called to Spirituality: The Evolutionary
   Organization   77

6. Shaking Off Addiction: The Recovering
   Organization   99

7. For the Betterment of Society: The Socially
   Responsible Organization   123

8. We Are Family! The Values-Based Organization   143

Part Four: A Plan for Spiritual Development

9. A Best-Practice Model   167

Appendix A: Questionnaire on Meaning and Purpose
   in the Workplace   187

Appendix B: Selected Quantitative Results   197

Appendix C: Detailed Dimensions of the Five Models   229

Notes   239

The Authors   247

Index   249

Foreword

Jay Gatsby, Scott Fitzgerald's legendary protagonist, is standing at his favorite bar when the bartender says, "I hear you lost all your money in the stock market crash."

"Yeah," Gatsby replies, "lost every last penny in the crash . . . but I lost all that was important to me in the boom." I was reminded of that passage not long ago when I was spending some time at one of those "hot" software companies in Silicon Valley whose employees are an anthem of our times: average age twenty-eight, average net worth over a million—more if you consider stock options. Stock options are great, no kidding, but these people were not happy campers. Their jobs were interesting, fulfilling—up to a point. When I asked them about their jobs and life, they were vaguely disconsolate, despairing—something "beyond words," one told me; "something missing."

A severe case of "affluenza," I thought. I also wondered: What was missing?

In this book, Ian Mitroff and Elizabeth Denton go a very long way in answering that question. What's missing at work, the root cause of the affluenza syndrome, is meaning, purpose beyond oneself, wholeness, integration. Mitroff and Denton demonstrate that we're all on a spiritual quest for meaning and that the underlying cause of organizational dysfunctions, ineffectiveness, and all manner of human stress is the lack of a spiritual foundation in the workplace.

I have to state up front that this is not one of those preachy, uplifting books on taking the soul out of the closet and making it OK for workers to pray on the job. The authors don't for a minute confuse spirituality with varieties of religious experience, though they do take religion very seriously. No, what makes this book unique, powerful, and something of a landmark contribution is that they base their findings—the first book to my knowledge that does this, thankfully—on an empirical and conceptual integration of spirituality in the workplace.

The heart of their argument is breathtakingly potent and it goes like this: Individuals and organizations that perceive themselves as "more spiritual" do better. They are more productive, creative, and adaptive. The people in these organizations are more energized and productive because work isn't solely about stock options and vacations and coffee breaks. Spiritual organizations are animated by meaning, by wholeness, and by seeing their work connected to events and people beyond themselves.

I think it's not an accident that as we approach the next millennium, the authors have written a work that will have enduring significance well beyond Y2K.

August 1999   Warren Bennis
                                     University of Southern California

Preface

We have worked in and around organizations most of our adult lives. We have also studied them extensively. Over the years we have tried all of the conventional techniques known to organizational science to help organizations change for the better and, we hope, to become more ethical. After years of study and practice, we have been forced to a painful conclusion: by themselves, all of the conventional techniques in the world will not produce fundamental and long-lasting changes. At best, conventional techniques produce only partial changes, which erode over time so that most organizations revert to their initial problem states, or they work for only a tiny fraction of organizations. In short, we believe that the field has failed to produce fundamental and long-lasting changes in the vast body of organizations. In fact, some of the most profound changes in organizations have occurred as the result of their own efforts and in spite of conventional academic knowledge.

We believe that the field of organizational studies faces a situation very similar to one faced by the eminent Swiss psychoanalyst Carl Jung. After trying unsuccessfully for years to cure alcoholism by means of psychoanalysis, Jung was forced to conclude that the problem was neither medical nor psychodynamic. It could not be treated by the techniques currently known to medicine or psychoanalysis. Jung finally concluded that the problem was deeply spiritual: the disease from which the alcoholic was suffering was spiritual emptiness. Furthermore, conventional religion had also failed repeatedly to fill the spiritual emptiness of alcoholics.

For Jung there was a crucial and fundamental difference between religion and spirituality—a difference that is so basic that we explore it continually throughout this book.

We believe that today's organizations are impoverished spiritually and that many of their most important problems are due to this impoverishment. In other words, today's organizations are suffering from a deep, spiritual emptiness.

The fact that spirituality has been avoided for so long by the field of organizational science as a serious topic for empirical and systematic study is damning evidence of the spiritual impoverishment of academia as well.

We believe that organizational science can no longer avoid analyzing, understanding, and treating organizations as spiritual entities. We not only believe that organizations must become more spiritual if they are to serve the ethical needs of their stakeholders, but we also have important evidence to support our beliefs. Indeed, our data contain some of the strongest statistical findings we have ever witnessed. At the same time, we are the first to acknowledge that our data are far from conclusive given the limited samples in our study. Nonetheless, the data suggest strongly that those organizations that identify more strongly with spirituality or that have a greater sense of spirituality have employees who (1) are less fearful of their organizations, (2) are far less likely to compromise their basic beliefs and values in the workplace, (3) perceive their organizations as significantly more profitable, and (4) report that they can bring significantly more of their complete selves to work, specifically their creativity and intelligence—two qualities that are especially needed if organizations are to succeed in today's hypercompetitive environment. On nearly every dimension in which we have made comparisons, those individuals and organizations that perceive themselves as more spiritual score better than those that perceive themselves as less spiritual.

Although our study is one of the first systematic studies of the beliefs and practices of high-level managers and executives with regard to spirituality in the workplace, by "systematic" we do not mean "definitive" or "final." Rather, we mean a *systematic beginning* of an *integrated* empirical and conceptual study of spirituality in the workplace, not a final product.

Also, we do not believe that topics as profound as soul and spirituality can be reduced to numbers checked off on surveys and questionnaires. For this reason we have employed a variety of techniques to study these phenomena.

First, we conducted more than ninety in-depth interviews with high-level managers and executives. Although our interviews followed a prescribed format so we could make systematic comparisons among them, they allowed us to range far afield so that we could pursue unanticipated issues. Thus, we collected both qualitative and quantitative data from the people we interviewed. We also mailed surveys to get a broader sampling of responses. Finally, we used interpretive techniques to analyze previously published articles and books on spirituality in general and on spirituality in the workplace in particular to enrich and deepen our understanding.

Because the findings of our study have important implications for the design and management of organizations far into the twenty-first century, we believe it is important to state our main results as succinctly as possible.

First, *contrary to conventional wisdom, the respondents in our study did not have widely varying definitions of spirituality.* Spirituality is not as variable a phenomenon as is commonly thought. Most of the people we interviewed had a rather definite notion of what it is and what it is not. There was nearly unanimous agreement on the definition of spirituality and on the importance it plays in people's lives. In brief, according to our respondents, spirituality is the basic desire to find ultimate meaning and purpose in one's life and to live an integrated life.

Second, *people do not want to compartmentalize or fragment their lives.* The search for meaning, purpose, wholeness, and integration is a constant, never-ending task. It is also a constant, never-ending struggle. To confine this search to one day a week or after hours violates people's basic sense of integrity, of being whole persons. In short, the soul is not something one leaves at home. People want to have their souls acknowledged wherever they go, precisely because their souls accompany them everywhere. They especially want to be acknowledged as whole persons in the workplace, where they spend the majority of their waking time.

Third, *our respondents generally differentiated strongly between religion and spirituality.* They viewed religion as a highly inappropriate topic and form of expression in the workplace. Conversely, spirituality was viewed as highly appropriate. Religion was largely viewed as formal and organized. It was also viewed as dogmatic, intolerant, and dividing people more than bringing them together. In contrast, spirituality was largely viewed as informal and personal, that is, pertaining mainly to individuals. It was also viewed as universal, nondenominational, broadly inclusive, and tolerant, and as the basic feeling of being connected with one's complete self, others, and the entire universe. If one word best captures the meaning of spirituality and the vital role it plays in people's lives, it is *interconnectedness*.

Fourth, *people are hungry for models of practicing spirituality in the workplace without offending their coworkers or causing acrimony.* They are searching for nonreligious, nondenominational ways of fostering spirituality. They believe strongly that unless organizations learn to harness the whole person and the immense spiritual energy that is at the core of each person, they will not be able to produce world-class products and services. Unlike reengineering, Total Quality Management, and other methods, spirituality is not a fad or a gimmick. People are hungry not only to express their souls but also to further the development of their innermost selves.

Fifth, *lacking positive role models of how to practice spirituality in the workplace, many people—not all—are terribly afraid even to use the words* spirituality *and* soul. Many of our respondents believed that more neutral words such as *values*, which carry less emotional baggage, are more acceptable and less threatening. However, an even larger percentage of the people to whom we talked felt strongly that to avoid using the "S-words" is a moral cop-out. They felt that unless one faces the phenomena of spirituality and soul head on, one is prone to moral relativism, as in "all values are equally good unless they hurt someone." Moral relativism, in turn, was seen as leading to even more fads and gimmicks. "Call it like it is and deal with it directly" was a common sentiment, expressed again and again.

Sixth, *one of the most significant findings that emerged from our research is the existence of a relatively small number of models for practicing spirituality responsibly in the workplace.* These models emerged from our respondents in the form of suggestive hints, and the few who suggested the models were unable to go beyond general labels or limited insights. No individual respondent was able to specify the complete details or underlying dimensions of any particular model. Most respondents were not even aware of the models. At best they had only sketchy knowledge of them. None of the respondents was aware of the full range of models. Furthermore, based on our knowledge of the literature, the models are also relatively unknown to students of organizations. Thus, an additional result of our research is the fleshing out of each of the models. To accomplish this, we performed a number of textual analyses of previously published articles and books on spirituality.

Seventh, *one of the major purposes of this book is to present the full range of models, along with an explicit discussion of their strengths and weaknesses, so that readers can make informed, intelligent choices regarding which, if any, of the models is most appropriate for their particular organization.* We cannot emphasize enough that prior to our research neither the models nor their underlying dimensions had been clearly identified. The models make it possible for managers, executives, and organization designers to make wiser choices. Not only can they choose which one of the "pure models" is best for their particular circumstances, but once the full range of models is identified they can also choose to build "hybrid models" based on a selection of the elements from the various pure models. In other words, it is difficult to make an appropriate choice among alternatives if the full range of alternatives is neither known nor spelled out explicitly.

Eighth, *there is an especially strong tendency in Western culture to identify spirituality exclusively as an individual phenomenon.* According to this way of thinking, spirituality is largely internal and subjective. As a result, Western culture tends to downplay as well as devalue the external, structural dimensions of spirituality. Western culture also tends to ignore that all of the inner spiritual development in the world may be for naught if we do not have the appropriate organizational and community structures that will allow the world as a whole to become a better place. This accounts for the emphasis that the present book places on both individual and organizational expression and interpretation of spirituality. The different models of practicing spirituality in the workplace are prime examples of the outer structural dimensions of spirituality. All the good words and feelings about spirituality are meaningless if we do not have structures for realizing those feelings.

Ninth, *those we interviewed did not, to their credit, see spirituality as a "soft phenomenon," or if they did, its softness did not matter.* The terms *hard* and *soft* are not only outmoded but irrelevant. As one senior executive we interviewed commented, "This so-called soft stuff is the hardest stuff I've ever had to deal with." What counts is that spirituality is vitally important regardless of whether it can be measured in numbers. In fact, most of the people we interviewed insisted strongly that spirituality could be measured. In fact, they believed that spirituality is one of the most important determinants of organizational performance. They also believed that people who are more highly developed spiritually achieve better results. In this sense, spirituality may well be the ultimate competitive advantage. However, herein lies a fundamental paradox: those who practice spirituality in order to achieve better corporate results undermine both its practice and its ultimate benefits. To reap the positive benefits of spirituality, it must be practiced for its own sake. If one practices spirituality without regard to profits, then greater profits can result.

Finally, *ambivalence and fear are two of the most important compo-nents of spirituality*. Contrary to conventional thinking, spirituality does not merely provide peace and "settlement"; it also profoundly "unsettles." The purpose of this unsettling is to spur us on con-stantly to improve the human condition. In short, the person who does not fear the tremendous power that is unleashed by spiri-tuality is not on the proper path to its attainment. Indeed, given its mismanagement over the course of human history, there is good reason to be wary of any attempts to manage spirituality in the workplace. Nonetheless, in spite of the tremendous fear associated with spirituality, the quest for it will not go away. Like it or not, the management of spirituality is one of the most fundamental of all management tasks.

Contents of the Book

Chapter One of this book discusses why spirituality is important and, as a result, why it cannot be left out of the workplace. Chapter Two, conversely, examines why spirituality has not received the se-rious, academic study it deserves in spite of its importance, and pre-sents key elements of the definition of spirituality that emerged from the views of our respondents.

Chapter Three presents the main qualitative findings from our interviews. It also presents selected quantitative findings in the form of statistical results. The chapter establishes unequivocally the ex-istence of the divided soul of corporate America. Current organiza-tions allow most people to bring only a tiny part of their entire selves to work, and at the same time the few parts that are allowed experi-ence severe wounding. The need for healing is thus substantial.

Chapters Four through Eight present the various models for fos-tering spirituality in the workplace that we have identified from our research. Each model is a way of healing the divided soul of corpo-rate America. Chapter Nine presents a "best-practice model." It also presents a series of critical questions that managers and execu-tives need to consider. Appendix A gives a full listing of the interview questions. Appendix B presents the results of detailed quantitative analyses of those questions, as well as statistical comparisons of the various groups of respondents. Finally, Appendix C contains a more detailed discussion of the underlying dimensions of the five models.

Acknowledgments

We wish to thank the following persons for helping to launch the study, for reading early versions of the manuscript, and for offering general advice: Herb Addison, Leo Braudy, Maxene Johnston, Irv Margol, Steve Piersanti, Lee Robbins, Gretchen Spreitzer, and Stephen Toulmin.

Elizabeth Denton especially wishes to thank Doug Webb, Myriam Orozco, and Pat Barrett for their love and support. She also wishes to thank Heidi Sherman, founder of the Professional and Business Forum, for her energy, humor, and support in the data collection part of the study.

Ray Anderson, Chairman of Interface, Inc., deserves special thanks and appreciation. He not only offered the perspective of his top management team but also opened his entire organization to our research. We thank the entire Interface family, especially Charles Eitel, president, for sharing his writing on leadership. Thanks are also due to Joyce LaValle, chief innovation officer, who became our "inside champion" to ensure data collection within Interface's large, decentralized, global environment.

Ian Mitroff expresses his deepest love for his wife Donna and his daughter Dana, and his appreciation for their continual, helpful words of encouragement. They are his guiding spirit.

We also wish to acknowledge the encouragement and constant help of our editors at Jossey-Bass, Cedric Crocker and Byron Schneider. Sincere thanks are also owed to Maggie Murray for her fine developmental editing.

Ken Wilber deserves a special word of mention. We cannot pay tribute enough to him for his tremendous influence on our work. We also appreciate his thoughtful and helpful comments on early drafts of the manuscript.

Finally, we would especially like to acknowledge and thank Warren Bennis. We doubt that this book would have been written without his constant help and encouragement. His editorial advice was especially welcome. He is the best friend any writer could hope to have.

August 1999

Ian I. Mitroff
Manhattan Beach, California
Elizabeth A. Denton
New York, New York

To our parents

A Spiritual Audit of
Corporate America

In our lifetime individualism has been so strong . . . that we may not yet have had the occasion to consider radically the notion of a truly common life. It wouldn't take much to conceive business as an enterprise in service of families and communities. It wouldn't take much imagination to connect work with individual calling and oriented towards the real needs of a community. Then we might discover to our surprise that money, business, commerce, and industry can all be part of our work of the soul.

—Thomas Moore, *The Education of the Heart*

A framework is that in virtue of which we make sense of our lives spiritually. Not to have a framework is to fall into a life which is spiritually senseless. The quest is thus always a quest for sense.

—Charles Taylor, *Sources of the Self*

Part One

Acknowledging
Soul and Spirit

Chapter One

Park It at the Office Door

The Unacknowledged Soul
of Corporate America

The great malady of the twentieth century,
implicated in all of our troubles and affecting us
individually and socially, is "loss of soul." When
soul is neglected, it doesn't just go away; it appears
symptomatically in obsessions, addictions, violence,
and loss of meaning. Our temptation is to isolate
these symptoms or to try to eradicate them one by
one; but the root problem is that we have lost our
wisdom about the soul, even our interest in it.
                    —*Thomas Moore*, Care of the Soul

As much and as surely as we are physical beings, we are also spiritual beings. It is a truism that our bodies require proper physical nourishment if we are to survive. It is also a truism, although it is far less acknowledged, that our souls require proper spiritual nourishment if we are to thrive.

Over the years, theologians and depth psychologists have pointed out that hope and love are the twin foundations on which all subsequent human experience and proper relationships are built.[1] Hope and love are also the twin foundations on which spiritual experience is built.

If hope and love are missing early in the development of the child, all of his or her future human relationships are put in serious peril, as is his or her spiritual progression. Proper spiritual development, nourishment, and expression are constant requirements throughout our entire lives. Furthermore, they are requirements of every setting in which we function.

The preceding ideas are some of the basic themes around which this book is built. As such, they stand in sharp contrast to the ideas with which current organizations are designed and managed. The feeding and care of the soul are critical to the development and sustenance of human beings; unfortunately, recognition of this is not the norm in current organizations. For instance, the following sentiments are typical of those that were expressed repeatedly by the corporate managers and top executives who were interviewed for this book:

> "I'm tired of having constantly to park my soul at the door before I go into my organization."

> "Organizations are constantly wanting and demanding more and more of us all of the time. But they can't have it both ways. They can't have more of us without getting and nourishing the whole person. Organizations must give back and contribute as much to the whole person as they want in return."

> "Organizations feel free to beat up on us forty to sixty hours a week. Then they put the burden entirely on us to repair ourselves on our own time so we can come back for more!"

Being forced to split off fundamental parts of oneself at work, being asked to give more of oneself without having one's whole self acknowledged in return, being asked to care for the soul and its concerns on one's own rather than on company time—these and similar laments were refrains we often heard throughout our research for this book. These negative feelings and perceptions exist in spite of the fact that the fears, the hopes, the dreams, the very essence—in short, the souls—of people accompany them wherever they go, including their places of work. With few exceptions, most organizations do not acknowledge the concepts of spirituality and soul. If we can assume that they cared in the first place, we can say that many organizations have lost sight of how to treat those who work for them as whole persons, as people with souls—and that they have lost sight of how to harness the tremendous energy that resides at the core of each of us. They have neglected to nourish this core, the source of all productivity and creativity in the workplace.

The Power and Potential Inherent in the Soul

What is the immense energy or potential that lies at the core of each of us yet remains largely unacknowledged and untapped in our places of work? The simplest definition of the metaphorical depth and potential of the soul was given over and over again by the various participants in our study: *The soul is precisely the deepest essence of what it means to be human. The soul is that which ties together and integrates all of the separate and various parts of a person; it is the base material, the underlying platform, that makes a person a human being.*

Unfortunately, rather than seeking ways to tie together and integrate the potential inherent in the soul with the realities of the workplace, most organizations go the opposite route. They seek to manage the cares and concerns of the soul by separating it from other realms, by walling it off as strictly as they can.

The usual way in which organizations respond to spiritual matters and concerns of the soul is by declaring them inappropriate or out of bounds. Conventional wisdom holds that spiritual matters and concerns are far too personal and private to be broached directly in the workplace, the most public and communal of settings. Moreover, because people differ sharply in their responses to such concerns, merely raising them will lead only to acrimony and division and not to the ultimate end of bringing people closer together at work.

Conventional wisdom also declares that spiritual matters have virtually nothing to do with the day-to-day demands of work, and even less to do with corporate affairs. As such, they are best dealt with outside of work, on employees' own time and in the particular way of their choosing. Armed with such rationales, most organizations kid themselves that by erecting a "Chinese wall" between the so-called private concerns of their employees and the public demands of their businesses, they can keep them strictly separated.

Regardless of how sincere or well-intentioned is the attempt to wall off so-called private issues from public ones, it not only fails as a general strategy but in a strange way actually helps to ensure that when spiritual issues are raised at work, they will be raised in ways that are inappropriate. By walling off such issues, we build up the pressure surrounding them. Thus, when the dam finally breaks, they are released with a vengeance in highly inappropriate ways, such as proselytizing for a particular religion. Besides, corporate America (which includes not-for-profits as well as for-profits, because both are big businesses) is hypocritical in ways that Chinese walls cannot disguise. On the one hand, corporate America declares spiritual issues strictly out of bounds, then on the other hand it tries sneaking them in through the back door and drawing heavily on them with calls for the unbridled energy and enthusiasm of its workers. At the same time, it fails to recognize and acknowledge that *enthusiasm* (from the conjunction of two Latin roots—*ens*, meaning "within," and *spiritus*, meaning "god" or "spirit"—literally, "the god or spirit within") is fundamentally a spiritual concept.

The worst thing about the wall, however, is that it is both an external and an internal division. It is external in that it walls off the organization from the deepest sources of creativity and productivity of its members. It is internal in that it produces a fundamental split in the souls of its members.

The Faustian Dilemma

The burden created by not acknowledging the souls of employees has created a deep ambivalence within corporate America. As we show in greater detail later, the employees, managers, and executives to whom we talked generally felt that they were caught in a basic "Faustian dilemma." On the one hand, they wished fervently that they could express more of themselves in the workplace, but they were afraid to do so. Indeed, many of those to whom we talked were terrified to do so. They were worried that if they did express their souls, they would end up selling them to their organizations. This fear is not unfounded. If the little of themselves that they currently expressed was being seriously abused by their organizations, what would it be like if they offered their complete souls? Would they be totally ridiculed, put down, and humiliated? On the other hand, if they didn't express more of themselves in the settings where they spend the vast majority of their waking time, then the development of their souls would be seriously stifled, possibly even halted. Given that the soul is precisely that aspect of human beings that cannot be confined and compartmentalized without severe repercussions, whichever path one takes is fraught with peril.

We disagree strongly with the perilous path that most organizations have undertaken, that is, separating spiritual concerns from the workplace. In fact, we disagree so strongly that our disagreement is the major impetus for writing this book. We believe that the workplace is one of the most important settings in which people come together daily to accomplish what they cannot do on their own, that is, to realize their full potential as human beings. For organizations to erect walls in the way of everyday spiritual development goes against the grain of deep human needs and puts an intolerable burden on individuals. This is precisely why organizations as wholes and not just individuals need to become more spiritual. Unless organizations become more spiritual, the fragmentation and ambivalence felt by individuals cannot be repaired. Unless organizations become more spiritual, they cannot reap the benefits of the full and deep engagement of their employees, their so-called most valuable resource. In the plainest terms, unless organizations not only acknowledge the soul but also attempt to deal directly with spiritual concerns in the workplace, they will not meet the challenges of the next millennium.

Healing the Divided Self: Models for
Spiritual Development in the Workplace

If organizations and not merely isolated individuals need to become more spiritual, then the fundamental question becomes, how can they accomplish it without offending or proselytizing their members? Are there any models that can be followed or adapted for the purpose of fostering spirituality in the workplace? In Chapters Four through Eight, we explore in depth five major and distinct models that constitute significant alternatives to the current policy of strictly separating spirituality from the workplace. Each model arises from a basic attitude of an organization and its members toward spirituality and religion. Each is a historically distinct and valid approach to the goal of finding meaning and purpose through one's work. Each has major strengths and, equally, major weaknesses. In addition, each has major benefits as well as costs. Though one or more of these models are in theory applicable to all organizations, some will most likely be rejected, at least in part, for reasons that will become apparent in the chapters ahead. Nonetheless, we believe that the decision to accept or reject a particular model of spirituality should be based on a clear understanding of what it is and what it entails.

Because one of the models we present, the *Religion-Based Organization,* is as close as possible to the picture of a complete takeover of a business organization for Christ (or any other particular god or deity), we want to make as clear as possible at the outset that the acknowledgment of spirituality in corporate America is not synonymous with compelling workers to accept an official company religion or forcing them to accept one of the world's major religions. Although many pure religious models do exist, it is important to acknowledge that there also exist many other possible routes to the acknowledgment of spirituality that are not based on the dictates or tenets of a particular religion.

For instance, one model that is identified positively with spirituality but not with any particular religion is the *Evolutionary Or-*

ganization, which begins its life with a strong identification or association with a particular religion and, over time, evolves to a more ecumenical position. Another model is the *Recovering Organization*, in which the principles of Alcoholics Anonymous (or some similarly designed recovery program) are consciously adopted as management principles. Typically, this model comes into being when there exists within the organization a "critical mass" of key executives who are in recovery for their addictions to alcohol, drugs, gambling, and so forth.

The *Socially Responsible Organization* is typically founded by a person or persons guided by strong spiritual principles or values that they apply directly to their business for the betterment of society as a whole. The heads of such organizations are typically more concerned with outside stakeholders than with the internal members of their organization.

Another model is the *Values-Based Organization*. The founders or heads of Values-Based Organizations are guided by general philosophical principles or values; they are not aligned with either religion or spirituality—indeed, they reject both of them in strong terms. However, as we show later, there is an underlying, implicit definition of spirituality in Values-Based Organizations, despite their strong denial.

To give a feel for the design of each model, we briefly present some of the underlying dimensions that are common to all five models:

• Each of the various models starts with a *critical or key precipitating event*, or what might be called a *key crisis event*. In most cases, this is a crucial crisis that either the founders or leaders of the particular organization face or that the entire organization faces. In certain cases, it is the result of a long stream of continuing crises. In every case, however, the initial desire to pursue a model of spirituality is born out of intense pain, out of the intense desire to confront and surmount major crises.

• Each of the various models possesses a fundamental, underlying *principle of hope* that expresses the basic optimism of the organization or, in somewhat different terms, expresses the object of its basic trust. For instance, most adopters of the various models believe that if they stick to their basic, underlying ethical principles and values, profits will follow and take care of themselves. Thus profits follow directly from being ethical, not the other way around. That is, one must be ethical no matter how large or small one's profits are. To become ethical once one's profits reach a certain threshold is to violate the spirit of ethics. An even stronger statement of this belief is the claim that if one is concerned with profits instead of with ethical principles, profits will suffer. In other words, organizations must be ethical for its own sake, not because it may lead to profits.

• Each of the models has its own distinct *fundamental texts*— that is, sources of wisdom for how to run a business ethically. These texts typically go well beyond the traditional texts that are used in most business and educational programs. Indeed, it is generally assumed by the developers and proponents of a model that most people have been greatly miseducated by the traditional texts of business, such as the texts of accounting, economics, law, and so forth. Each model thus broadens considerably the notion of "fundamental text." For example, in the Religion-Based Organization the additional texts are the Bible as well as various fundamentalist interpretations. In the other models, the alternate texts are often derived from the works of the great ethicists and philosophers. These works supply principles other than pure economic ones for running an organization.

No matter what their underlying alternate texts, all of the models speak a language that is very different from that of the typical traditional business. Although they continue to use the ordinary terms of business, such as *profits and losses, market share*, and so on, they also use such terms as *caring, heart, love*, and *trust*. In addition, they use such terms without shame or self-consciousness.

• The existence of a business language different from the ordinary makes for another underlying principle: each of the models makes spiritual talking and listening, or what is called *active listening* in the organizational development literature, a vital requirement. This principle arises out of the need to get others to embrace the founding values, religious basis, or innovative spiritual message of the organization. The Religion-Based Organization assumes that prayer is the single most powerful form of spiritual talking and listening; it is seen as the ultimate communication channel, open to everyone twenty-four hours a day, 365 days a year, and for eternity. Other models work from the belief that the capacities to talk and listen spiritually have to be developed. These organizations are proactive in retraining their employees in new forms of spiritual conversation.

• Another underlying, or core, principle has to do with an organization's recognition of and attitude toward its stakeholders. Stakeholders are any individuals, groups, or even whole institutions that affect or are affected by the policies of an organization. The models range in attitude toward stakeholders from considering a small number of them relevant, as in the Religion-Based Organization, all the way to acknowledging future generations and even the entire planet as stakeholders, as in the Values-Based Organization.

• All of the models have an articulated guiding or ultimate-purpose-of-business principle that helps in limiting greed—be it the unlimited accumulation of money or the unrestrained pursuit of power—and that specifies the purpose of one's profits. Is the organization in business to do good or to make money? Is making money a means or is it an end unto itself? In addition, each model grapples seriously with size and the relationship of size to the ultimate purpose of business: Can an organization be ethical or spiritual if it grows beyond a certain size?

• Last but not least, each model demonstrates to a greater or lesser extent which existing business functions are spiritualized by the adoption of a particular model and which ones are added to the organization. The traditional functions, in most cases, are preserved, but attempts are made to transform them or infuse them with strong religious or other values. The Socially Responsible Organization goes further than any other model to inculcate a whole new business design.

These core principles are a helpful framework for allowing us to make systematic comparisons across the models. Still other principles are uniquely identified with one or two of the models or help distinguish them from the rest of the models. For instance, the time frame in which a business evaluates itself is particularly significant for the Evolutionary Organization. It may be spread over many generations or it may be compressed into a few years; in each case different kinds of tensions are created within the organization.

The principle by which an organization frames its competition can also be unique. For the Religion-Based Organization, the competition, or enemy, is literally the Devil. For members of the Recovering Organization, alcohol and other harmful addictions are the enemy and the competition. Some of the models are distinct in how they use the vocabulary of spirituality; others have a distinct management style or overall governing metaphor. We take a close look at the unique dimensions, or underlying business principles, of each of the models, along with the common and core principles, in the chapters that pertain specifically to the models.

Also, given the present state of our knowledge, it is vitally important that we stress that we do not discuss operational specifics in this book. Instead, we discuss the broad, underlying principles by which most organizations are run. When things are running smoothly, most of these principles are largely taken for granted. They are rarely examined, and one can even argue that they do not need to be examined. However, when an organization is contemplating, or requires, fundamental change, it is absolutely vital to examine as systematically and as explicitly as possible the organization's fundamental, underlying principles.

For far too long the principles by which traditional organizations have been run have been taken for granted. Because the principles that underlie spiritually based organizations are so radically different, we must undertake the most fundamental examination of all: the systematic uncovering and challenging of traditional principles. Thus we believe that the most important contribution we can make in this book is not only to challenge old principles but also to illuminate new ones.

Closing Reflections

It is a normal human—and hence organizational—instinct to try to preserve the status quo. Thus it is tempting to continue the management of spirituality by separating it completely from places of work. Indeed, separation is a tempting management policy for all sorts of situations. When something becomes especially difficult to control, the temptation is always strong to relegate it to other realms, to place the burden elsewhere. Separation, however, is only one available management policy out of many.

Separation was a valid management policy at an earlier stage of human history. As Ken Wilber argues so brilliantly in *A Brief History of Everything*,[2] a key characteristic of virtually all the earliest stages of human development was that critical elements were so fused together that they literally had no separate existence, let alone separate identities. In Wilber's description, they were so completely fused as to be contaminated. Thus, first for survival and eventually for the sake of evolutionary development, the key elements had to be separated from one another in order to develop into more mature forms and stages.

At the present stage of human development, however, we face a new challenge. We have overseparated key elements from one another. Yet as Wilber points out so cogently, the answer is not to go back to an earlier, primitive state of fusion but instead to forge a more mature and robust integration.

The task of integration is particularly important in today's world. Today there is no aspect of human existence that is not influenced by the most disparate and improbable elements from the far ends of the earth. This is truly a systems age, wherein a host of complex elements and systems interact constantly and significantly with other equally complex elements and systems.[3] This age calls out for a new "spirit of management." For us, the concepts of spirituality and soul are not merely add-on elements of a new philosophy or policy of management. Instead, they are the very essence of such a philosophy or policy. No management effort can survive without them. We refuse to accept that whole organizations cannot learn ways to foster soul and spirituality in the workplace. We believe not only that they can but also that they must.

Chapter Two

A Strange but Formidable Alliance

Barriers to Studying and Defining Spirituality

> It is impossible to define precisely what the soul
> is. Definition is an intellectual enterprise anyway;
> the soul prefers to imagine. We *know intuitively* that
> soul has to do with genuineness and depth, as when
> we say certain music has soul or a remarkable
> person is soulful. When you look closely at the
> image of soulfulness, you see that it is tied to life
> in all its particulars—good food, satisfying
> conversation, genuine friends, and experiences that
> stay in the memory and touch the heart. *Soul is
> revealed* in attachment, love, and community, as
> well as in retreat on behalf of inner communing
> and intimacy [italics added].
>
> —*Thomas Moore*, Care of the Soul

If spirituality is in large part what defines us and if work also plays a large role in our definition of who we are, why then has there not been more systematic study of spirituality as it relates to the workplace? The short answer is that a strange alliance of influences— from conventional academics to New Age thinkers to guardians of U.S. culture and history—have all put strong barriers in the way of the serious study of spirituality. As a result, before there can be any attempt to break down these barriers, we need to confront this strange but formidable array of obstacles.

To begin, however, one point needs to be made clear: it is not that there have not been studies of spirituality—to the contrary. One has only to walk into any bookstore to be overwhelmed by the number of books with *spirit* or *soul* in their title.[1] A growing number of these books even pertain to business.[2] Most of the books on spirituality and business, however, are based on personal, anecdotal accounts of a single author's experience with a few organizations. They are not based on the systematic study of the actual experiences of a wide range of managers and top executives. This is not to say that these books are worthless. It is only that their validity is limited because it isn't clear how applicable they are to a broad range of executives and organizations.

Major Obstacles from Academe

Strange as it sounds, probably the major impediment to our knowledge of spirituality in the workplace comes from the institutions expressly devoted to furthering knowledge: business schools in particular and the academic community in general. It is imperative that we understand why the acknowledgment of the soul and its proper treatment are conspicuously absent from business schools and, by extension, from the organizations they serve.

In today's business world, an MBA is a virtual prerequisite for success. (To reach the highest pinnacles, a degree from one of the top business schools not only helps but is a virtual necessity.) Business schools, it is important to understand, are populated mainly by academics, not by actual business practitioners. Like academics everywhere, they have been shaped by their education to conform to strict standards regarding acceptable research topics and methods. If one peruses the academic business journals, one finds countless studies of the quantifiable aspects of business: size, structure, market share, and so on. One also finds countless scientific hypotheses, including computer and mathematical models, purporting to explain the relationship between such variables.

Almost exclusively, the variables in such mainstream studies are either *cognitive* (people are presumed to be calculating machines guided solely by their rational self-interest) or *structural* (for example, the number of layers in an organization and the physical barriers to communicating between them.) A small number of studies are concerned with ethical variables, but they are most likely to be found in fringe journals at the edge of the profession. An even smaller number of studies are taken up with aesthetic variables, such as the "style," "color," or "texture" of an organization. Conspicuously absent altogether are studies dealing with soul or spirituality.[3]

Why are the variables of soul and spirituality absent from the teaching and research agendas of business schools? What does it mean that these vital variables are missing from general theories of business?

Unfortunately, most academics have been trained to believe that unless something can be measured precisely, it is not a legitimate topic for scientific investigation. An even stronger statement of this belief is the contention that unless something can be measured precisely, it is without meaning. In the extreme, some go as far as to say that unless something can be measured, it cannot even be said to exist.

In addition to not lending themselves to scientific measurement, issues of soul and spirituality often get tagged as "soft and fuzzy" or "touchy-feely." Any association with such topics is the literal kiss of death in the academic world. Thus, if such inherently soft and fuzzy topics are to be dealt with at all, they are someone else's responsibility and should be addressed outside of work, and definitely outside of traditional scholarship.

If traditional academics are at one end of the spectrum, New Age proponents are at the other. Whereas the standards of traditional academics are too tight, the standards of New Agers are too loose. Whereas essentially nothing spiritual qualifies for study by traditional academics, almost anything does for New Age practitioners. This is not the place to delve deeply into New Age standards

of inquiry, but a brief excerpt from a New Age book is suggestive of
the substitution of feelings and emotions for conventional methods
of science:

> Let me start by summarizing my conclusions. No one can prove it,
> but I strongly suspect that the answer [to the question, Is reincarna-
> tion literally true?] is yes, no, and maybe. While the evidence both
> for an against reincarnation is inconclusive, the idea certainly ap-
> peals to me. And no matter what other explanations can be offered
> for what seem to be past lives, there is no way to diminish the ther-
> apeutic benefit that many people have had from undergoing what
> seem to be regressions into past lives.
>
> . . . If you find a therapist who does past-life regressions, put
> them to the same test you would any other potential health care
> provider. Ask about their training, request references, interview
> them and then add your intuition to what your research provides.[4]

Contrast the preceding with a traditional business article ex-
plaining the profitability of an organization in terms of the size and
structure of its industry—the differences are striking indeed. At the
same time, notice the appeal to traditional standards in terms of re-
questing references and so forth. (What in the world, however,
would possibly count as legitimate evidence of past-life regressions
or the legitimate credentials of past-life therapists?)

In short, whereas academics tend to be dominated by their
brains, New Agers tend to be dominated by their emotions. Because
academics are suppressing their hearts, their writings are wooden
and cold; because New Agers are suppressing their brains, their
writings tend toward sappiness.

Obstacles from U.S. History and Culture

There are of course many other reasons besides academic and educational ones for why spirituality has not been studied systematically. The most significant reason may be the cultural and historical

legacy of the United States. From its very beginnings, the United States has insisted on a strong separation between religion and government. This separation is enshrined in our constitution: "Congress shall make no law respecting an establishment of religion" (Amendment 1). Religion is to remain a private relationship between an individual and his or her maker. The separation between religion and government has carried over virtually to all other institutional arrangements in American life. From the separation of religion and government it is but a short step to the separation of religion and business. Removing that separation, even to study it, is viewed as a major invasion of privacy, if not an outright violation of constitutional rights.

In a corollary fashion, the current emphasis on "political correctness" and its minimization of all possible sources of offense have also retarded the study of spirituality. It is unfortunate but true that many people who regard themselves as liberal equate spirituality with religion, a taboo topic, and because religion is out of bounds as a legitimate topic, so is spirituality.

Despite the many cultural injunctions against the revelation of private issues, most people, we found, are eager to talk about feelings of spirituality and the need for spirituality in the workplace. Their eagerness is an expression of their deep hunger for acknowledgment of or attention to matters of the soul in the settings where they spend so much of their waking time. Interestingly enough, we have also found that those who are opposed to introducing spirituality into the workplace are also eager to talk about their reasons.

Language Barriers

A different kind of barrier exists in the approach that tends to be taken by writers on spirituality. Often there is a serious mismatch between their language and that of business practitioners. Correctly or not, the language of many writers on spirituality is perceived by business practitioners as airy, or ethereal, as planes above the harsh realities of everyday practice.

Unfortunately, a good example of the mismatch is David Whyte's *The Heart Aroused: Poetry and the Preservation of the Soul in Corporate America.*[5] We say "unfortunately" because this book is both admirable in content and extremely well written. It has much to offer practitioners in the way of valuable and relevant conclusions for business. But Whyte's highly innovative approach of using poetry—specifically the great epic poem *Beowulf*—to demonstrate the nature and power of soul and spirituality does not connect stylistically with many of the practitioners we surveyed. In its own way, its style is as off-putting to practitioners as much New Age writing is.

The issue is not any particular sense of disconnection that readers may feel with Whyte's work or with poetry in particular or art in general. Poetry and art are, in fact, two of the most important ways in which spirituality and the soul are known and treated. But in our experience, poetry and art are needed to supplement, not replace, conclusions based on the actual experiences of people in organizations. (We believe that Whyte would agree with us on this point.) Without models or guides for fostering spirituality, the language divide is otherwise too great for most managers and executives to bridge.

Barriers of Definition

The barriers to studying spirituality and its underlying accompaniment, the soul, are not entirely cultural. They are also due to factors other than professional and political narrowness and the difficulties of language. They are philosophical—barriers raised by definitions and the assumptions behind them. To many people, the mysteriousness of spirituality and the soul make them impossible to define—and if you can't even define something, how can you attempt to study it? It is amazing how widespread this belief is, given that it is erroneous, as explained shortly. But that's precisely why it may be so widespread.

At the opposite end of the spectrum is the equally erroneous belief that spirituality has too many if not an infinite number of definitions. According to this viewpoint, there are as many definitions of soul as there are people. Thus, whereas the one attitude declares that spirituality is impossible to define and thus essentially meaningless, the second assumes that definitions of soul are unique to each person.

Both attitudes are at once seriously flawed yet worthy of a deeper look.[6] To say that soul and spirituality are inherently elusive does not mean that they cannot be discussed in meaningful ways. Furthermore, to say that each person's soul is unique is not the same as saying that the definition of soul is completely arbitrary, unique, or meaningless. Because each soul is by definition unique does not mean that the concepts or the words we use to describe soul are necessarily unique as well. According to this brand of thinking, there is at least one general property that all souls possess, namely, their uniqueness. Thus there is at least one thing we know to be universally true of all souls.

To say that each person practices spirituality in his or her own distinctive fashion does not mean that the number of different ways of practicing is infinite. As a matter of fact, there are a surprisingly small number of definitions that capture the range of meanings that people have for a concept that is so vital to their lives.

Overcoming the Barriers of Definition

It is possible to get beyond the barriers of defining soul and spirituality by first exploring what *soul* and *spirituality* mean to most people. That is, asking people what *soul* and *spirituality* mean to them is a way of eliciting their underlying definitions of the terms. Indeed, finding the meaning that a particular concept has within the total context of a person's life is one of the best ways of securing a definition of that concept.[7] More to the point, a good or adequate definition of a significant concept is one of the most important outcomes of a research study. Contrary to much conventional wisdom, a good or adequate definition is not the initial starting point for research.

When the people we interviewed were asked, What *meaning* does spirituality have for you and you alone, even if no one else agrees with you? Certain ideas were offered repeatedly. (Notice that we did not ask each person how they would define *soul* and *spirituality*):

- Spirituality is highly individual and intensely personal. You don't have to be religious to be spiritual.
- Spirituality is the basic belief that there is a supreme power, a being, a force, whatever you call it, that governs the entire universe. There is a purpose for everything and everyone.
- Everything is interconnected with everything else. Everything affects and is affected by everything else.
- Spirituality is the feeling of this interconnectedness. Spirituality is being in touch with it.
- Spirituality is also the feeling that no matter how bad things get, they will always work out somehow. There is a guiding plan that governs all lives.
- We are put here basically to do good. One must strive to produce products and services that serve all of humankind.
- Spirituality is inextricably connected with caring, hope, kindness, love, and optimism. Spirituality is the basic faith in the existence of these things.

Certainly not everyone with whom we talked articulated, or agreed with, every element of these preliminary notions of spirituality. Nonetheless, most endorsed the notions of a supreme guiding force and interconnectedness as fundamental components of spirituality. Some did not even try to define the soul directly but merely assumed its existence. In that respect, they often came close to paralleling the thoughts of leading thinkers and writers on the topics of spirituality and soul.

Respondents' Definitions of Spirituality

By examining the notions of spirituality and soul held by the participants in our study, we were finally able to produce the following definition of spirituality. It's not that defining spirituality is sufficient to tell us how to bring it about within the workplace and other meaningful settings, but it is an important first step. Because of the importance of this definition to all that follows, certain elements of it are worth commenting on in some detail:

- *In contrast to conventional religion, spirituality is not formal, structured, or organized.* Organizations and formal structures are not critical ingredients of spirituality. Although spirituality is often associated with a particular religion, and hence realized through its rituals and dogmas, it is not inherently part of any formal, organized religion.

- *Spirituality is not denominational.* It is not even interdenominational. It is both above and beyond denominations. If anything, it is profoundly nondenominational. Thus spirituality is not Christian, Hindu, Jewish, Muslim, or any other particular faith. At the same time, however, spirituality is Christian, Hindu, Jewish, and Muslim in the sense that these are all historically important ways in which it has been experienced and celebrated.

- *Spirituality is broadly inclusive; it embraces everyone.* Spirituality is universal and nonproselytizing in the sense that it does not promote a particular way of being spiritual. It is inclusive in the best possible sense of the term. It embraces everyone no matter what their age, beliefs, creed, gender, race, religion, sexual orientation, and so on. Furthermore, it does not attempt to convert everyone to a single way of believing or celebrating their spirituality. The essence of spirituality is the embrace of all ways of experiencing and practicing it without condoning or endorsing a particular way. Nonetheless, a clear preference is expressed toward the most universal ways of expressing and practicing spirituality.

- *Spirituality is universal and timeless.* It is more general and universal than particular individual values, which vary with place and time. In this sense, it is neither relative nor absolute. It is not relative in the sense that it is a general yearning on the part of most people. Further, there is strong agreement between the most diverse people as to its meaning. Conversely, it is not absolute in the sense that there is not one and only one final meaning of the term. At the same time, it is an integral part of the universe. It was there prior to and subsequent to creation.

• *Spirituality is the ultimate source and provider of meaning and purpose in our lives.* It satisfies a deep hunger and yearning in all of us for meaning and purpose. This sense of personal meaning is reinforced by the notion that the universe itself is not meaningless, that it is not devoid of purpose, that there is a supreme being who is the source of all life, existence, meaning, and purpose.

• *Spirituality expresses the awe we feel in the presence of the transcendent.* It recognizes the mystery that is at the core of the universe and of life itself. It asserts that there is a transcendent power that is responsible for the creation and care of the universe. Spirituality also asserts that this power, whatever it is, is beyond full human comprehension—hence the awe and reverence toward all creation.

• *Spirituality is the sacredness of everything, including the ordinariness of everyday life.* The concept of sacredness is a fundamental part of spirituality. Not only is the sacred found in the starry heavens above us, but it is also present in the everyday, ordinary things of life.[8] From this perspective, everything is sacred. Thus a god, or higher power, is also imminent in the world—in other words, not only transcendent but also present everywhere.

• *Spirituality is the deep feeling of the interconnectedness of everything.* Not only is everything related to and affected by everything else, but stronger still, everything is part of everything else. The universe is seamless. Although our everyday lives may be compartmentalized and fragmented, the universe is not. The universe is calling out for us to undo the fragmentation and compartmentalization of our daily lives. To be spiritual is to examine the connections between one's products and services and the impacts they have on the broader environment. This recognition of interconnectedness constantly forces one to expand one's vision.

• *Spirituality is integrally connected to inner peace and calm.* One attains this inner peace and calm by being related to the world, not separate from it. One attains peace and calm by doing good.

- *Spirituality provides one with an inexhaustible source of faith and willpower.* It gives one the power and the will to persist in the face of seemingly hopeless and insurmountable odds. It provides the strength to carry on the good fight for righteous causes. It allows one to persevere no matter what. It provides an abiding sense of hope and optimism. Spirituality is the ultimate end in itself.
- Finally, *spirituality and faith are inseparable.* One does not believe in or practice goodness because one can prove that its effects will add to the bottom line. Instead, one believes in and practices goodness for its own sake, that is, as an end in itself.

An Apparent Contradiction

Careful readers will have undoubtedly noticed an apparent contradiction. Earlier in this chapter we were critical of the so-called standards accepted by the New Age writer on reincarnation and past-life therapy. But in accepting our respondents' definitions of spirituality and using them to formulate our own, haven't we in effect substituted one uncritical notion for another? Like the author who earlier debated the merits of past-life therapy, our response is yes and no. Although we ourselves may not endorse the existence of reincarnation, or although we may give limited credence to past-life experiences, as students of spirituality we must acknowledge that such feelings are one of the major forms that spirituality takes. In short, we have to explore the many forms of spiritual beliefs, as well as the functions that such beliefs serve, without necessarily condoning them.

A further point is even more fundamental. *One can believe in spirituality without believing in past-life experiences, or any other particular form of spiritual experience. However, one cannot believe in spiritual experience of any kind without first believing in spirituality.* To be sure, belief in something does not guarantee its existence, but that is precisely our point. We are not interested in proving spirituality any more than we are interested in proving the existence of a god or higher power. Instead, we are interested in understanding what a belief in spirituality confers in people's lives.

The serious study of spirituality and the soul does not mean the abandonment of critical thought. To admit the phenomenon of spirituality, or to go beyond admitting it to believing in it, does not mean that one ceases to engage in legitimate criticism or rational thought.

Concluding Reflections

To further such rational, critical thought, it is helpful to contrast the definition of spirituality derived from our respondents with that of one of the best contemporary analysts of spirituality, Ken Wilber.[9] On the basis of an extensive analysis of spirituality across a broad array of world cultures, Wilber proposes that two dimensions are sufficient both to sort and to understand the varieties of spiritual experience. The first dimension is *inner* versus *outer;* the second is the *individual* versus the *group, community, or society.* Putting the ends of the two dimensions together in all possible combinations results in four distinct orientations toward spirituality: (1) inner-individual, (2) outer-individual, (3) inner-communal, and (4) outer-communal.

The *inner-individual* orientation is what most people, including the majority of our respondents, mean by spirituality. The inner-individual approach stresses that spirituality is a purely inner, subjective phenomenon. Furthermore, it is potentially unique for everyone in that spirituality is experienced in terms of each person's innermost feelings and emotions, and each person's alone.

The *inner-communal* dimension underscores that spirituality is a group phenomenon. How spirituality is experienced is a function of the particular culture in which a person is reared and lives. In short, spirituality is a function of the deep beliefs, values, rituals, and celebratory acts that constitute the deep meaning of a society. Indeed, culture is such a powerful force, it virtually "creates people."

The *outer-individual* position holds that spirituality is a function of—that is, is known by—the actions of a person and the effects those actions have on others. According to this position, spirituality is not some mysterious inner force but rather the net effect of a person's acts with regard to others and the world.

Somewhat similarly, the *outer-communal* position stresses that spirituality is revealed in the structures—that is, the organizations and institutions—that a society enacts and maintains to help the poor and less fortunate. It is also revealed in a society's celebration of the arts and its places of beauty.

It is Wilber's particular genius to have first recognized each of these four orientations with regard to spirituality, and then analyzed how a robust approach to spirituality demands the integration of all four approaches. In other words, not only is each of the four orientations incomplete without the others, but also, and more importantly, each depends on the others for its basic existence and sustenance.

Few people are as adept as Wilber at recognizing and integrating all four positions. Certainly our study participants mainly stressed the two inner positions. Very few made any mention at all of the other two positions. When they did, it was to note the presence of a higher force or power. This makes good sense, because it is precisely the outer expressions of spirituality that are the subject of the various models for fostering spirituality in the workplace, and these models were virtually unknown to our participants.

Wilber's four positions also help to shed additional, needed light on the extreme separation between conventional notions of science and spirituality. Western science concentrates almost exclusively on the outer dimensions of reality; Western spirituality focuses almost exclusively on the inner dimensions. Western science so elevates the outer that it defines it as the only proper object of study. In doing so, it not only downgrades the importance of the inner life, but it also essentially regards it as meaningless. Only the outer is worthy of the term *objective reality*. The inner is reduced to the purely subjective, which by definition is beyond proper scientific study. We disagree emphatically with this notion as we turn to our scientific findings in the next chapter.

Part Two

Auditing Soul and Spirit

Chapter Three

The Divided Soul of Corporate America

Faith is not what today is so often called a "mystical
experience," something that can apparently be
induced by the proper breathing exercises or by
prolonged exposure to Bach (not to mention
drugs). It can be attained only through despair,
through suffering, through a painful and ceaseless
struggle.

—*Peter F. Drucker*

In this chapter we present a general overview of the findings from
our interviews and surveys. (Interested readers can find some of the
data that was collected, as well as the detailed questionnaire and interview questions, in the appendixes at the back of the book.) Before we begin, however, it is important, we believe, to speak of the
general mind-set with which we approached our study of spirituality in the workplace. Although the initial goal was to conduct a systematic study of spirituality, we were forced due to the complexity
of the phenomenon to regard our study merely as a systematic beginning, not as a final, definitive product. Given the barriers to the
systematic study of spirituality described in the previous chapter, we
wanted to conduct research that would help open up and explore
new territory, not with people who are primarily academics, or spiritual thinkers, but instead with people who are on the firing line in
their organizations.

Purpose and Development of the Design of Our Research

The major consideration guiding the development of our interview questions and mailed surveys was to pursue the notion of spirituality as it relates to the workplace. The need to feel whole is integral to spirituality in virtually any setting where people attempt to find meaning. To ascertain respondents' sense of their wholeness—and its antithesis, split—we explicitly formulated questions having to do with how much and which parts of themselves people felt they could bring to their workplaces. We asked these questions so that respondents' notions of their wholeness could emerge from both the qualitative responses to our mailed questionnaires and from our in-person interviews. We also used various quantitative assessments that asked people to circle numbers with regard to how much and which parts of themselves they felt they could bring to their organizations. The results allowed us to perform systematic comparisons between different types of organizations and helped us to find out whether organizations that have an explicitly declared spiritual orientation allow people to bring more of themselves to work than traditional organizations.

Questions as Probes

The in-person interviews were designed as much to be conversations as to be structured, systematic explorations of specific topics. With this in mind, we used our questions as probes to open up and explore new issues.

Each interview began with a set of questions designed primarily to put the person at ease (see Appendix A). They were also intended to capture preliminary information such as where the interviewee was born and went to school, job history, how many people he or she supervised, and so on. Next, the interviewees were asked to indicate the top three things that gave them the most meaning and purpose in their jobs. They chose from a list of items such as being associated with an ethical or good organization, doing interesting work, being of service to others, making money, realizing their full potential, and so on. The interviewees were then asked to state the basic values that they believed guided them in making important decisions in their lives. They were also asked how often and under what circumstances they were forced to compromise their basic values in making important decisions at work.

Then they were asked to paint a picture of their organizations. They rated them on a variety of dimensions such as happy versus sad, ethical versus unethical, autocratic versus democratic, profitable versus unprofitable, caring versus uncaring, worldly versus spiritual, sane versus insane, tolerant of gays and minorities versus intolerant, and so forth. The interviews then moved into high gear with questions about whether, how often, and where they and their families attended church, whether they prayed, and if they believed in a deity.

Once these more sensitive issues were broached, we were ready to ask the respondents questions that explored the main topics: What meaning does religion have for you and how important is it in your life? (This question allowed us to secure each respondent's implicit definition of religion.) What meaning does spirituality have for you and how important is it to you? What differences do you perceive between religion and spirituality? Is spirituality a relevant concern and appropriate topic for discussion in the workplace, or is it best dealt with outside of work? Respondents were asked about their feelings about spirituality compared to their feelings about the more neutral topic of general philosophical values. They were also asked whether they were aware of any methods that organizations could use to foster fruitful discussions of spirituality without causing people to feel violated or creating dissension.

The interviewees were then asked how often they felt joy or bliss in the workplace and for what reasons. Had they ever had an epiphany or a strong spiritual experience at work? Had they ever cried, felt depressed about their job or their organization?

To get an idea of respondents' notions of their own wholeness, the next part of the interview asked questions about how much and which parts of themselves people felt they could bring to work, such as How much of your self, your soul, your intelligence, your creativity, and your humor can you bring with you to your job?

Next we asked participants if they ever prayed at work and what they prayed for if they did. To wind down the interview, we asked what their organizations had done that they were most proud of and, conversely, what their organizations had done that they were most ashamed of. They were asked to name an organization that they considered a role model in fostering spirituality in the workplace. We also asked for a brief inventory of the various intervention programs their organizations offered to employees, such as alcohol treatment, counseling, and so on. Finally, we asked if they agreed with the basic contention that long-term organizational success demanded that organizations learn how to foster spirituality in the workplace.

Although some of these questions have certainly been asked before, most have not. To our knowledge, managers and executives have not been asked directly whether and to what extent they experience joy in their places of work. Depression, crying, and indeed full emotional expression have certainly not been explored to any systematic extent.[1] Also, to our knowledge, previous studies have not explored how much and which parts of themselves people feel comfortable expressing at work. These questions certainly have not been asked systematically of a wide array of executives across a variety of organizations.

The Respondents

Our sample was composed of five different groups. (See Appendix B for the demographics of the various groups.) The largest group consisted of 131 individuals who returned mailed questionnaires. Two thousand questionnaires were originally mailed to human resource (HR) managers and executives primarily on the West Coast, to whom we had access via a special database. HR managers were chosen because, of all the various corporate functions, their function is most specifically charged with handling a broad range of human problems and emotions in the workplace. Thus, we reasoned, they are the ones most likely to be sensitive to such issues as spirituality.

For every completed questionnaire returned, at least two were returned unopened because the party was no longer at the address and left no forwarding address. Thus we had an effective sample size of 2,000 − (2 x 131) = 1738. Out of 1738 questionnaires, 131 responses is a return rate of approximately 7.5 percent. Out of 2,000 questionnaires, 131 responses is a return rate of approximately 6.6 percent. We recognize that neither of these two percentages is especially high. As best as we can ascertain, the response rate was low because of the length of the survey and the sensitivity of the topics.

In general we found that it was much easier to obtain cooperation in face-to-face interviews than in mailed questionnaires. Indeed, no request for a face-to-face interview was declined. Therefore we recognize that those who responded to the mailed questionnaires may not be typical of the general population of HR professionals. Conversely, the responses from those HR professionals who were interviewed were not different from the responses of those who returned the mailed questionnaires.

The second group consisted of the entire echelon of fourteen senior executives of an East Coast manufacturing company known for taking an explicitly positive stance toward spirituality in the workplace. This group was interviewed by Elizabeth Denton.

The third group consisted of eighteen individuals who were members of new business alliances and professional associations formed explicitly to promote spirituality in the workplace. The members of this group were thus active supporters of spirituality, and for this reason were particularly important to our study. They, too, were interviewed by Denton.

The fourth group consisted of thirteen senior managers and executives of a single West Coast utility, a traditional, profit-making organization. This group proved invaluable in allowing us to make comparisons with organizations that hold nontraditional viewpoints. It was interviewed by Ian Mitroff.

The last group consisted of twenty-three individuals from various for-profit and not-for-profit organizations. This group was also interviewed by Mitroff.

In addition to these formal interviews, we also conducted twenty or so partial or informal interviews with people at various conferences and in other settings. Because the data from these interviews was partial, they could not be included in our formal statistical analysis. Nonetheless, they provided important background information.

It would take far too much space to discuss all of our research findings in detail. It is also not possible to relay all of the differences between the various groups. Fortunately, it is possible to get a feel for the overall qualitative results merely by reporting on Mitroff's selected interviews. This group contains employees of the West Coast utility, Mitroff's partial interviews, and the ten or so informal Mitroff interviews. At the end of the chapter, we present limited, but the most important, quantitative comparisons between all of the groups.

Qualitative Results

What Gives People Meaning in Their Work

The hands-down, first choice of everyone we interviewed regarding what gave them the most meaning and purpose in their job was "the ability to realize my full potential as a person." In extremely close second place was "being associated with a good organization" or "being associated with an ethical organization." Because most people saw *good* and *ethical* as the same, it did not matter to them whether they picked a good organization or an ethical organization as their second choice. The third choice was having "interesting work," while a distant fourth was "making money." Tied for fifth place were "having good colleagues" and "service to humankind." In sixth place was "service to future generations." In seventh place was "service to my immediate community." (See Figure B.18 in Appendix B. The responses from the mailed questionnaires were essentially the same as those from the interviews.)

These results are in general agreement with previous findings. When asked directly, most people do not list money as the most important thing about their jobs. Of course this depends on whether or not one is employed as well as on how well-paying one's job is. In any case, beyond a certain threshold higher needs kick in. The desire for "self-actualization," as psychologist Abraham Maslow called it, becomes paramount.

Parts of Themselves That People Can Bring to Work

It is interesting as well as revealing to compare the results from the early parts of the interviews with those from later portions. When asked how much and which parts of themselves they were able to express at work, many respondents noted that they were able to express their intelligence and creativity significantly more than their feelings, soul, and humor. The overall indication is that people are more comfortable expressing their intelligence than their emotions or feelings at work. (Figures B.22 and B.23 give needed quantitative support to the qualitative findings from the interviews.)

This finding is neither surprising nor shocking because it is in tune with the prevalent design of and expectation in current workplaces. Although it was unfortunate, it was not surprising to find that the separation that people experienced between their thinking and feeling sides contrasted sharply with what they said was the number one thing that gave meaning in their jobs: the opportunity for each person to realize his or her full potential as a human being. Unless *full potential* is defined narrowly, which in the broader context of our interviews it clearly was not, this result means that most people will not realize their full potential at work.

Although they were not explicitly conscious that they had provided conflicting responses in different parts of the interview, most people nonetheless sensed that they had. If only vaguely, they realized that they had to separate and compartmentalize significant parts of themselves at work. To be sure, not everyone wants to express all of themselves at work, or anywhere else for that matter. Many people want to keep a certain, if not a significant, part of their self private, that is, there are things they will share with no one else. It is clear, however, from the total context of the interviews that a decisive majority wished that they were able to express and develop their complete self at work. Even more fundamental is the notion of choice. That is, although many people want to keep a significant part of themselves private, the decision to share or not to share is something that virtually everyone wishes were under their control.

Basic Values That Govern People's Lives

When asked to list the basic values that govern their lives, most people responded with a common set of basic virtues: integrity, honesty, building and maintaining good relationships, keeping one's word, trustworthiness, being there for one's family and for others, and so on. A few listed more metaphysical or spiritual values, such as "being in harmony and in touch with the universe." The overwhelming majority of respondents also indicated that they rarely, if ever, had to compromise their basic values in making important decisions at work. Unfortunately, this did not always hold up in statements of the facts. For example, in response to later questions in the interviews, the chairman of one of the largest and most important organizations in his particular industry bemoaned that he could not criticize the greed that is so rampant in corporate America because if he were to do so he would offend some of his biggest clients. This acknowledgment stood in sharp contrast to his earlier claim that as chairman and founder of his organization he was exempt from compromising his deepest values. When the discrepancy between his remarks was pointed out, his silence spoke volumes.

How People See Their Organizations

With so much evidence of compartmentalization and split, it is equally important to note the areas in which our respondents saw little or no contradiction. Almost everyone interviewed saw their organization as being caring, ethical, and profitable all at the same time. They saw no contradiction in this. This view is especially significant because a majority of Mitroff's interviewees were from for-profit organizations (see Figure B.9). Those from not-for-profits were in agreement with those from for-profits in seeing no contradiction between being profitable and being ethical. (Figures B.20 and B.21 further corroborate this alignment.) Unfortunately, we have no data other than the opinions of the respondents on this link. All we can say is that most of our respondents saw no contradiction between the two. It would of course be an important study in itself to see whether there is any systematic linkage between actual profitability and beliefs.[2]

Views of Religion and Spirituality

Approximately 30 percent of our respondents had a positive view of both religion and spirituality (see Figure 3.1). A very small percentage, roughly 2 percent, had a positive view of religion and a negative view of spirituality. Roughly 60 percent, or the majority of those to whom Mitroff talked, had a positive view of spirituality and a negative view of religion. Finally, 8 percent had a negative view of both religion and spirituality. (These results are almost in exact agreement with those from the mailed survey; see Figure B.27.)

Definitions of Spirituality

Although the definition of spirituality given in Chapter Two was the dominant response, there were some differences. In general we observed four distinct orientations toward spirituality (shown in Figure 3.1):

**Figure 3.1. Four Orientations Toward
Religion and Spirituality**

Spirituality

		Positive	Negative
Religion	Positive	30% Religion and spirituality are synonymous and inseparable; source of basic beliefs/universal values.	2% Religion dominates spirituality. Religion is a source of basic beliefs/values.
	Negative	60% Spirituality dominates religion; spirituality is the source of basic beliefs/universal values.	8% Neither religion nor spirituality are primary. Universal values can be defined and attained independently of religion and spirituality.

1. A number of respondents framed their definitions of religion and spirituality in terms of both spirituality and religion, not in terms of spirituality versus religion. It was a case of both/and instead of either/or. For these respondents, the terms *religious* and *spiritual* have exactly the same meaning. Both terms reflect a positive, direction-giving set of beliefs that guide a person's life. A belief in a god or higher power is both central and a prerequisite. A specific dogma, principles, and tenets are followed and are used to guide one's day-to-day decisions and important choices in life. These respondents appear in the upper left-hand cell of Figure 3.1.

2. For the majority of respondents, there was a clear difference between the meanings they gave to the terms *religious* and *spiritual*. Nearly everyone who differentiated spirituality from religion viewed religion in negative terms. The descriptors used most often were *narrow, prescriptive, dogmatic, restrictive, closed, exclusive,* and so on. The same respondents had a much more positive view of spirituality. To describe it they used such terms as *essence of life, spirit, soul*

expression, meaning, connection, interconnectedness, creative, creation, universality, cosmic oneness, and so on. This group appears in the lower left-hand cell of Figure 3.1.

3. Another set of respondents defined spirituality with no reference whatsoever to religion. Rather, spirituality was expressed in terms of the "human spirit." For these people, it is taken-for-granted as a fact that everyone is a spiritual being and that spirituality is an integral part of humankind's basic makeup. This group differentiated between the physical world and the world of spirit. Repeated references were made to the human spirit, humanity, humaneness, life force, creativity, the motivation to express oneself, the expression of self, relating deeply to others, our common humanity, soul, self-actualization, and so forth. This group expressed a negative orientation toward religion and a positive orientation toward spirituality, as indicated in Figure 3.1, where they also appear in the lower left-hand cell.

4. The definition of a fourth group centered around the notion of consciousness. Being spiritual means being more fully conscious than one who is not spiritual. A person who is conscious acts more from awareness than from habit or cultural conditioning. Many who resisted talking about spirituality in business were quite verbal and accepting of the need for greater consciousness in the workplace. They felt that both individuals and organizations would benefit greatly from more conscious leadership and decision making. In addition, there were others in the group who, although they were quite comfortable with the term *spirituality*, felt that the word *consciousness* didn't carry as much negative weight and was therefore a better word to describe what they were talking about.

Somewhat paradoxically, this group had an implicit definition of spirituality that emphasized values. Thus they used the word *spiritual* but in a peculiar and idiosyncratic way. For this group, values were an all-important consideration. For them, the identification, clarification, and "living" of one's values are spiritual in that they are fundamental expressions of one's self. According to this group, underlying all behavior and actions is some fundamental value that is being expressed, consciously or otherwise. A prime value of this group was the belief that all living and even nonliving things have fundamental value. The following questions were basic: Is one acting in congruence with one's values? Does one embody integrity and respect for all living things?

This group of respondents talked a great deal about such virtues as authenticity, honesty, integrity, and respect. Spirituality was seen as not only an expression of the best of a person, but also an expression of the whole person himself or herself. Spirituality was based on the process of becoming conscious of humankind's higher values and committing oneself actually to living them. In short, for this group spirituality was nothing more than an expression of a person's values. The views of this group thus correspond most closely to a negative orientation toward religion and a negative orientation toward spirituality, as shown in the lower right-hand cell of Figure 3.1. Perhaps the best characterization of this group is that they were simultaneously positive and negative toward spirituality.

The participants represented in the upper right-hand corner of the figure were more concerned with the rituals of their religion and the shared community it offered them than with spirituality, toward which they were negative.

Emotions at Work

Most of those who were interviewed did not experience strong emotions at work. The feeling of joy was the strongest of any feelings cited. Crying, feeling depressed, or having an epiphany were almost nonexistent. Even joy was usually experienced in rather commonplace ways, for instance, in accomplishing an important task. Less often, joy was experienced in response to others, such as when a coworker or a subordinate accomplished something significant, or at the birth of a child.

Belief in a Higher Power or God and Its Presence at Work

Almost everyone who was interviewed believed in a higher power or god. However, when it came to feeling the presence of that power or god at work, there was a strong and sharp split, with the vast majority of responses clustering at the extreme ends of the spectrum. In other words, an almost equal number of respondents reported having infrequently experienced the presence of a higher power in the workplace as those who reported having strongly experienced the presence of a higher power in the workplace. These same general findings hold as well for praying and not praying at work. (It is beyond the scope of this book to show that these differences can be used to construct different intensities of religious belief and spirituality.)

What People Pray for at Work

People indicated rarely praying or meditating at work, but when they did it was mainly to prepare themselves for difficult situations and for general guidance in making tough decisions. On occasion they prayed for coworkers who were going through difficult times. Very infrequently people prayed "to get me through the day" and "to give thanks for something good that happened."

Spirituality as a Relevant Topic in the Workplace

Most people felt moderately strongly that spirituality was relevant as a topic in the workplace. When it came to the appropriateness versus the inappropriateness of spirituality, they were in the middle. They also leaned moderately toward the position that spirituality should be dealt with outside of work. With regard to general philosophical values, people felt very strongly that it was both relevant and appropriate to discuss them at work and that they should be dealt with at work. (Once again, the results from the mailed questionnaires lend strong support to the results from the interviews; see Figure B.28.)

The total context of our interviews provides a somewhat different interpretation of the seeming inconsistencies. From the interviews it is clear that a positive and much greater role for spirituality in the workplace is an ideal. Presently, general philosophical values represent the best currently attainable real option. Thus there is not necessarily a conflict between the different responses. Given the respondents' general unawareness of any viable models for fostering spirituality in the workplace, they fall back on general philosophical values as the only viable option.

Feelings of Deep Ambivalence

One of the strongest findings from the interviews is validation of a theme raised in Chapter One: Most people wish there were ways in which their spirituality could be expressed in the workplace. At the same time, most people are extremely hesitant to do so. Many wonder what advantage will be taken of them if they do address this issue where they work. Many also have strong doubts that they could do this without offending their peers. The overriding experience is a deep and abiding ambivalence with regard to spirituality.

Some of the fear and accompanying ambivalence are due, undoubtedly, to people being unaware of any positive models that could guide the expression of spirituality in the workplace, such as the alternative models and their dimensions that were introduced in Chapter One and that are the central topic of the next five chapters.

This last finding is borne out by the fact that almost the entire set of respondents was unable to mention at least one organization that they regarded as a role model in fostering spirituality. The few organizations that were mentioned—and even these cites were rare—were the tried-and-true ones, such as The Body Shop and Ben & Jerry's Ice Cream, which have received considerable media attention. In a few cases, respondents mentioned the names of organizations of which the general public is unlikely to be aware.

No matter which questions were asked and which areas of their lives were probed, the ambivalence toward spirituality surfaced in some clearly recognizable form. For instance, an extremely common response ploy was a game of "you go first." For example, supervisors who were interviewed said, "If a subordinate were willing to initiate a conversation about spirituality, then as his or her superior I would be willing to listen and participate." Subordinates, of course, said the exact same thing, only in reverse, "If my superior were willing to open up or initiate the conversation on spirituality, then I would be willing to share and participate." Thus a game is being played whose unwritten rules are clear to all the players. Each player is waiting for the other to make the first move, and neither is willing to make the first move. Clearly, to play the game is to make no moves and remain in ambivalence.

Stories: The Total Context

It was extremely common for the respondents to relate to the different questions by means of stories that tended to integrate all of their feelings. In other words, the respondents did not view the individual questions in isolation. Instead, they told stories that not only cut across the individual questions but also tied them together. The following are typical. Indeed, they are composites drawn from the responses of different individuals. Not only do the stories help illustrate the general themes of this book, but they also give the reader a direct feeling for the deep sentiments and emotions that were expressed in the interviews.

Charles

Charles (not his real name) is a typical CEO of a midsize, highly successful manufacturing business on the East Coast. In his early fifties, in good physical shape, and happily married with three "great kids," he has an enormous zest for living and for life in general. He is quite proud of the entrepreneurial skills that enabled the creation of his business and that have kept it fresh, exciting, and highly competitive over the years. Nonetheless, it didn't take long in the interview for a deep wound in his soul to surface:

> A few years ago, I had an epiphany. I realized—or better yet, I could
> no longer deny—that the chemicals I was using to manufacture
> and treat the furniture I was making were highly toxic. They were

extremely dangerous to the environment. To my dismay, I realized that I had become an unwitting agent of evil. Needless to say, this does not fit at all with my self-concept.

Although I long ago abandoned the religion in which I was raised, my spirituality, on the other hand, has steadily grown over the years. Organized religion never had much appeal or meaning for me. It's more concerned with maintaining itself. It cares more about the organizational aspects of religion and about ritual and dogma than about serving people irrespective of their beliefs. Spirituality, on the other hand, is intensely personal. Not only do you not have to be religious to be spiritual, but it probably helps if you are not religious, especially if you want your spirituality to grow and be a basic part of your life.

Spirituality is the fundamental feeling that you are a part of and connected to everything, the entire physical universe and all of humanity. It is also the belief that there is a higher power or god— whatever it is and whatever we call it—that governs everything. Spirituality is not only *believing* that everyone has a soul, but *knowing* this and being in constant communication with one's own soul.

The epiphany I had was: How could I proclaim myself to be spiritual, to believe that everything is fundamentally connected to everything else, that we are put here on earth basically to increase goodness and not just make money, and yet continue to make things that were basically harmful to the world? Ever since that realization, I feel as if I'm carrying a spear in the middle of my chest. It's a constant reminder of the pain I felt when I realized what I was doing. I struggle every day to pull that spear from my chest.

While not always as articulate as Charles, most of those to whom we spoke had experienced some form of "wounding of the soul" as a result of working in organizations. This was the case whether the organization was for-profit or not-for-profit, dispelling the myth that not-for-profits are necessarily better environments than for-profits. In fact, one can make the case that not-for-profits exploit their workers just as much as for-profits. Some not-for-profits rationalize the lower salaries they pay in terms of the "high psychic rewards" derived from working for an organization with "lofty goals."

It is also interesting to note that contrary to conventional wisdom, working in a not-for-profit does not automatically make one more spiritually inclined. Many not-for-profits have highly specific political goals, such as the inclusion of the disenfranchised, minorities, recent immigrants, and the poor in the political process. As a consequence, such organizations are even more concerned than many for-profits with obtaining "hard results" in the secular world. Whether an organization is more or less spiritual depends on the specific organization, not on its profit status per se.

One thing, however, is clear and applies to all organizations no matter what their status. A general wounding of the soul or the experience of a severe crisis is an important and necessary stimulus for embarking on the search for spirituality.

John

John is another typical executive. He is the CEO of a major social service organization. Although the organization is officially not-for-profit, John is responsible for raising and managing millions of dollars annually if he and his organization are to serve its needy clientele. Like many of the CEOs we have interviewed, he is a complex blend of realism and idealism. He is tough and tender, worldly and spiritual. His very presence exudes confidence. He is on a first-name basis with the power elite of his city. He moves easily and confidently between the highest and the lowest social strata. In sum, he experiences little tension or contradiction between what many would see as irreconcilable opposites.

Charles, John, and their counterparts challenge many of the myths or opinions about top executives. For instance, while John has extreme disdain for New Age terminology with its "gushy, sloppy language and thinking" as well as its paraphernalia, such as crystals and beads, he is also not afraid to talk openly about his spirituality and the vital role it plays in his life and work:

I pray every day for guidance in making tough decisions, especially at work. I also pray to renew myself. I find that whenever I allow myself to be in contact with my spirituality for an extended period, then something good always happens. The grants and money I've been worrying about frantically suddenly materialize. [This theme is repeated over and over again throughout our interviews.] Every time I have let myself be in touch with my spirit, I've been able to ignore the advice of my closest advisors, to the benefit of my organization. It always works out better than I expected.

Like the majority of the CEOs and top executives who were interviewed, John is extremely skeptical of organized religion:

I have little place for organized religion in my life or work. I view it as dogmatic, closed-minded, and generally intolerant of other points of view. It divides more than it unites. It is more exclusive than inclusive. Religion is more concerned with perpetuating itself than with helping humankind. Spirituality, on the other hand, is personal and individual. You don't have to be religious in order to be spiritual. [John thus echoes the earlier sentiments of Charles. In fact, virtually all of our interviewees expressed similar sentiments.] For me, the essence of spirituality is connectedness with everyone and everything in the universe, to the whole of humankind and the physical universe itself. It is feeling the awe and the mystery of being. It is also knowing that there is a supreme being or higher power that guides everything. I believe strongly that religion should not be discussed in the workplace. On the other hand, I believe not only that spirituality can be discussed in such a manner without dividing people, but also that discussion of it is absolutely key if we are to create and maintain ethical, truly caring organizations. All organizations, for-profits as well as not-for-profits, need to learn how to harness the immense spiritual energies of their members if they are to become both ethical and profitable over the long haul. Any organization can make money in the short run by exploiting and maltreating its employees, but if it wishes to be profitable over the long haul, it needs to learn how to be spiritual.

Selected Quantitative Results

Figures 3.2 and 3.3 summarize some of the most significant quantitative results. With a few notable exceptions, on every dimension organizations that identify themselves as more spiritual are superior to their less spiritual counterparts.

Figure 3.2 shows the results obtained from two of our sample groups: group 2 (G2) consisted of the senior executives of an East Coast manufacturing company known for taking a positive stance with regard to spirituality in the workplace. This organization's orientation toward spirituality in the workplace emanated from the very top; at the same time, the organization had strong for-profit goals. Group 4 (G4) consisted of the senior managers and executives of a West Coast utility that followed a traditional economic orientation. This orientation does not mean that the organization was unethical; indeed, it had a strong base of ethical values, which it practiced. Nonetheless, on nearly every dimension these two organizations were at the extreme ends of the responses for all the sample groups. Furthermore, separate analyses of variance (ANOVAs) show that the differences between all of the groups are statistically significant on ten of the total of fourteen scales. In addition, the differences are extremely significant on seven of ten scales.

For instance, although all of the organizations perceived themselves as "warm," the two organizations that perceived themselves as "more spiritual" also perceived themselves as the "warmest." Also, G2 perceived itself as the most profitable, followed closely by the West Coast utility. At the same time, the remaining group with a strong spiritual orientation perceived itself as being the least profitable. Thus, being more spiritual does not in itself automatically guarantee higher profitability. Nonetheless, the results are highly suggestive.

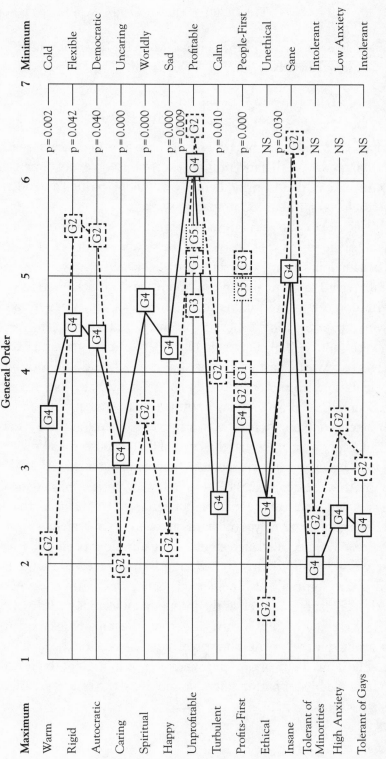

Figure 3.2. Organization Profile

General Order

G1: mailed questionnaires (N = 131); G2: East Coast manufacturer (N = 14); G3: Denton partial interviews (N = 14); G4: West Coast utility (N = 13); G5: Mitroff partial interviews (N = 24)

p = level of statistical significance; NS = not statistically significant

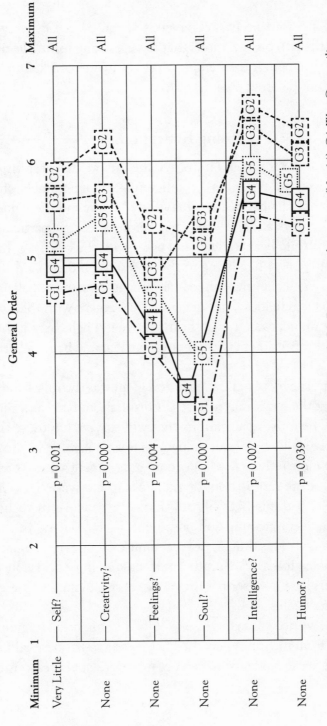

Figure 3.3. How Much of Yourself Can You Bring to Work?

G1: mailed questionnaires (N = 131); G2: East Coast manufacturer (N = 14); G3: Denton partial interviews (N = 14); G4: West Coast utility (N = 13); G5: Mitroff partial interviews (N = 24)

Figure 3.3, conversely, is completely unequivocal. On every dimension, the two organizations that have a strong spiritual orientation allow or permit their employees to bring more of themselves to work than the other organizations do.

Closing Reflections

A final indicator from our findings of the importance of spirituality—and even, in some cases, of religion—is that a number of respondents noted a connection between religion and the value it conferred on work and the workplace. For instance, one participant observed, "While I generally do not agree with the beliefs of those who are religious, I like being in their presence more than I [like being] with nonbelievers. While I may not agree with the beliefs of those who are religious, I am in general agreement with their values. Furthermore, even though I can't prove it, I believe that there is a direct connection between being spiritual and being a better, more ethical worker."

Perhaps the most telling reflection of all was the following: "I believe that there is no alternative to organizations becoming more spiritual. The only organizations that will survive are those that have a deep value base. But values are not enough. It has to be something more universal. Most of corporate America doesn't realize it, but we are running out of gimmicks to motivate the workforce. The only thing that will really motivate people is that which gives them deep meaning and purpose in their jobs and in their lives in general. This thing is not a gimmick. Whatever you call it, it is spiritual at its base." "Spiritual at its base"—in fact, "deeply religious at its base"—describes the model of spirituality we present in the next chapter.

Finally, we need to mention one of the most important findings to emerge from the interviews. In a few cases a respondent alluded to an underlying model by which organizations could responsibly practice spirituality in the workplace. In those rare cases, the model alluded to was extremely sketchy. It was nothing more than a hint or suggestion. As we show shortly, starting with the next chapter, we took these suggestions very seriously and sought out previously published books to see if we could use them to flesh out the various models. Much to our surprise, we found that we could. Even more to our surprise, we found that we could illuminate underlying dimensions of the various models that those who had written about them were not aware of. Thus we were able to work back and forth between our data and the data provided in previous writings on spirituality.

Part Three

Models for Fostering Spirituality

Chapter Four

Taking Over Your Company for Christ

The Religion-Based Organization

An enthusiastic missionary as a young man, at
age 42 [Jon Huntsman] was asked to serve as a
"[Mormon] mission president" for a group of
220 young proselytizers in Washington. He took
leave from his company and moved his wife and
nine children with him. When his stint was up,
they headed back to Utah, and Huntsman
resumed building the $5 billion, 10,000-employee
Huntsman Chemical Corp., which he owns
outright. Ten years ago, Huntsman shifted his
company's mission from pure profit to a three-part
priority: pay off debt, be a responsible corporate
citizen and relieve human suffering. Thus far his
company has donated $100 million of its profit to a
cancer center at the University of Utah. It has also
built a concrete plant in Armenia to house those
rendered homeless by the 1988 earthquake, and it is
active in smaller charities ranging from children's
hospitals to food banks. Since the shift, says
Huntsman, "we have a far greater spirit of
accomplishment and motivation. Our unity and
teamwork and corporate enthusiasm have never
been higher." And he still puts in his 15 to 20 hours
per week as a lay clergyman. He concludes, "*I find it*

impossible to separate life and corporate involvement
from my religious convictions" [italics added].

—David Van Biema

The model with which we begin our discussion of developing spirituality in the workplace is the Religion-Based Organization. Because it is the most extreme of the models, it is likely to be judged the most objectionable. The question, of course, is why start with an extreme case that is not representative of the vast range of organizations?

One of the most compelling reasons is that extreme portraits allow us to observe with greater clarity both the benefits and the dangers inherent in a particular phenomenon. They often do more to illuminate than to obscure the phenomenon under study. Another reason is that this particular model is based on a relatively small, unified, and clear set of strong and exacting principles. Their very certainty and forcefulness offer a clear standard by which to evaluate and judge other models. Ideally they can be used to chart a course between desirable limits on religious expression in the workplace and policies of tolerance.

Another reason is that we do no service to the study of spirituality in the workplace by ignoring or rejecting its more extreme—some would even say its "dark"—aspects. In addition, as we show, the principles that guide the Religion-Based Organization are not unique. Many of the same principles are present, in appropriately modified form, in other models and environments. This shows again why it serves our purpose to begin with the Religion-Based Organization. Let us start, therefore, with the threshold set by Christian organizations with an extreme religious basis: the complete takeover of a business for Christ.

The Ultimate Goal: A Religious Takeover

A few of our interviewees were practicing ministers with active congregations. Like the Mormon owner of Huntsman Chemical (see this chapter's epigraph), they spoke for those who find it impossible to separate their corporate involvements from their religious convictions. It is significant that whether they were affiliated with a nonprofit or a for-profit organization, their outlook was much the same. The following is a composite of their strongly held beliefs:

> I am an ordained minister. On the weekends I am the pastor at a local church. However, the organization in which I work during the week is my main ministry. I not only believe that the goals and mission of the organization are meaningful in themselves, but also that they happen to coincide with my religious beliefs.
>
> Although we have to make a profit in order to support ourselves, we exist primarily to serve the needy, the disadvantaged, and the poor. Doing good is our ultimate goal, not making money.
>
> There is another reason why this organization is my ministry. It is the best vehicle for reaching the largest number of people and, as a consequence, serving Christ.
>
> I have another goal as well. Most people who work here know that I am a minister. If someone asks me why I am a Christian, I do not hesitate to tell them. However, even though I see it as a fundamental part of my mission to convert the entire organization to Christ, I am very careful to conceal this.

The mission statement is unmistakable: to bring religion into the workplace and to take over the entire organization for Christ.

Unfortunately, when most people are asked to think about organizations that are "spiritual," a rigid and stereotypical image along the lines of the following often emerges: a spiritual organization is one in which a person is under tremendous pressure, at least subliminally, to accept the tenets of a particular faith or religion. Notably, too, whether the particular religion pictured is Christian, Hindu, Jewish, or Muslim, it is almost always perceived in highly fundamentalist terms. Indeed, a few of our respondents described employment in a religious organization as being isolated on a tiny island inhabited by a group of "true believers" who are in sole possession of "the Truth."

It is little wonder that most people react so negatively to the idea of spirituality in the workplace. How could they react otherwise? Such a controlled and controlling environment would be a nightmare, the embodiment of our worst fears.

Indisputably, strongly religious organizations do exist, making the pages of news magazine and business media. ("The top beef ranch in the world is not the King Ranch in Texas," reports *Time* magazine. "It is the Deseret Cattle and Citrus Ranch outside of Orlando, Florida. It is owned entirely by the Mormons. The largest producer of nuts in America, AgReserves, Inc., in Salt Lake City, is Mormon-owned. So are the Bonneville International Corp., the country's 14th largest radio chain, and the Beneficial Life Insurance Co., with assets of $1.6 billion.")[1] These organizations, then, are not mere figments of the imagination or the projection of our worst fears. However, although they are real, they are not the only designs or models by which to foster spirituality or practice it in the workplace.

Paradoxically, one of the best ways of countering our negative reaction to this type of organization, or at least of putting this type of organization into perspective, is to examine the basic principles that underlie so extreme an example. Examining the assumptions, practices, and principles behind a particular model shows clearly what the model, if followed as intended, forces us to accept. Careful analysis of underlying principles is also one of the most powerful means of knowing how to limit a model's impact, or to keep it from gaining control over an entire organization.

Our Method of Analyzing the Religion-Based Organization

In scrutinizing the pure Religion-Based Organization, we are guided not only by the results of our own surveys and interviews but also by our broad study of previously published materials. Fortunately there are books that serve as virtual manuals or primers for the complete takeover of a business organization for Christ, or any other deity. Such books are extremely valuable in helping to identify and observe systematically the set of principles that underlie the Religion-Based Organization. The book we chose as our primary guide through the relatively few but certain principles of the Religion-Based Organization is *Transforming Your Workplace for Christ*, or *TYWFC*, by William Nix.[2] We chose this book because it is one of the clearest and strongest statements to be found not only of the principles but of the zeal behind them. Though it is obvious from the title that *TYWFC* is primarily a Christian manual, the reader should bear in mind that similar treatises exist for other religions.

A word on how we have incorporated ideas and excerpts from *TYWFC* into this chapter: We have approached *TYWFC* as if it were a coherent and consistent set of beliefs about a Religion-Based Organization that form a unified belief system. We quote directly from Nix's book when its language helps to illustrate the power and meaning of these principles to those who abide by them. In addition, we have taken the radical and controversial step of interpreting the book as a quasi-management or business text for running a Christian-based business or for transforming an organization into such a business.

The Principles of the Religion-Based Organization

There are more principles in *TYWFC* than those we have chosen for discussion. We have tried to capture the more salient principles, those that allow for systematic comparison with the principles of the four other models presented in this book, as well as some that convey the unique features of the Religion-Based Organization. We begin with what seems to be the dominant principle of such organizations: management by the Word of God.

The Word of God as the Ultimate Business Text

I heard the arguments in favor of letting Barbara go, but I was not convinced this ultimate employment action was necessary or fair, much less honoring to our Lord. That's right! *I believe we must filter all business decisions through the Word of God* [italics added]. His word is applicable even in personnel-related matters. In fact, His word is applicable *especially* in personnel-related matters [italics in original].

. . . A biblical response awaited me the next morning. These words of the apostle Paul sum up the supervisor's response: "Warn those who are idle, encourage the timid, help the weak, be patient with everyone" (1 Thess. 5:14). Barbara was warned to improve her work. She was given training in certain areas to shore up her weak spots. Later she transferred to another area of the company and now she is doing a great job. Patience saved the day and made a Christ-honoring difference in Barbara's life.

. . . At times it seems that we too must exhibit *unlimited patience* [italics added] in a world that desires to have it all today. In many workplaces Barbara would have been released on the spot. If someone in the ranks cannot measure up, then cut them loose.[3]

A hallmark of the Religion-Based Organization is its strict governance by the "Word of God" as defined by the text or texts of a particular religion. God's Word, not corporate policy, is thus the ultimate test for the soundness of any business action or decision. In the vernacular of business, the Word of God is the "ultimate text of business."

Fundamentalist Christians believe that the Word of God is given by the Bible. To them, the Word is literally, not metaphorically, true. As social critic Bruce Bawer points out in his book *Stealing Jesus: How Fundamentalism Betrays Christianity*, the literal interpretation of God's Word tolerates no opposition.[4] Other interpretations are considered falsehoods, and those who hold them are cast literally as the Devil. This particularly black-and-white position is not surprisingly among the hardest for outsiders to accept.

By looking to the Word of God as the ultimate source of business wisdom, the Religion-Based Organization either greatly amends or wholly substitutes a different set of texts for those found in traditional business programs or practicing businesses. As innocuous as this may sound, the consequences are profound and far-reaching. For one thing, because the Word of God governs, God himself, not a human CEO, is considered the supreme leader of the organization. For another, because God's Word is considered eternal, the time line by which a Religion-Based Organization evaluates itself and conducts its affairs is completely shifted from that of the non-religious organization. The time frame is literally extended to eternity—needless to say, the longest time span imaginable. Thus the Religion-Based Organization does not manage for only the next quarter or for short-term profits.

God as Supreme Leader and Business Owner

> Our relationship with God is vertical; He is on top and we are on the bottom. This picture suggests a chain of command. He is first and we are second. He is in charge, and we are to serve Him and follow His orders. It is not my theory; it is God's command.[5]

A further consequence of the predominance of the Word of God in Religion-Based Organizations is a strict hierarchical structure. The vertical chain of command makes possible yet another fundamental principle: work flows from God, not from people. In the language of business, God is not only the *supreme supervisor* but also the *supreme designer* of the jobs in an organization. To take it a step further, God is the *ultimate owner* of any business. The fact that God is owner makes it not merely appropriate but a demonstration of honor that he be acknowledged and discussed at work. *TYWFC* provides an answer to the question, Is it appropriate to discuss Christ at work? "God gave your work for the purpose of building His Kingdom and a civilization that honors Him. *God created work. He owns it* [italics added]. My question is, why is it not appropriate to discuss Christ at work? The philosophy driving capturing your workplace for Christ is that you must demonstrate you live for Christ in and through your work before your words will be heard. Decisive Christ-honoring action is needed. You are God's envoy in your place of employment."[6]

Having God as both CEO and owner transforms the Religion-Based Organization into a unique corporate entity, because in most organizations the owner or owners are not the same as the CEO. It also redefines the role of employees. Those who work in Religion-Based Organizations are there to act as God's servants; they serve only at his pleasure.

Satan, the Major Competitor

> Satan roams the landscape looking for weak moments. We are his prey. Be self-controlled and alert. Your enemy the Devil prowls around like a roaring lion looking for someone to devour (1 Pet. 5:8).[7]

Every organization faces competition, but the Religion-Based Organization faces the greatest competitor of all. In the language of business, Satan is the supreme competitor or competition.

As previously noted, fundamentalist Christians take their terms literally and not metaphorically. Thus, for them the Devil actually exists and his presence is everywhere. The requirement is to be ever vigilant. As Bawer puts it:

> To be a committed [fundamentalist] Protestant is to have a powerful, black-and-white sense of the conflict of good and evil. A former fundamentalist described the mind-set to me as follows: "There is no more gray. You're separated from this world and at the same time inhabiting an unseen world, in which you're fighting an unseen battle against the unseen enemy. . . . Satan is a constant, overwhelming presence, the same yesterday, today and forever. It's a whole different mentality," the ex-fundamentalist explained. "You not only

think about God all the time, you think about the Devil all the time. Everywhere you go in every encounter with other people, you ask yourself whether this is of the Devil. He is under every bush."[8]

The wily Devil can appear in the most unexpected guises, including internal organizational programs, in the name of change. To the Religion-Based Organization, management fads and buzzwords that come and go are other manifestations of Satan, who is extremely clever in tempting us constantly with false solutions to all our problems. God, of course, is the ultimate guarantor, ensuring that we will be able to resist the most seductive fads and pressures for quick change.

The Principle of Hope

One of the key underlying sentiments of TYWFC is that everything is possible through God and that God makes everything possible. Although not a direct quote, this one statement embodies the "principle of hope" or "principle of optimism"—in short, the ultimate principle that justifies the placement of trust in the Religion-Based Organization by those who believe in it. But if hope is a gift received directly from God, people are obligated in return to perform religious service. Indeed, religious service is one of the highest goals in the Religion-Based Organization. To be sure, other goals are present as well, depending on whether the organization is for-profit or not-for-profit. In our research, however, we found that such organizations did not differ radically in their goals. In the not-for-profit sector, a primary goal was to give employment to those who could not find it in the private sector. These organizations were willing to hire people who were essentially unemployable anywhere else. This same concept of service was also present in Religion-Based Organizations in the private sector. Although eminently desirable, making money was not the primary goal. Rather, the primary goal was to provide ethical goods and services that would benefit humankind. Making money was also an important goal for the religious organizations that hosted or sponsored such goods and services, but only so they could carry out their religious mission.

As this chapter's epigraph notes, the Mormon-led Huntsman Chemical Corporation made a public shift in its corporate mission from a pure profit orientation to redistributing profits toward relieving human suffering. For this particular for-profit company, this change was the result of a deliberate decision to cultivate service for ethical reasons alone and not because it might lead to profits.

The Anything-Is-Possible Principle

> Faith says God has a terrific plan for all of us. . . . Faith holds fast to the knowledge that God is in control. Faith believes that with God anything is possible. . . . Faith is the fuel of an encouraging intervention.[9]

Given the locus of hope of the Religion-Based Organization, it is not surprising to encounter this highly optimistic principle, one of the most interesting of all of the principles presented here. Most managers and executives have good reason to believe, on the basis of their experience, that the best-laid plans do not guarantee their own eventual implementation. Indeed, the goodness of a plan is rarely the key to its translation into practice. In the Religion-Based Organization, however, there exists a fundamental belief that all barriers to implementation are removed once people give themselves over to God. In other words, faith in God is the ultimate guarantor of implementation. Put somewhat differently, through God the best plans are implementable. But how to engage the ear of God? The following closely related principle tells how.

Prayer: the Ultimate Communication Channel

In all five models—those with a religious basis as well as those with a spiritual basis—engagement in spiritual talking and listening, or what might be termed *spiritual conversation*, is not left to chance. In the pure Religion-Based Organization, spiritual conversation takes place between human beings and God in the form of prayer, and prayer is not optional but an absolute requirement. As described in somewhat militaristic language in *TYWFC*: "Your workplace cannot be transformed for Christ unless and until you fall to your knees in prayer. The battle for the hearts and minds of your co-workers belongs to God. The power to represent Him comes as you know His will and as you allow Him to change you. Knowledge of His will and experiencing Christ-like change come through the work of prayer."[10]

According to this principle, prayer is required for the transformation of any organization into a fully religious one. Indeed, prayer is a binding constraint on management's behavior: top management must literally fall to its knees if they are to manage the organization successfully. Furthermore, in the language of business, prayer is not only a binding constraint on management's behavior but also the *supreme channel of communication*. Unlike human communication systems, God's channel is always informative, ultimately transformative, and always available: "Prayer is our spiritual satellite system. We voice our concerns, fear, apologies, and requests to God, and He beams back His perspective and will for us. God will take our finite and human perspective on another's life and miraculously transform it into a Christ-honoring, selfless, forgiving spirit. Through prayer we gain God's perspective."[11]

The Precipitating Crisis Principle

Religious or spiritually based organizations are founded in the wake of a precipitating event or crisis. Often the precipitating event is severe dysfunction of the business or a series of repeated financial failures. Social injustice, or a long history of social crises, can also lead organizations to reevaluate the terms of success. Very often, too, the personal history of a company's founders or the angst experienced by its top leaders plays a major role in meaningful change.

All organizations are influenced by the personal crises of their
top executives, and the pure Religion-Based Organization is no exception. It is quite clear from our research that the deep appeal of
Religion-Based Organizations arises from a personal need to resolve
inner conflict and turmoil. The author of *TYWFC* tells of the extent to which he was stirred to action as a Christian by witnessing
multiple problems in the workplace:

> The Executive Vice President of a large banking company felt God
> urging him to transform his workplace for Christ. His company al-
> ready enjoyed the Thursday morning visit of a local pastor who of-
> fered a devotional thought and prayer. These Thursday morning
> meetings had become a weekly highlight for many employees.
>
> As time passed, this senior manager wanted to take his employ-
> ees deeper. He wanted to see persons come to know Christ person-
> ally. This boss witnessed divorces, addictions, abuse, and other
> serious consequences of sin. He also found pettiness, jealousy, and
> anger in his workforce.
>
> He began to pray that God would show him how to honor his
> Creator in the workplace. With an insight as clear as if he had been
> studying for weeks, this manager developed a program to teach
> Christ-like values to his employees. . . .
>
> That Executive Vice President is me [William Nix]. I have been
> humbled to see God work in our place of employment. God used
> this experience to teach me the real burden of management. Mem-
> bers of the management team are stewards of the time, talent, and
> future of those we serve, our employees. The manner in which man-
> agers who are Christian choose to respond to this unique opportu-
> nity reveals what they believe about God.[12]

Why some executives turn to the constrictive framework of the
Religion-Based Organization rather than to other kinds of frame-
works to help them through their personal crises we may never fully
know. Perhaps it is the bedrock stability of the Religion-Based Organization that attracts such people. Perhaps such individuals are

already familiar and identify deeply with the crises that were an integral part of Christ's life and through which he was transformed; the stories, beliefs, and symbols associated with religious revelation are nothing if not deeply affective and powerful. Or perhaps it is because the Christian church offers ideas and beliefs that are eternal, that lie outside time at work, human history, or even time itself. Through participation in a Religion-Based Organization, the executive's life acquires meaning beyond himself or herself. The executive takes part in a universal, if not eternal, drama. In this way, the executive becomes a major stakeholder in the religious enterprise, along with Christ.

Stakeholders of the Religion-Based Organization

The term *stakeholders* once meant exclusively "stockholders" (those whom Milton Friedman in an earlier era called the primary, if not the only, stakeholders in an organization). The term has come to mean any and all individuals, parties, organizations, and institutions that either affect or are affected by the policies of an organization. The highly evolved modern corporation has a multitude of stakeholders to whom they are beholden or whom they must seriously consider, including labor unions, competitors, the federal government, mass media, financial institutions, workers, middle management, top management, security, the police, fire departments, surrounding communities, other multinational corporations and governments, and so on. Beyond this basic list, even special interest groups, animal rights activists, and the tabloid press may be considered stakeholders, because they can either make or break an organization.

One of the distinguishing marks of a Religion-Based Organization is the exceptionally small number of stakeholders it considers relevant to its situation. These relevant stakeholders coincide with the version of reality put forth by the Religion-Based Organization. Thus the principal stakeholder is God, who is equivalent to the "Big Boss" or CEO and also owner and at the top of the hierarchy.

Satan, who is after all the main competition, is another prime stakeholder, along with the individual self, the Christian soul, whose salvation from hell is at stake. In addition, coworkers and families are considered stakeholders. To say the least, this list is very different from the typical list of parties that most organizations and institutions consider to be stakeholders.

This deliberately limited list of stakeholders serves a vital function: it provides the Religion-Based Organization with another strong and identifiable source of certainty, clarity, and simplicity, even at the expense of departing from normal business reality. The certainty accorded these stakeholders also justifies the necessity of intervening in the spiritual life of others in the workplace. The notion of this necessity is derived from of a sense of mission: that to save souls from an eternity in hell one is obligated as a member of a Religion-Based Organization to confront one's colleagues in the workplace to turn their eyes toward God. In the language of business, one has an obligation at work to become an *active intervener* or a *stakeholder for Christ*.

The Principle of Spiritually Managed Growth

> The world says to grow your business regardless of the circumstances at home. God's Word said you should be devoted to one another. My Dad knew he could not remain devoted to his family and employees if he chose to grow [his] business. Maybe others can properly balance such a heavy load and, if so, then keep building. But remain devoted to one another.[13]

We have reserved for last one of the more admirable principles of Religion-Based Organizations—and in fact, of spiritual and value-driven organizations in general: the conscious choice to limit growth and manage greed. This choice comes about through explicit recognition that the accumulation of profits or anything else can get out of hand and become addictive. Growth beyond reason, especially growth rationalized in the name of reason, is dysfunctional.

The choice to limit growth is strongly connected in Religion-Based Organizations to the principle of spiritual connectedness—the notion that all underlying organizational principles, as well as business actions and decisions, are interconnected, that they form a tightly integrated system. There is no alternative in such a system but to foster and protect this interconnectedness through controlled and balanced growth.

Subsidiary Principles and Clever Tactics

There is no doubt whatsoever that the ultimate goal of the pure religious model is the complete takeover of the organization for Christ. Nonetheless, there is a fair amount of subversiveness, even duplicity, surrounding how to go about it. This approach is reflected in subsidiary management principles, or creative tactics, that are played out beneath the surface of the organization.

Even though direct intervention in the name of Christ is not only justified but mandated in the Religion-Based Organization, there is also the recognition that a direct frontal assault is likely to turn off all but the most avid of employees. Thus, according to TYWFC, one is advised to proceed quietly and cautiously, as follows:

> As you begin inspecting your workplace through the eyes of Jesus, you should keep quiet about what you are doing. I say this for three reasons: (1) This is the time to "be still." Let God reveal the needs around you. (2) Others will mask their behavior if they know you are watching. You must discover their true need. (3) Your intentions may cause misunderstanding among your peers. Some people will incorrectly see your effort as an attempt to browbeat your colleagues.[14]

One passage of TYWFC goes so far as to recommend that one act like a "stealth bomber" in all efforts to "capture" one's workplace for Christ.[15]

Another, more subtle tactic is to keep a "spiritual Rolodex"—this is a direct quote!—in which one lists the needs of one's coworkers and the "spiritual progress" one is making in turning them toward the Word of God. Other recommended strategies involve adopting clever biblical names for personal e-mail addresses and using portions of scripture as screen savers on personal computers.

It must be recognized that all such tactics are in service of a coherent, consistent, and integrated set of principles. It is also evident that the principles are made on a bedrock of certainty, clarity, and simplicity that justifies the use of such tactics.

To most people, and to most organizations, however, the price to be paid for certainty, clarity, and simplicity is too high. The adherence to such principles both requires and reinforces an extremely homogeneous workforce that is willing to abide by a strict social contract. (Indeed, one Religion-Based Organization of which we are aware actually counts the number of times Jesus is mentioned in a preemployment application and uses the information in its selection process.)

The greatest price of certainty, however, as many see it, is the danger that the Religion-Based Organization may be a thinly disguised cult. This is indeed one of the criticisms leveled frequently at organizations run by the Mormon Church. There is little doubt that cultish organizations discourage the very diversity of the workforce that is required to function in a complex world. Homogeneous workplaces and organizations function best only in extremely stable and invulnerable environments. Today's work environments are anything but this.

Closing Reflections

The primary intention of this chapter has been to evaluate critically the underpinnings of the Religion-Based Organization. Whatever one thinks of its underlying principles (the policy of limiting growth and greed is likely to be seen as admirable while a dedication to total transformation of the workplace is likely to be seen as insupportable), they help us to realize this model's benefits and limitations. The handful of individuals in our study who either were or had been members of Religion-Based Organizations echoed these polarities in describing their experiences, with comments ranging from the extremes of "wonderful" to "absolutely suffocating."

The benefits of working in a Religion-Based Organization are many: one is an active and respected participant in a coherent and cohesive belief system, one is a member of a community bound together by deep feelings and emotions, there is a prevailing sense of spiritual oneness and connectedness, life-long friendships are encouraged and nourished, a sense of harmony is fostered between one's work and all other aspects of one's life, a common language is used, and most of all, there is the satisfaction that one's beliefs are grounded in ultimate truths. Conversely, all these benefits have to be balanced against the weaknesses attendant in homogeneous workplaces in general and in religious ones in particular: the dominance of a single viewpoint, the restrictions imposed on actions and decisions, and the expectation of conformity in all matters, to name a few.

To most readers, the principles of the Religion-Based Organization will probably, on the whole, be strongly unacceptable. Although the majority of our respondents did not clearly articulate the principles as we've expressed them here—indeed, as we've indicated, most of our respondents were aware of neither the various models nor their underlying principles—a general sense of awareness was operating nonetheless in the general feeling that any and all expression of religion in the workplace is highly inappropriate. We are inclined strongly to agree with them, even though we realize it may be difficult to ban all religious talk because it can be construed as protected speech. Nonetheless, in spite of the legal difficulties, the vast majority of our respondents felt that it was highly desirable to set clear limits on religious expression and talk in the workplace. Many felt even more strongly that zero-based tolerance policies should be set. In other words, no religious talk at all should be tolerated. However unfortunate this attitude may be, it means that employees who consider religion extremely important in their lives will not be able to realize their full potential in most work environments. The most desirable if not the only alternative may be for them to seek employment in expressly religious organizations.

In assessing the benefits and limitations associated with Religion-Based Organizations it can be helpful to see them in terms of a very particular state of religious development. In a remarkable book entitled *Stages of Faith*, theologian James Fowler presents a developmental theory of religious faith modeled after the work of Harvard psychologist Lawrence Kohlberg on the stages of moral development in children.[16] Although Fowler's work does not explicitly address organizations, it is possible to draw parallels between his stages of individual religious development and those of organizations. A direct inference from Fowler's work is that the Religion-Based Organization, as it currently exists, is at an early, if not "primitive," stage of religious development. This stage is, in Fowler's words, one of the "mythic-literal faith . . . in which the person begins to take on for him- or herself the stories, beliefs and observances that symbolize belonging to his or her community. Beliefs are appropriated with literal interpretations, as are moral rules and attitudes."[17] The parallels to the principles of Religion-Based Organizations are apparent.

This stage in which symbols are "taken as one-dimensional and literal in meaning"[18] is also a stage in which we are invested in our own "cosmic stories" or dramatic narratives. But as Fowler points out, this is not a stage in which we "step back from the flow of stories to formulate reflective, conceptual meanings. For this stage, the meaning is both carried and 'trapped' in the narrative."[19] Organizations at this stage are trapped in the belief that their version, or story, of religion or their style of management, and theirs alone, is the only true path to God.

As a final note, it is important to stress that not all Religion-Based Organizations are as extreme as the portrait drawn in this chapter. (Indeed, we were fortunate to be able to interview members of more moderate and tolerant Religion-Based Organizations.) Not all Religion-Based Organizations believe the myth that their religion and theirs alone is the only true path to God. As with all things human, there is a wide spectrum to be found.

Many Religion-Based Organizations are much more ecumenical than the one described here. For this reason, the model in this chapter is probably better described as a Fundamentalist Religion-Based Organization. More ecumenical Religion-Based Organizations are more closely aligned with the models in later chapters. For this reason, we have deferred discussion of them until later in the book.

Chapter Five

Called to Spirituality

The Evolutionary Organization

Larry M. Rosen, the current head of the Los Angeles chapter of the Young Men's Christian Association (YMCA), is a Jew. He is the only Jew ever to head a major chapter in the history of the organization. In Ian Mitroff's interview with him, Rosen referred to the significance of this fact. "Because the YMCA had a long history as a religious organization from its mid-nineteenth-century origins, and because it has been steadily *transformed* [emphasis added] during the twentieth century from an essentially evangelical Protestant Christian organization to a more ecumenical one, it is extremely comfortable talking about spirituality. The fact that I am a Jew and was appointed head of a major YMCA is not only proof of how far the YMCA movement has come, but also of how ecumenical it is."

It is to Rosen that we owe the idea of the model of the Evolutionary Organization. In effect, Rosen suggested that the YMCA evolved over the course of its history from a Religion-Based Organization to an Evolutionary Organization. However, he was unable to spell out the details of this transformation or the details of the evolutionary model.

In this chapter, we explore two very different organizations—the YMCA and Tom's of Maine—and how they evolved from rather traditional religious bases into organizations with much broader and more ecumenical outlooks. On the face of it, these two organizations could not be more different from one another with regard to mission, purpose, size, and scope of operation. The YMCA is a not-for-profit organization that exists to meet the social and spiritual needs of individuals, communities, and even whole societies. It has hundreds of entities and employs tens of thousands of paid workers and volunteers. Its reach is virtually worldwide. In contrast, Tom's of Maine[1] is a small, privately owned, entrepreneurial business headquartered in northern New England. It manufactures and promotes environmentally friendly hygiene products such as toothpastes, soaps, and shampoos. One organization is a giant institution, the other is a small company—yet both are prime examples of the Evolutionary Organization.

The YMCA and Tom's of Maine are striking examples of different modes and time frames of evolution, or reactive versus proactive responses to change. The YMCA evolved over decades of changing social times and all manner of institutional crises. Tom's of Maine evolved over a short but intense period of personal crisis and subsequent organizational change. Comparing two such vastly different examples helps give a sense of the variety of types that lie along the spectrum of Evolutionary Organizations.

In purely chronological terms, the YMCA evolved over a period of some 150 years, while Tom's of Maine evolved over a 5- to 7-year period. In the YMCA's case, as we shall soon show, the relatively long time frame reflects complex interactions between forces inside and outside the organization. It also reflects the YMCA's characteristic mode, as an institution of reactive change, of intervening in response to changing needs and circumstances.

Tom's of Maine evolved in a very short time, primarily by actively seeking out and courting change. This was possible only because, unlike the YMCA, it had a single leader, Tom Chappell, and because it experienced different crises and interventions. Whether relatively long or short, however, the element of time reflects both the strengths and the weaknesses of the Evolutionary Organization.

A major strength of the Evolutionary Organization is the endurance of its efforts. The time invested in change helps to ensure that the changes produced will be deep and long-lasting, rather than superficial and transitory, as is the case with the vast majority of organizational change efforts. Conversely, the length of time invested, as well as the nature and number of crises and interventions, places severe constraints on those choosing to adopt this model. A great many individuals and organizations are bound to feel unwilling or unable to make the commitment and sacrifices required.

Another consideration is that the long investment in realizing a mission, as the YMCA as an institution sought to do, or in answering a calling, as Tom Chappell did as an individual, is potentially the best test of the mission's worthiness. But the evolutionary nature of the process can also act to change the mission substantially before it can be realized, as happened more than once over the YMCA's long history.

The YMCA: Changing Times and Changing Missions

For ease of discussion, the history of the YMCA can be divided into three overlapping phases: (1) from its founding in 1844 to the 1920s, (2) from the 1920s to the 1960s, and (3) from the 1960s to the present.

The Founding Phase Turns Radical

In its founding phase, the YMCA was governed by a single, major mission: to aid the hordes of young men and women leaving the farms, first in small numbers and then in droves, to come to the cities in search of work. *Aid* meant a number of things: facilitating the transition from farms to factories, easing the stresses of the Industrial Revolution, providing a safe haven from the licentiousness of city life, shoring up Christian values threatened by exposure to wide varieties of sin, providing inexpensive room and board for young people working for subsistence or near-subsistence wages, and seeing that proper Christian values were maintained by its clientele, thus providing businessmen and factory owners, many of whom were on YMCA boards of directors, with a virtuous and willing workforce. The YMCA also felt that it was necessary to perform all of these tasks in such a way that the established churches would not feel that the YMCA was encroaching on their missions. Indeed, the association between the YMCA and the official Protestant churches was so strong that in 1869 the YMCA adopted an evangelical test "stipulating that active association members had to be members of a Protestant congregation."[2]

Thus the YMCA sought to regulate the social lives and preserve the Christian mores of those in its care. But social life rarely conforms to the best-laid plans of mice or men. Providing a safe haven for young men and women and helping them maintain their meek Christian values was attractive to employers, but it had quite another outcome than what was intended. Working for wages that barely sustained them and being taken advantage of by ruthless employers had the ultimate effect of radicalizing the young men and women who were first attracted to the YMCA. At the risk of over-simplification, the YMCA steadily came to be in league with factory owners and leaders of business in opposing the cause of organized labor. However, its opposition helped bring to the verge of action those whom it tried to keep innocent for service in abusive factories and businesses.

The YMCA finally came to realize that if it wanted to keep its clientele, it had to rethink and reshape its mission. It had to do much more than quietly minister to young people's moral, religious, and spiritual needs. It had to begin serving their secular needs as well, including equipping them to confront abusive employment practices. Events forced the YMCA to respond increasingly to secular social forces. Unexpectedly, its responses to external events did much to change the YMCA's religious identity. Thus, in admittedly shortened form, a series of social forces and repeated crises proved instrumental in the YMCA's evolution to the second and reactionary phase of its development.

A Long Period of Backlash

Whereas phase one of the YMCA's history was marked by the transition of the indigenous U.S. farm population into the large industrial cities, phase two was marked by the arrival in waves of European immigrants, their difficult integration into U.S. life, and the ensuing changes this brought to U.S. culture. Much as the founding phase ended in a backlash brought on by the many unforeseen and unintended effects of the YMCA's policies, so did the second phase. The backlash was equally strong, but of a different kind.

The waves of new European immigrants bore no resemblance to the earlier groups of mainly white, Anglo-Saxon, Protestant emigrants from U.S. farms to the cities. The new arrivals were certainly not Anglo, let alone Protestant. An increasing number of the new Y members were Catholics and Jews. Some came from rural areas of their homelands, but many had lived in cities.

The influx of immigrants put new pressures on the YMCA. In addition to continuing demands to champion the needs of young Christian men and women for better wages and working conditions, the newcomers were clamoring for entrance into all phases of American life.

At the same time, another force, heretofore silent, was gathering momentum. Blacks were becoming a more powerful, vocal presence in the cities of both the North and the South, demanding racial justice. Founded on the spirit and mission—indeed, the very words—of Christ, the YMCA could not without substantial contradiction ignore the rightful demands and pleas for social justice by blacks. Although it maintained "separate but equal" chapters well into the twentieth century, the YMCA nonetheless became a significant, and more often than not the only, training ground for black leadership. In time, blacks would even assume prominent places of leadership in the YMCA, though not without considerable resistance by the white majority.

Its sensitivity to the plight of blacks notwithstanding, the YMCA was still open to charges of racial discrimination. Its policies and governing structure largely mirrored the attitudes and overrepresentation of the dominant white culture. In the charged political climate of the 1950s and 1960s, evidence of racism in the YMCA and other major institutions of U.S. life began to take on more inflammatory and symbolic meaning. Godless communism and socialism were being proclaimed as among our most dangerous enemies by many of the most powerful and influential members of American society. If America and her institutions, of which the YMCA was one of the most prominent, were to stand up to communism and socialism, then not only democratic but both democratic and Christian ideals and commitments had to be honored. If Christ truly represented universal tolerance and brotherhood, then racism could not be tolerated in any institution that invoked him. Racism was no longer just a blemish; it was totally unacceptable. The YMCA, as a result, was forced to take strong stands on civil rights and social injustice.

The responsive new leadership taking shape at the YMCA no longer represented the interests of businessmen and powerful economic institutions alone. More and more, the interests of the poor and downtrodden were represented. Significantly, this period stands out as one of the few in the YMCA's history in which it was proactive in courting, if not actively leading, the way to change. From the press of the period came a report of the new leadership eschewing "religious exclusivity and embracing the redefinition of Jesus along the lines of a rebel, a figure to be respected, not for his divine parentage, but for the intensity of his social commitment."[3]

Initially, the new leadership was carried along by the momentum associated with the great social upheavals that have occurred throughout U.S. history. Those spearheading these efforts believed honestly and deeply, if not somewhat naively, that significant and long-lasting changes could be made in the fabric of American life. When such changes proved harder to materialize, and even harder to take root, than was hoped, the inevitable result was the disillusionment that began the YMCA's third phase.

More Unexpected and Unplanned Change

Disillusionment over the changing social fabric reached its apex nationally with the late stages of the Vietnam War. As this conflict grew to crescendo, manifesting in increasingly unrestful or violent ways, profound social and economic changes of another sort were going on. Reacting to the extreme difficulty, if not impossibility, of a single wage earner providing for the economic needs of a family, women thronged to the workplace in record-setting numbers.

The impact on the YMCA was one it had experienced repeatedly over its history. Unexpected, unplanned, and even unwanted social changes worked to change the YMCA far more dramatically than any of its own plans and policies. As the pressures of work life increased sharply for both men and women, they sought a safe haven to which they could escape and relax. The YMCA responded to this new need, becoming well-appointed health clubs and recreation centers for the increasingly affluent middle class.

One after the other, the YMCA's founding principles led to unintended and even undesired social consequences, either immediately or in later phases. For instance, from its founding the YMCA had housed young men and women separately to control sexual entanglements, but this later led to the YMCA's becoming a testing ground for sexual exploration with members of the same sex. In the 1960s, the YMCAs were well known nationally as places where homosexuals could "cruise" with relative ease and safety. The YMCA's sexual policies provided a perfect environment in which gays could meet and conduct sexual encounters.

Changing Business Principles of the YMCA

From even this brief sketch of the YMCA's long and complex history, contrasts between its business principles and those of the Religion-Based Organization begin to emerge. Recall from the last chapter that the main business text of the Religion-Based Organization is the Word of God. Though this may have been the main text with which the YMCA started, over time it was strongly amended by the "Word of Society," or social forces. In other words, the main text became conditioned by external secular forces.

Other principles connected with the YMCA's original religious basis, such as ownership by God and competition from the Devil, also underwent alteration. In the fundamentalist religious organization, God is both CEO and owner, as realized through the figure of his Son, Jesus Christ. This embodiment took on a very different meaning in the YMCA as Christ became more and more identified with his earthly role of exemplary social activist or reformer. The Devil as chief competition likewise changed face over the course of the YMCA's history. Originally construed as the sinfulness of city life to which young people fresh off the farms were exposed, over time and through the reformists' eyes the Devil took on the guise of unscrupulous business owners who exploited workers, unscrupulous labor leaders who exploited their members, and eventually racists who resisted the inclusion and equal treatment of blacks.

Even though the YMCA was never, even initially, as zealously fundamentalist as the organization portrayed in *Transforming Your Workplace for Christ*,[4] it is sadly apparent that in its evolution from being a Religion-Based Organization, something basic and profound has been lost. Although it may have evolved into a more ecumenical, secular, and spiritual organization, the YMCA seems to have let go of much of its former energy. It is visibly less soulful at its core. Its mission, too, is no longer as clear, as distinct, or as freshly appealing as it was early in its history. In short, it has become just another secular organization competing to help overstressed Americans deal with the day-to-day business of their lives. Whether this is the inevitable fate of all organizations that survive the evolution from a religious base to a more ecumenical one is unknown at this point. Although the YMCA may be better able to speak the language of spirituality because of its long religious history, it remains to be seen whether this newfound "spiritual language" has a fundamental purpose to serve in today's world.

None of this, however, should be taken as diminishment of the ease with which the YMCA can and does speak a spiritual language. As an organization, it is extremely comfortable with its brand of spirituality, neither fostering it nor imposing it on anyone. Those who are attracted to the YMCA and to its ecumenical mission and environment likewise appear comfortable and unself-conscious in talking about spirituality, especially as it relates to the meaning to be found in work and in everyday activities.

Tom's of Maine: A Short Course in Evolution

The evolutionary history of Tom's of Maine is an altogether different story from that of the YMCA. In the first place, it is the compressed story of a single individual activated by the immediacy of crisis, not the tale of an entire social institution subject to changing times and circumstances. Second, it is far from an impersonal narrative. It is a story told through the eyes of Tom Chappell himself, owner of Tom's of Maine, with the immediacy and fervor but without the detachment and perspective of a more distant observer.

Tom Chappell relates the story of his own and his company's evolution in his book entitled *The Soul of a Business: Managing for Profit and the Common Good.*[5] He writes in candid terms of a time before the changes wrought by his spiritual "awakening," when he seemed to have achieved everything he could want out of life—a successful business, a large salary, a strong marriage and family, a big house, a big boat, and all manner of material possessions. But he goes on to tell of having awakened one day to feelings of deep disappointment, depression, and disillusionment, and furthermore, being utterly mystified as to why. In equally revelatory language, he writes of the sudden dawning of insight, of realizing that in the course of meeting his wants he had lost the most valuable thing of all—his soul.

Interestingly, particularly in light of his eventual actions, Chappell looked to his minister rather than to a therapist or clinician for guidance. His minister proclaimed vociferously that there was indeed a way out of Chappell's depression and it was through embracing his business—Chappell's business was his ministry and his calling. However, the minister's words only confirmed Chappell's belief that his basic problem was the loss of his soul. Where could he go and what could he do to regain it?

Naturally entrepreneurial, Chappell had the innate means to find answers to his own questions. Yet in a move that surprised even himself, he paid a visit to the Harvard Divinity School, became convinced of the need to study theology in a nondenominational setting, and decided that this departure was the only way he could regain his soul.

Chappell's journey of study and discovery is instructive at the same time that it makes for interesting reading on a number of levels, including an allegorical one. In allegorical terms, in heeding the call to regain his soul and embrace his ministry, he embarked on the classic odyssey of the hero, captured so well by Joseph Campbell in *The Hero with a Thousand Faces*.[6] Upon hearing the call, heeding it is crucial. If a person receives a calling but doesn't follow it, not only will that person stay depressed, but his or her soul will remain undeveloped.

Next, having heard the call and having decided to heed it, Chappell had to convince others, namely the board of directors of his company, of his need for a four-year partial leave of absence—the benefits of which were far from clear at that point and not at all quantifiable—to pursue his calling. Chappell eventually succeeded in convincing his board with the argument that he would continue to manage and oversee his business while on leave at Harvard. With this last hurdle overcome, he embarked on his journey with great enthusiasm.

Chappell's book provides a new philosophical rationale and foundation for running a spiritually based business that stems from his reading of the great philosophers while at Harvard. He takes careful note of the fact that the basic language of utilitarians—the philosophers of business—is that of benefits versus costs. The fundamental utilitarian principle is, Do what is best for an organization as a whole, even if it means hurting individuals. *Best* is defined as those actions whose benefits are greater than their associated costs.

At Harvard, Chappell was also exposed to another language or tradition in ethics, one based on rights, duties, and obligations, as well as on the universal commandment to do what is right and eth-

ical even if it doesn't always translate into greater profits or immediate benefits to one's business. Armed with his new concepts and
language, he recounted being able, for the first time, to stand up to
his internal voices of competition, or his "Devil within," as well as
to external voices (the accountants, the professional managers, and
the members of the board of directors of his company). He argued
as many times as was necessary to convince them that a business
based on the quality of its products and on doing what is right for
the customer would not only survive but prosper.

Chappell's utter conviction is crucial because, as Joseph Campbell points out, the most difficult part of the hero's journey occurs
when he returns from his quest, not when he starts out. He then has
to persuade those who have not gone on the journey of the new realities he alone has been privileged to apprehend. In Chappell's
case, he had to convince everyone in his organization, from executives on down, to adopt the new spiritual mission and integrate it
with every other aspect of running the company.

As anticipated, Chappell was met with fear, anger, and uncertainty—all various expressions of resistance to the unknown—from
all ranks of his company. Executives and subordinates alike had to
be won over slowly through hours of patient listening and continual involvement. Chappell calls this process the "circle of listening," and it remains a vital underlying principle of his business. At
the same time, he had to continue to affirm and integrate traditional business principles into his new vision. This meant that employees would still be made responsible and held strictly accountable
for results. Indeed, they were going to be held even more accountable now that the company was going to produce products that
were ethically viable.

Along the way, and in keeping with the classic hero motif,
Chappell's new vision was constantly and severely tested. At the
same time, it was continually bolstered by new spiritual insights and
epiphanies. To deepen the sense of shared mission and validate the
revamped nature of his company, he repeatedly invited colleagues
and teachers from the Harvard Divinity School to talk to his board

and employees. Not only did these outsiders successfully instruct the board members and employees, but they eventually charmed and won them over to their style of spiritual thinking.

Principles of the Evolutionary Organization

A Series of Essential Crises

In Evolutionary Organizations such as the YMCA and Tom's of Maine, the "crisis principle" is paramount. If the Evolutionary Organization is to transform itself, a crisis—better yet, a series of crises—is absolutely necessary.

There are elements of crisis in the fundamentalist organization—that is, the precipitating events and personal angst of executives described in the last chapter. But the central assumption of the Religion-Based Organization is that through God everything is possible, including the weathering of crises. This does not mean that such organizations are free of major crisis—indeed, the biggest crises are often those that revolve around personal failures to receive Christ—but only God, not the testing done by crisis, is the way to deep, lasting change.

Crucial as it is to the Evolutionary Organization, a major crisis is not by itself generally sufficient to bring about transformation. It is well known that people and organizations go through crises all the time without real change taking place.[7] More often than not, the typical reaction to a crisis is, oddly enough, to apply more of the same principles that led to the crisis in the first place. This is done in the mistaken belief that confronting the crisis can thus be avoided.

It is the rare individual who confronts a crisis by embarking on the hero's journey, the unknown road to change. It is the rare company that overcomes uncertainty and becomes a role model for others to follow. It thus seems a necessary corollary to the crisis principle that a deep crisis of meaning must first be experienced without knowing whether a solution is possible or even exists. This leads to the next principle, readily seen in the foregoing example, of spiritual openness to change.

The Principle of Spiritual Openness

This principle, which calls for a deep but accessible openness to change, is a distinguishing feature of both the Evolutionary Organization and the Recovering Organization (see Chapter Six). A ready and open response to crisis, such as Tom Chappell's response, embodies interesting paradoxes. The individual must be open spiritually to exploring the unknown, without having fully developed yet the spiritual capacities to see the exploration through. The individual whom Joseph Campbell calls the hero must possess a strong will that is ready to be tapped, a readiness to explore a promising but complex future beyond the ordinary.

It is equally critical that the potential hero exhibit spiritual leanings early on in his or her life. The groundwork for the Evolutionary Organization is almost always laid early on and through traditional religious means. Chappell, who was raised Episcopalian, notes early in his book that the Episcopal Church and religion have always played an important role in his life.

Likewise, stirrings about something beyond traditional religious manifestations also occur at an early age. For the most part, these stirrings remain dormant while the hero goes off on other quests. Following the stages of the classic journey, the hero's first task in life is to gain technical mastery over the material aspects of his life. This is necessary before he can undertake the much more serious and perilous task of developing his spiritual side.

The Main Business Texts:
The Works of the Philosophers

In the Evolutionary Organization, the traditional utilitarian-based texts of business are not abandoned altogether. However, they are greatly supplemented and amended.

In contrast to the fundamentalist Religion-Based Organization, where the Word of God alone is the text, the Evolutionary Organization makes a wide range of nonreligious, philosophical texts the basis of the new curriculum. Works by utilitarian philosophers such as Jeremy Bentham, nonutilitarian ethicists such as Immanuel Kant, and religious thinkers such as Reinhold Neibuhr and Martin Buber[8] make up the business canon at Tom's of Maine.

Kant, whose ideas strongly influenced Chappell, believed in an altogether different basis for business ethics than profit projections and cost-benefit calculations. Of utmost importance are Tom's of Maine's stakeholders, whose numbers are to be extended and who, as human beings, are to be treated with utmost dignity and respect. From Buber, who believed that utilitarianism reduces customers to objects, things, or "its," Chappell derived the belief that the relationship between a company's leaders and workers and its customers ought to be one of "I-Thou," not "I-It." Indirectly from Buber, perhaps, came Chappell's emphasis on the need for close spiritual listening, to be taken up in a later principle.

Future Generations: Fundamental Stakeholders

The limited set of stakeholders that helps define the Religion-Based Organization is greatly expanded in the Evolutionary Organization. God continues to be a partner and an important stakeholder, but the Kantian influence is evident in the greater number and type of stakeholders now considered. It is of great significance that future generations, whose importance is not diminished merely because they are not yet born, are counted as stakeholders. Unlike in traditional companies, in the Evolutionary Organization the principle of discounting future generations does not apply. In other words, future generations are not considered less valuable merely because they are in the future (much as future dollars are discounted against those currently in hand). Chappell leaves no doubt whatsoever where he stands:

Once confused about my priorities, I am now very clear: The ultimate goal of business is *not* profit [italics in original]. Profit is merely
a means towards the ultimate end of affirming the health and dignity
of human beings and their families, affirming aspirations of the
community, and affirming the health of the environment—the common good. If our air is polluted, our communities and people polluted, how can our business really prosper? . . .

Is there anyone—or any company—who can argue that the future health of the planet is not in their interest? Are you willing to
say to your children or grandchildren that you don't give a damn
about the condition of the world you will leave them?[9]

Not only does Tom's of Maine extend its list of stakeholders,
but it also allows for inevitable, even desirable, tension to exist between them. The tension that originally arose between Chappell
and his professional staff and board of directors is now expected
and even encouraged by the company as necessary for its ongoing
development. Thus tension between stakeholders is seen as more
than something to be expected and managed—it can be argued
that it is also needed to ensure that the traditional economic concerns of the business are both taken into account and enmeshed
with the new principles. This concern is in keeping with another
principle of the Religion-Based Organization: a conscious restraint
on the size and growth of a company.

The Ultimate Goal: Development, Not Growth

Recall, if you will, the deliberateness with which the Religion-
Based Organization manages growth, its conscious choice to set
limits on size and greed. In the less absolute world of the Evolutionary Organization, the same limitations are acknowledged but
given more play. The Evolutionary Organization is more likely than
the Religion-Based Organization to experience how easy it is to be
led by values and to get trapped by size.

Chappell, like the entrepreneurs of Ben & Jerry's Ice Cream (see Chapter Eight), had an explicit policy of giving more money to outside charities and worthy organizations than most businesses. He reasoned, therefore, that if his organization grew even larger and made more money, he would be able to give even more to worthy causes. Although well-intentioned, his reasoning is faulty. Interestingly, Chappell's better instincts led him away from this thinking and in another direction early on.

In his book, Chappell notes that as part of the process of shifting away from being a traditional utilitarian organization toward being a more ethical and spiritually based one, he and his entire company assembled under a large tent near the manufacturing area to engage in dialogue. Though neither we nor Chappell can offer exact data to support it, there may well be clear constraints or limits on the manageable size of a spiritually based company. In calling his whole company together, Chappell seems to have intuitively realized that if an organization becomes large, it must then be subdivided into units in which people can continue to interact face-to-face. Some have set this number at somewhere between 150 and 300. Certainly this numerical range has not escaped astute observers of human interaction throughout history. For instance, it is hardly accidental that the size of an army company is around 150 soldiers. Certainly no organization, including the Catholic Church, has demonstrated how to maintain a spiritually based economic entity whose participants number in the thousands.

It appears, then, that 150 to 300 is the maximum size of the human unit in which people can still interact on a one-to-one basis and with personal knowledge of one another. Beyond this point, people shade into statistical abstractions—and if anything seems critical to the Evolutionary Organization, it is that people not be treated as numbers or abstractions.

Russell Ackoff, one of this country's premier thinkers and writers on strategy and systems thinking, offers what may be the best and most cogent explanation of the soundness of this management principle.[10] He notes that growth and development are not the same. Many organizations, including biological and physical phenomena, grow without developing—for example, cemeteries and nuclear waste dumps. The point is that Evolutionary Organizations may have to limit growth consciously so they can develop. In such organizations, the governing principle is "less is more." We say more about this principle in succeeding chapters because it is probably the least understood of all the principles underpinning spiritually based organizations.

Spiritual Listening: Absolutely Essential

Alluded to earlier by Chappell, the principle of spiritual listening derives from the Religion-Based Organization. In that model, as you may recall, the listening channels are tuned to receive the Word of God. In this model they are tuned to communication taking place at all levels of the organization.

Chappell writes that he was too far in front of his internal stakeholders for them to absorb his message. He learned painfully that for communication to happen he had to engage his board, his managers, and his employees continually in concentrated "active listening." He had to spend countless hours patiently and willingly listening, not responding in reaction to anything that was said, in order to absorb fully and attempt to allay the anxieties and fears of his colleagues. Although the current term in the organizational development literature is *active listening, spiritual listening*, with its implication of engagement at the deepest layer of being, better fits the philosophy at Tom's and like-minded organizations. A tradition of seminars, personal study and reflection, circles for listening, and other forms of training are in keeping with the communication style and set of beliefs of the Evolutionary Organization.

Hope and the Ultimate Purpose of Business

Hope and purpose—what the business puts its faith in and what it makes its ultimate goal—are closely allied principles of the

Evolutionary Organization. Because a shift to a broader spiritual outlook is taking place, hope and optimism lie in the outcome of evolution itself. Evolution toward a more spiritual basis and a more ethical operation is not merely hoped for but altogether possible when measured by a different yardstick of success. Evolutionary Organizations recognize explicitly that profits are only a means, not the end, to fulfilling a company's true purpose. The true end, and ultimate aim, is doing good for one's customers. If this occurs, profits will follow. Provable or not, this principle is the fundamental belief of an ethically based business.

In a strikingly worded passage, Chappell notes that the bottom-line "habits" of traditional business no longer drive his company. The choice of the word *habit* is deliberate, indicating his belief that it takes serious and sustained work to break the hold of traditional rules and standards by which one's business has been measured. As his remarks suggest, as much as tremendous energy and will are needed to develop and maintain a traditional business, even more are needed to build and sustain a nontraditional business. Contrary to common expectation, the road to building a spiritually based business is not easier. Indeed, in many ways, it is harder. Not only are there skeptical stockholders, board members, and professional managers to face, there are also employees who expect and demand more of an ethically based organization, and of whom, in turn, more is demanded, both in performance and in toleration of a wide range of emotions.

Toleration and Expression of Deep Emotions

The toleration of a wide range of emotions is such an exceptional and accepted part of the Evolutionary Organization, it is important to explore it as a principle. One of the reasons that such organizations may be so difficult to create and maintain is that their emotional expectations are set extremely high. Companies like Tom's of Maine are as invested in cultivating a deep and free range of emotional expression as they are in cultivating respect for the environment and spirituality. To put it mildly, this can be extremely scary and anxiety-inducing for many employees, especially men, who have been taught and learned extremely well how to put a tight lid on their emotions, especially at work.

The emotional range of this model takes in both negative and positive extremes. Expressions of joy and loss are likely to extend well beyond everyday events at the office to profound and difficult matters outside it, such as illness, death, recovery, and family turmoil. At one point, Chappell recounts in detail a time during which his company grieved together, as a family, in response to an employee's sudden loss of his wife's relatives in a car accident.[11]

This is not to say that such acts of emotional support and mutual sharing do not go on in traditional organizations. They frequently do. Indeed, many of the principles characteristic of Evolutionary Organizations can be found in other types of organizations as well. Generally, however, only one or two of these principles exist and operate to any great extent in traditional organizations. What is so distinctive about the Evolutionary Organization is the combination, reinforcement, and interaction of principles as a total system. Moreover, the Evolutionary Organization has a strong sense of itself as a tightly integrated and interconnected system, expressed quite often in ecological terms. Tom's of Maine has been called, and has called itself, an *ecosystem:* a system that must maintain a delicate but crucial balance.

Subsidiary Principle and Relations with Employees

Like the Religion-Based Organization, the Evolutionary Organization has subsidiary principles that further distinguish it as a model. It is known for how it relates to its employees and for the standards it sets for their performance.

To begin with, the Evolutionary Organization has an explicit subsidiary principle for valuing the whole person. Not only are employees given permission to bring their souls to work with them, but they are expected to do so. There is every recognition that one can never fully leave one's personal issues at the office doorstep. They are intertwined with everything one does.

Also, given the Evolutionary Organization's recognition of the wholeness of individual systems and their interconnectedness, not surprisingly this model employs a much broader and more personal vocabulary than other models. Its vocabulary is not rooted in impersonal utilitarian terms such as *costs and benefits*. It is not afraid to speak openly of caring, dignity, hope, integrity, love, optimism, sharing, and trust. Further, these qualities are not simply abstract ideals, but an integral part of the organization's spiritual infrastructure.

The heavy emphasis on spiritual values and a spiritual infrastructure, however, does not allow for less than high-level performance. For employees to think otherwise is sheer folly. Evolutionary Organizations are, if anything, even more demanding of their employees' performance than other organizations. High-sounding words like *excellence* and *spirituality* do not cut it without visible evidence of their realization. To raise expectations of a higher-than-ordinary level of performance and then not deliver on them is to court disaster.

Spiritually based organizations do not shrink from difficult tasks like firing employees who are not up to the standards demanded by their jobs. They also do not shrink from expecting their members to continue their spiritual progress. For the evolving organization to prosper, all of its employees must be perpetual students. Those who are unable or unwilling to adhere to this standard will not be ministered to as they are in the Religion-Based Organization; they will be let go in the most humane ways possible. High standards, in both idea and practice, are indicative of a final principle, the necessity of spiritual autonomy.

The Principle of Spiritual Autonomy

This is a definitive principle of the Evolutionary Organization and poses a greater challenge than it appears to on the surface. Chappell makes it clear that he and his wife together control more than

50 percent of the stock of Tom's of Maine. Retaining a controlling share may be absolutely crucial for the Evolutionary Organization if it is to remain master of its fate and controller of its destiny. Time and again Chappell relates how he has been approached by much larger organizations wanting to take him over. They just "don't get it," he is wont to exclaim, when it comes to understanding the principles on which his business is based.

The preservation of the integrity of principles through financial and spiritual autonomy may be a further limitation on the size of the Evolutionary Organization. It remains to be seen whether large organizations, especially multinationals, can be spiritual in other than isolated pockets.

Closing Reflections

The organizations portrayed in this chapter are but two representatives along a broad continuum of Evolutionary Organizations, and Evolutionary Organizations represent but one way or model of becoming spiritual.

In both examples, transformation was brought about through sustained hard work. There should be no illusions whatsoever about the systematic and sustained effort required of an organization to become more spiritually based. Without this effort, no organization will develop sufficient spirituality or be able to maintain it.

The differing nature of the events and time frames at work in transforming these two organizations also helps account for the specific ways in which they each practice their spirituality. As noted earlier, the YMCA is at once unself-conscious and explicitly self-conscious about its practice. Its expressions of spirituality have come to be a natural, taken-for-granted part of its culture. This is probably one of the best ways for an organization to practice and renew spirituality. But the YMCA is equally self-conscious in its care not to express spirituality in denominational terms. It has learned how to make spirituality available in ways that are open to the widest possible number of people.

The views that evolved at Tom's of Maine are somewhat different. Because its transformation was accomplished over a much shorter period and through the medium of internal efforts, it is fairly conscious and explicit about its underlying business principles, even if they have not been examined as systematically or presented as overtly as we have done in this chapter.

We want to state again our impression that the YMCA may have become so comfortable with its form of spiritual language that it has fallen into a "slumber zone" with regard to its practice. The passion toward its spirituality appears to have waned. Tom's of Maine is evolving, at least for now, in a different direction. Given its youth, it has greater energy, enthusiasm, and passion. Its spirituality is alive and sparkling, even if its genesis quite naturally invokes skepticism mixed with wonder.

If it is necessary for company leaders to undergo divinity school, or an equally strong reeducation, the applicability and adoption of the Evolutionary Organization throughout corporate America will obviously be limited. If, however, Tom's of Maine is exemplary of the kind of change that can be achieved through the investigation and practice of ideas that are sharply at variance with today's business education, ideology, and practice, then it is on target as a valuable corporate model. What we can hope to take from Chappell's example is not that divinity or any other type of schooling is necessary to make a lasting transformation, but rather that a prolonged and sustained reexamination of the principles on which one's business is founded is warranted.

Finally, in closing we must note that many of the principles in this chapter are vague, especially compared with those that define the Religion-Based Organization. The evolution of the spiritually based organization is still taking place; its leading examples are still so early in their infancy that we are lacking the specificity that we would like. At this juncture of the development of these organizations, the principles must remain more in the form of guidelines than as exact and detailed operating principles. Even so, they illustrate unequivocally the tone or spirit of the Evolutionary Organization.

Chapter Six

Shaking Off Addiction

The Recovering Organization

I dropped out for two months last year. I went to
Colorado and took off my watch, I just dropped off.
I was astonished at how much stress I had been
living under for the last 35 years. The stress just
peeled off and peeled off and peeled off and the
adrenaline drained out of me. . . . I've got to learn
to live at a much lower adrenaline level and be
happy with myself. I've got to learn not to be
totally *addicted* to a schedule of rapid interaction
with others, to be *addicted* to how others see me,
something which unfortunately, is extremely
important in terms of running a business [italics
added].

—*Bhavin Shah*

On more than one occasion we were fortunate to interview individuals who had been or were currently in Alcoholics Anonymous
(AA). Spirituality is a central feature of AA, so these people had a
specific model, an explicit guide, for talking about spirituality in
ways that were neither offensive nor threatening to others. A few
of our respondents had even tried on their own to adapt and practice isolated features of AA in their organizations. They had consciously tried to use some of the aspects of AA (such as the Twelve
Steps; see Table 6.1) as management principles. They had thus tried
to extend AA from the individual to the organizational level. Most

of these people took care not to mention to their coworkers the source of their new management principles; others were quite open and aboveboard about what they were doing.

AA as a Model for Spirituality in the Workplace

The most dramatic example of the use of AA as a model for fostering spirituality in the workplace occurred in a not-for-profit, social

Table 6.1. The Twelve Steps of Alcoholics Anonymous.

Step	Statement
1.	We admitted we were powerless over alcohol—that our lives had become unmanageable.
2.	We came to believe that a Power greater than ourselves could restore us to sanity.
3.	We made a decision to turn our will and our lives over to the care of God *as we understood Him*.
4.	Made a searching and fearless moral inventory of ourselves.
5.	Admitted to God, to ourselves, and to another human being the exact nature of our wrongs.
6.	Were entirely ready to have God remove all these defects of character.
7.	Humbly asked Him to remove our shortcomings.
8.	Made a list of all persons we had harmed, and became willing to make amends to them all.
9.	Made direct amends to such people wherever possible, except when to do so would injure them or others.
10.	Continued to take personal inventory and when we were wrong promptly admitted it.
11.	Sought through prayer and meditation to improve our conscious contact with God *as we understood Him*, praying only for knowledge of His will for us and the power to carry that out.
12.	Having had a spiritual awakening as the result of these steps, we tried to carry this message to alcoholics, and to practice these principles in all our affairs.

Source: Alcoholics Anonymous World Services, *Alcoholics Anonymous Comes of Age: A Brief History of AA* (New York: Alcoholics Anonymous World Services, Inc., 1985), pp. 59–60.

service organization where Ian Mitroff had the good fortune to interview most of the members of the senior staff. In the course of being interviewed by Mitroff, the director of the organization mentioned casually that, along with most of his senior staff, he had been in AA for years. As a result, he and his colleagues were extremely comfortable talking about their spirituality with anyone in the organization. They were able to do so in nonsectarian, nonproselytizing terms. Their spirituality was a well-developed, well-practiced, taken-for-granted skill. It was part of their everyday being.

The fact that the director and most of his executive staff were associated with AA meant that the organization had a critical mass of key personnel who were not only extremely comfortable but also highly schooled in talking about spirituality, as well as in translating it into the organization's day-to-day behavior. Even so, it was apparent from their responses to the interview questions (see Appendix A) as well as from their descriptions of their organization's behavior that the translation and practice were more implicit than explicit.

Despite the relatively long history and widespread diffusion of the systematic application of the principles of AA to the design and management of organizations, we still do not have significant examples of the Recovering Organization. Nonetheless, there are strong indications that people are starting to think seriously about such applications.[1] Among all the models for fostering spirituality, the Recovering Organization has the most explicitly developed set of rules for talking about spirituality in ways that are acceptable to the largest number of people. This feature alone makes it extremely important.

AA is peculiar in that it both is and is not an organization. It certainly is not an organization in the traditional or typical sense of the term. There are no permanent leaders at either the local or the national level. It has no formal or hierarchical structure. It supports no political causes or outside social interests. Furthermore, people are free to come and go from particular AA groups as they desire. They are also free to start new groups when and if they desire.

Conversely, if one interprets the word *organization* to mean a group of individuals who are dedicated to helping one another no matter how long it takes, then AA is an organization. Better yet, in its own words, it is a "fellowship" dedicated to one and only one goal: helping individuals in their lifelong battle to recover from alcoholism.

The words *cure* and *final recovery* are absent from AA's vocabulary. There is no complete or final cure for alcoholism. Recovery is a never-ending process. It is not a final state or event.

Our analysis of AA and its extension to organizations is not merely the result of an examination of the relevant published literature on AA.[2] It is also based on extensive personal observation of AA meetings and on observing other recovery groups that are based on AA's principles—the Twelve Steps and Traditions—such as Marijuana Anonymous, of which Mitroff's youngest brother, Michael, was a member until his untimely and premature death. In addition, we have attended numerous AA meetings with close friends and colleagues who were "working the program."

AA's Principles

AA is not a religious organization per se, but its principles explicitly embody a strong spiritual outlook. In addition, the principles are remarkably similar to those of the other models we have encountered.

AA's principles are frank and unequivocal. They leave no doubt whatsoever that, left to their own devices, individual addicts are totally unable to cure their addictions. Although individual willpower is necessary, and hence required, there is also the fundamental recognition in AA that something more or greater than oneself is also required. This something greater is referred to as a "higher power."

In terms of the depth of commitment to belief and absolute faith in a god or higher power that is required for recovery, AA's principles are extremely close to those of the Religion-Based Organization. Yet in some ways AA's principles are even stronger and pose even tougher challenges. For one thing, AA places clear and strong constraints on "managing addictive impulses" through its severe and exacting principles as well as its tradition of Twelve Steps. In addition, the guiding principles and the Twelve Steps form an integrated system of beliefs and actions. In essence, AA is a *total ethical management system*—a system for managing not only alcohol or other addictive substances but also underlying and more frankly raw addictions to greed, power, and compulsion.

As unique as AA is among organizations, its general principles—principles of hope, response to crisis, ultimate sources of wisdom, spiritual talking and listening, management of greed, attention to various stakeholders, management of size, and so forth—are again remarkably similar to those found in other models of spirituality in the workplace. This does not mean that AA's principles necessarily appear in the same order or are expressed in the same language as the principles of other models. Nor is there necessarily an exact, one-to-one correspondence of principles between models. However, on the whole, the same general kinds of spiritual principles—at times modified, softened, or as in this case, made more acute—appear over and over in various forms.

PRINCIPLE 1: The addict is totally unable to control or manage greed and compulsion; he or she is totally powerless with regard to his or her addiction.

The first and foremost of AA's Twelve Steps (see Table 6.1) is that the addict makes the brutally frank admission that he or she is powerless to manage alcohol, or whatever form his or her addiction takes (gambling, drugs, sex, the acquisition of power, and so on) and as a result, that his or her life is totally out of control. By whatever path an individual arrives at it, this first step toward recovery requires that the addict acknowledge without any qualification whatsoever that he or she is an addict, and furthermore, that his or her life has been ruined by addiction. Because this step is generally so difficult, it is very rare that a person can acknowledge his or her addiction without considerable pain and a great sense of failure.

To admit to addiction is to admit to other mistakes as well, most notably a life of delusion. As one recovering alcoholic put it, "An alcoholic lives in 'sincere delusion' that he or she can handle alcohol."[3] Another delusion is the belief that addiction is a matter of degree—in other words, that it is possible to be only a "little bit" addicted. As a result of such self-delusion, the addict has to experience not a single failure but repeated failures to control his or her drinking, drug use, gambling, and so forth. Only after repeated and extensive failure—though sometimes not even then—is the addict able to take the difficult step outlined in the first principle. Only after the addict has been humbled by successive failure might he or she be ready to embark on the difficult road to recovery.

Notice how similar this pattern of severe failure followed by deep humbling is to the crisis experienced by Tom Chappell, the founder of Tom's of Maine (see Chapter Five). Here, as there, a major crisis is absolutely necessary in order to produce major changes in a person's life. By itself, however, one major crisis is not sufficient. The alcoholic, for example, is unable to learn from a few bad experiences or from logical arguments that alcohol is dangerous, because the learning mechanisms of the addict are seriously defective. As a consequence, a single crisis is rarely, if ever, enough to prompt major change. Even a major crisis such as a near-death experience is often not enough.

PRINCIPLE 2: No human entity is capable of controlling the addict's behavior; only a nonfinite, nonhuman power can help the addict recover.

The second principle is the recognition that the addict must first exhaust every conceivable human means of controlling his or her undesirable behavior before he or she is willing and able to turn to other avenues of help. Up to this point, the addict may have tried every means currently known to medical science, alternative medicine, psychology, psychotherapy, and so on, without success. It is only after the repeated failure of all known human means of controlling alcoholism that the addict is ready to turn to a means that is nonhuman and nonfinite.

In reading the book known as the "Big Book of AA"[4]—or in the language of this book, AA's major "alternative text"—one is constantly struck by the profound nature of the insights of AA's founders. These insights are essentially spiritual epiphanies. What is also striking is how close many of the insights of AA's founders are in tone and inspiration to the ideas of the great seventeenth-century French philosopher and mathematician René Descartes, especially as expressed in his *Meditations*.[5]

Descartes was governed, if not obsessed, by a single goal: to establish a certain and secure foundation for all knowledge. He was motivated by what he regarded as the flimsiness of what passed for knowledge in his day. Except for the propositions of mathematics, all other forms of knowledge, according to Descartes, were seriously deficient. He was thereby determined to doubt everything he had been taught, in the hope of discovering something he could not doubt, and hence which could serve as a secure foundation or platform for all knowledge.

It is not necessary to retrace the labyrinth of Descartes' complex philosophical arguments. It is also unnecessary to discuss in detail the major defects of his thinking, which have been pointed out by generations of successive philosophers. What is important for our purposes is a critical strand of his argument, one that is highly similar to arguments used by AA's founders. At a critical juncture in his work, Descartes needed not only to prove the existence of God but also to show that God is not a malicious deceiver of human beings.

Descartes observed that, by definition, God is not finite but infinite. In addition, not only does God possess an infinity of attributes, but he and he alone possesses each attribute without limit. In other words, God is unbounded and attains the highest possible "score" on each attribute. Humankind, conversely, is most certainly finite, which raises the question of the origins of human knowledge of the infinite. Now, the notion of the infinite (God) comes either from humankind (from the finite) or from outside humankind (from the infinite). Descartes argued that because we are finite creatures, the concept of the infinite, which is much greater than us, could not have originated within us. Therefore, the notion of the infinite must have been planted in us by the infinite, or God himself. Whether or not one takes issue with this argument is somewhat beside the point, because it is seriously flawed. (The great German philosopher Hegel was to point out that the concept of the finite implicitly involves the infinite. That is, the finite invariably stands in sharp contrast to what is not finite, that is, the infinite. The point is that each concept invariably depends on its opposite for its definition. Each implicitly makes reference to the other. From this standpoint, one could thus also say that the concept of the finite could not have been planted in humans by themselves.)

The founders of AA also used arguments that are strongly Cartesian. One cannot prove for all time that no human means will ever be found that will cure humans of alcoholism. Indeed, no one can claim to have investigated all human means of accomplishing anything. All one can say is that currently known means are limited or imperfect.

To go from the idea that all currently known human means of curing alcoholism have failed to the idea that all human means whatsoever in the future are doomed to fail is, to put it mildly, a gigantic leap of faith. To then go further and embrace the idea that only a power greater than humans can cure us of addiction is an even bigger leap of faith. But faith is precisely what is operating.

The founders of AA were convinced by their own experiences of having tried every conceivable human means to no avail that a nonhuman power was all that was left to help them. Their argument was not so much a demonstration of logic, as Descartes' was, but a matter of deep faith and belief. Underlying this belief was the more fundamental conviction that the disease from which the addict was suffering was spiritual. The root cause, if there was only one, was not physical or psychological, and consequently it would not respond to physical or psychological treatments; rather, the root cause was profoundly spiritual.

PRINCIPLE 3: God is nondenominational; everyone is free to conceive of God, or their Higher Power, as they see fit.

AA is strongly rooted in Christian, Protestant, Anglo-Saxon values. Nonetheless, from its very beginnings AA made God widely accessible and acceptable by emphasizing that each person was free to embrace God in whatever way he or she conceived of him. In other words, AA evolved from an initial religious affiliation with Christianity to a nonreligious, spiritual ecumenicism.

Some analysts contend that despite its claims to the contrary, AA still retains its Christian underpinnings. Others contend that AA is in a category all by itself. It is both religious and not religious at the same time; it is also neither. Instead, it is a quasi-religion.[6]

From AA's standpoint, what is important is that one believe in a higher power, not that one have any particular conception of it. Indeed, belief in a higher power is seen as absolutely essential for recovery.

AA recognizes explicitly that many people have been turned off, if not offended, by their earliest religious experiences. For this reason, each person is asked to accept God *as he or she conceives of him*, and not according to any particular religious connotation. Dennis Morreim expresses the point well:

> Many surrendered alcoholics are not ready for a clear and more definite concept of God other than "Higher Power." When one first enters the program, there may be a lot of anger and resentment toward God. As I go to different treatment centers to lecture, I can sense hostility and anger from some recently admitted clients when I tell them that I am a pastor. They may have experienced rejection from the church, from a pastor, or from "those Christian people who think that they are better than everyone else." All this is interpreted by the alcoholic as judgment and condemnation by God. "If these

people have nothing to do with me, then God, too, must have nothing to do with me!'"[7]

PRINCIPLE 4: Recovery necessitates that one's entire being be given over to one's higher power.

As noted earlier, addiction is not a matter of degrees. Neither is belief in a higher power. It is not enough simply to believe that a higher power is necessary for recovery. It is absolutely essential to give one's entire being and soul over to it. Nothing less than a complete, absolute commitment will do.

A related belief or principle is that the only absolute and essential requirement for membership in AA is the sincere desire to stop drinking. Nothing else matters. No one is excluded from membership in AA based on their social standing, race, religion, age, sex, and so on. Although these things may matter in the outside world, they are completely irrelevant in the world of AA.

PRINCIPLE 5: God is the ultimate authority.

One can say that God, or one's higher power, is the CEO or owner of the work of recovery. This principle is similar in spirit to that of the Religion-Based Organization, where God is both the CEO and the owner of the enterprise. This principle also emphasizes that God is at the top of the recovery chain. In addition, one can say that God is also at the bottom of the chain, because God is the foundation on which recovery is built. Without God, recovery is not possible.

PRINCIPLE 6: Recovery is possible through God and the program of AA.

Principles 4 and 5 express the idea that belief in God and the complete turning over of one's will to God are absolutely necessary for recovery. Principle 6, conversely, comes extremely close to expressing the idea that complete belief in and the complete turning over of one's will to God are sufficient for recovery. That is, if one completely turns one's will over to God, recovery is not only possible but will necessarily follow.

Principle 6 can also be interpreted as AA's principle of hope. If anything, the addict has been totally without hope of ever getting better. Principle 6 expresses the notion that recovery is not only possible but also attainable through the program. Deep personal transformation is eminently possible through AA.

AA's principle of hope is also amazingly similar to the principle of the Religion-Based Organization that through God anything is possible. AA's principle is stronger, however. AA holds out the promise that if one "works the program" religiously, then miracles will occur. Good things that one could only have dreamed of before now happen mysteriously and miraculously.

PRINCIPLE 7: One and only one goal is allowable.

AA allows for one and only one goal. This goal is the same for each individual addict, for the various groups of which he or she is a member, and for the organization of AA as a whole. This goal is the recovery of the individual addict. All other goals are secondary and to be kept strictly separate from the program. For this reason, AA is tenacious in not affiliating or associating itself with any outside political groups or social causes, however worthy they may be. The uncompromising singularity of goal and mission is a strong and distinguishing element of this model.

PRINCIPLE 8: The Big Book is the bible or the word of AA; the broader text also consists of personal stories of its members.

The Recovering Organization relies almost completely on its own alternative sources of wisdom. The Big Book is the alternate business text of AA.[8] It is to AA what the Bible or the Word of God is to the fundamentalist Religion-Based Organization. It contains the founding principles of AA and how they were arrived at, along with the original Twelve Steps and Traditions, which have been adopted by many other programs of recovery.

The Big Book of AA also contains the personal stories of its founders, as well as those of scores of individuals who have been helped by the program. It is thus important to realize that members of AA think of their "text" as more than just a book to which everyone can refer. Just as important as what is published are the literally thousands of personal stories of AA's members that are told over and over again at meetings and gatherings. Thus, the "whole text" of AA is both that which is contained in print and that which is part of the living, oral tradition.[9]

That every AA member, irrespective of age, race, sex, or social position, partakes of the same tradition and shares the same stories is one aspect of the organization that makes it so powerful. It enables the individual addict to appreciate that he or she is neither alone nor unique. It also helps individual addicts to make connections to others, and often, for the first time in their lives, to form healthy interpersonal relationships.

PRINCIPLE 9: The Devil is alcohol.

The Big Book puts it well: "Remember that we deal with alcohol—cunning, baffling, powerful! Without help it is too much for us. But there is One who has all power—that One is God. May you find Him now!"[10]

One of the defining attributes of the Devil is that he is able to assume the most cunning shapes and disguises in order to tempt humans. His power rivals even that of God. Thus, although it doesn't call alcohol by that name, AA sees the Devil as equivalent to alcohol.

The Devil also assumes another form. In the process of recovery, the addict comes to recognize that in his or her extreme obsession with alcohol, to the exclusion of all other desirable things in life, he or she was "insane." He or she did things that were "crazy."

SHAKING OFF ADDICTION **111**

From this standpoint, the Devil can also be regarded as planting insanity in humans, if not as having created the insane state itself.

It is important to understand that in the Recovering Organization, unlike in the Religion-Based Organization, the Devil is to be interpreted metaphorically, not literally. Just as the notion of God may be interpreted more broadly as one's Higher Power, so may the Devil be interpreted as the "Supreme Lower Power," although this term is not used in AA.

PRINCIPLE 10: One has to be trained to talk and listen spiritually.

AA does not assume that everyone knows how to talk and listen spiritually. Although the basic capabilities of talking and listening may be inborn, the ability to do these things at a high spiritual level has to be developed through extensive practice. This ability also has to be constantly maintained lest it atrophy. As a result, AA has developed a special set of rules or guidelines for talking and listening spiritually. These rules govern discourse in AA meetings. According to Klaus Mäkelä:

> On the basis of observations of meeting and interviews with members, the main rules of speech can be spelled out as follows:
>
> 1. Do not interrupt a person speaking.
>
> 2. Speak about your own experiences.
>
> 3. Speak as honestly as you can.
>
> 4. Do not speak about other people's private affairs.
>
> 5. Do not profess religious doctrines or lecture about scientific theories.
>
> 6. You may speak about your personal problems in applying the AA program but do not attempt to refute the program.
>
> 7. Do not openly confront or challenge previous turns of talk.

8. Do not give direct advice to other members of AA.

9. Do not present causal explanations of the behavior of other AA members.

10. Do not present psychological interpretations of the behavior of other AA members.[11]

The first two rules are the most crucial. The first rule supports the nonconversational turn-taking system. The second rule restricts turns to speaking of one's own experiences. In AA parlance, members tell self-narratives. Regardless of whether the topic of the meeting is a step, a tradition, or a personal story, speakers are expected to cover it through their own experiences. Although the use of turns is restricted to self-narrative, the content is open. This leads to a great variety of themes. In practice, the notion of personal experience is sometimes interpreted very broadly. It may be possible to get around the ban on political topics by discussing one's political feelings.

PRINCIPLE 11: Recovery demands a complete reversal of one's prior belief system.

Rarely is a single thing the complete cause of another. Although belief in a god or higher power is absolutely essential for recovery, many other things are required as well.

Principle 11 is equivalent to the notion that although planting an acorn is necessary for the production and growth of an oak tree, by itself it is not sufficient. In addition to planting the acorn in fertile soil, one must also provide proper moisture and sunlight.

The metaphor of the acorn and the oak tree applies to AA. In addition to the necessity of giving one's will over to God, recovery also demands that one completely overturn and reverse one's entire belief system. A trivial modification of the addict's belief system will not do. The addict got into trouble in the first place not because one or two isolated beliefs were wrong, but rather because a whole, reinforcing belief system was faulty. For this reason, the trivial or slight modification of one's beliefs will not do. Nothing less than the collapse and overturning of the entire faulty belief system is required. The surgery required for recovery is radical, not minor.

PRINCIPLE 12: The principles and program of AA are systemic; they form an integral whole.

Table 6.1 presented the Twelve Steps of AA. These steps can be roughly divided into three groups. Steps 1 to 3 are loosely called the "decision steps"; Steps 4 to 9 are called the "action steps"; and Steps 10 to 12 are called the "maintenance steps."

One of the most interesting features of these steps is that many of them have appeared in innumerable programs throughout human history. Thus, it is not necessarily the novelty or the newness of the steps that constitutes the uniqueness of AA; instead, it is the combination and integration of the steps along with the principles of AA, of which this chapter has stated merely a few.

Step 1 says that one has lost power over alcohol—or metaphorically, the Devil. To admit one's powerlessness over alcohol means that one has taken the important step of brutal frankness. One has cut through the enormous wall of denial that encapsulates the addict and his or her support system.

The second step can be interpreted as coming to see that hope is possible, that a cure is available. Furthermore, the characteristics of the cure or curing force also become evident. The curing force is neither finite nor human. Instead, it is an extraordinary power. Given the overwhelming power that alcohol has over the addict's life, it is not surprising that an equally powerful, if not stronger, force is required to overcome it.

Step 3 expresses the important principle of making a decision to turn one's entire being and soul over to one's higher power. One is not merely dipping one's toes or fingers into the water. Instead, a total immersion is required. Furthermore, it is not necessary to make a commitment to a specific deity or particular religion. What is required is for the individual to give himself or herself over to a higher spiritual power as he or she conceives it.

Step 4 can be interpreted not only as a searching and fearless moral inventory, but also as a searching and fearless spiritual audit. To say the least, very few of us undertake such an activity. Step 5 indicates that it is not merely enough to make an audit or an inventory; it is also absolutely necessary to act on it. Step 5 also expresses the notion that the audit, as well as the actions designed to correct one's situation, are possible only through a deep, ongoing relationship with others. In pursuing the devil of alcohol, the addict has become isolated not only from others but also from himself or herself.

Step 6 can be construed as the readiness to implement new actions. The addict is thus ready and willing to remove all roadblocks or obstacles to implementation. As we noted in Chapter Four, on the Religion-Based Organization, this is rarely the case for most individuals, let alone for organizations.

Step 7 can be construed as asking one's higher power to give one the blessing to correct one's wrongdoings, if not change altogether. This step continues the process of rebuilding one's relationship to his or her higher power.

Step 8 is a continuing audit. It is to make a list of all the persons one harmed while one was an addict. It is also a direct expression that one is willing to make amends to those one has hurt in the past. Because the addict was previously lacking in self-reflection, the importance of reflecting on one's behavior is emphasized explicitly throughout the steps. For this reason, a single audit is not sufficient. Step 9 is the implementation of those actions designed to make amends and improve one's relationships with those one has harmed in the past.

Step 10 expresses the notion that a moral and spiritual audit are never complete. They must be carried out constantly. Because we are finite, not only are we doomed to make mistakes, but if we are fortunate enough to follow the program, we can also learn from them.

Step 11 can be construed as the desire to improve continually our relationship with our higher power, and as a result, participate in the program.

Step 12 can be interpreted as a further generalization or a systemic principle. Even though AA eschews any formal contact with social causes or other political movements, in effect Step 12 says that there are no walls or boundaries between one's participation in the program and the rest of one's affairs.

A Stakeholder Analysis of AA

A stakeholder analysis of AA is extremely revealing. While one is in the grip of addiction, there is essentially one and only one stakeholder of any consequence, namely, the addict himself or herself. All other stakeholders are ignored in the pursuit of one's addiction. In somewhat different terms, the stakeholder can be viewed as the insane mental state in which the addict operates. To say that the addict is extremely self-centered is to put it mildly.

Another way to look at the process of recovery is as follows: by "working the program," the addict learns to expand his or her universe of stakeholders. This is a direct consequence of the Twelve Steps, many of which are devoted to rebuilding damaged relationships.

The Extension of AA to Organizations

The extension of AA to organizations, and hence to the Recovering Organization, consists of two parts. The first part is the adaptation and extension of the philosophical principles of AA, which were formulated primarily for individuals, to whole organizations. The second part consists of the development of specific techniques for the actual management of organizations according to Twelve Step principles.

The extension of the basic underlying philosophy, principles, and steps of AA to business organizations is not difficult theoretically. The difficulty, in other words, does not lie in the cognitive or intellectual realm. Rather, it lies in the affective or emotional sphere.

To our knowledge, Lee Robbins has done the most systematic thinking on the application and extension of the Twelve Steps and the principles of AA to organizations. His Ph.D. dissertation involved the application of the Twelve Steps to organizational learning as well as the comparison of the Twelve Steps to other methodologies.[12] Robbins's ideas are captured in Tables 6.2, 6.3, and 6.4. Table 6.2 shows the translation and modification of the original Twelve Steps into a form that is appropriate for organizations, Table 6.3 shows how the principles for solving problems that derive from AA run counter to currently existing conventional strategies, and Table 6.4 shows some more detailed applications and translation of the principles and steps of AA for organizations.

Because most of the items in Tables 6.2, 6.3, and 6.4 are self-explanatory, we do not comment on every one of them. However, a few points bear emphasizing. First, notice that no explicit reference is made in the tables to spirituality per se. If one likes, one can view the application of AA to organizations as a profound value shift. Although this interpretation is certainly valid, we would nonetheless resist it strongly. We do not believe that all reference to spirituality can or should be avoided. However, major differences of opinion do exist.

For us, the greatest value of Robbins's tables is that they reinforce principles of openness and inseparability, that is, breaking down barriers and walls between individuals, departments, and the various aspects of a person's life. Another point is the extreme emphasis that is put on limiting the size of working units. Size, probably more than anything else, is responsible for the formation of new AA groups. Once a group reaches a critical size, it is more a matter of feeling that the group is too large to carry on spiritually than a matter of rational calculation. The same principle applies to organizations, although a precise measure of how big is too big cannot be given at this point. For AA groups, the number seems to be between twelve and twenty. As we mentioned in Chapter Five, the number for organizations has been estimated to be between 150 and 200.

The first step of AA is difficult for individuals, but it is probably even more difficult for organizations (which are composed of groups of individuals as well as the innumerable interactions among them)

Table 6.2. Application of Twelve Step
Fellowship Characteristics to Business Firms.

Twelve Step Fellowship Characteristics	Application to Business Firms
1. Pragmatism for the fellowship, working groups and individual recovery programs.	Emphasis is on results not rules; improvement through persuasion not coercion.
2. Replication rather than enlargement as size increases.	There is a limit on the maximum size of the unit.
3. Simplicity of organizational goals and forms.	Stated concisely for all members; ties closely to above.
4. Quality of rewards for all members.	Intrinsic rewards, pay for individual skills, attention to quality of work life.
5. Strong perceived linkage of organizational individual goals.	*Optional* participation in planning and policy setting at all levels.
6. Few paid staff, informal acceptance of authority within specialized spheres, emphasis on peer control and recognition.	Managers as facilitators and joint selection by "subordinates" and "higher" managers, as well as lean management.
7. Overlapping responsibilities.	Union-management joint ventures.
8. Rotation of roles, multi-skilling of leaders.	Widespread training of facilitation skills as well as technical skills including use of peer teaching.
9. Sponsorship.	Mentorship.
10. Explicit shared stakeholder control.	Inclusion of employees and others as stakeholders in addition to owners for decision making.
11. Protection for minorities and dissidents.	Ombudsmen and economic employment opportunity officers and functions.
12. Minimization of control and dependence by other units of the organization.	For example, use of the profit center concept.
13. Clarity of objectives, compelling but sparsely written policies.	Clarity of and agreement upon mission, and lean policy manuals.

Source: Robbins, L. P., "Learning in Organizations: The Effects of Interactive Planning and Twelve Step Methodologies," unpublished Ph.D. dissertation, University of Pennsylvania, Philadelphia, 1987.

Table 6.3. Counterintuitive Fellowship Techniques.

Solution Difficulty	Conventional Solution	Counter-Intuitive Methods
If the solution doesn't work	Do more of the same, harder . . .	Do less of the same—back off—"turn it over"
Uncertainty	Gather more data, wait, plan . . .	Take action, see what happens
Solved problems reoccur . . .	Get an expert . . .	Avoid experts, find others to "share the experience"
Problem-solver IS the problem	Focus on others, make them change	Focus on self
Circular, unproductive discussions . . .	Increase feedback	Decrease feedback, listen
Emotional involvement . . .	Increase emotion . . .	Express emotion

Source: Robbins, L. P., "Learning in Organizations: The Effects of Interactive Planning and Twelve Step Methodologies," unpublished Ph.D. dissertation, University of Pennsylvania, Philadelphia, 1987.

because it requires that they admit that by following well-accepted rules of conventional business practice, they are in danger of failing.

One of the most difficult of all aspects of AA is that it requires individuals to admit that they, as well as their entire family systems, are dysfunctional. In the case of the Recovering Organization, this requires admitting not only that the entire organization is dysfunctional, but also that it is in effect a dysfunctional family.

In addition, organizations must also recognize and admit that a slight modification only of current business practices will not make things better, but that it will actually make things worse. For this reason, the notion of a higher power as a transformative principle is absolutely necessary. A legitimate interpretation of the concept of a higher power that is applicable directly to organizations is that a different, higher, ethical set of business principles, practices, and standards are required if the organization is to become more effec-

Table 6.4. Adaptation of Fellowship Methods to Business Firms.

1. Limit organizational units to 100–150 members.

2. Focus units on clear specific purposes measurable by and chosen with participation of members.

3. For higher level policy-making, utilize overlapping teams from multiple units and unit representation in the central policy-making body.

4. Minimize differentials and rewards for status; allow units to divide profits.

5. Limit coercive pressures, use self selection in group decision methods.

6. Leaders to be selected, or at the very least, confirmed, by those led.

7. Aim toward multi-skilling in technical and leadership skills of all willing employees.

8. Support socialization on and off the job.

9. Provide open access to information about the unit and the firm.

10. Use mentorship extensively with confidentiality protected.

11. Support voluntary groups for individual transformation with no penalties for information shared in group.

12. Visit "open meetings" of AA and other fellowship groups to learn from the experience of the organizations.

Source: Robbins, L. P., "Learning in Organizations: The Effects of Interactive Planning and Twelve Step Methodologies," unpublished Ph.D. dissertation, University of Pennsylvania, Philadelphia, 1987.

tive. One can thus downplay the emphasis on the notion of a higher power or god and still assert that what is needed is an emphasis on a more ethical set of principles. The rest of the steps of AA can then be reinterpreted as consistent with performing a moral and spiritual audit of how the organization has operated in the past and how it has, as a result, harmed its internal and external stakeholders. The principles can also be interpreted as processes for correcting past wrongs against stakeholders. It must be borne clearly in mind, however, that the organization is required to do more than conduct conventional "climate and culture surveys" of its employees and customers. In addition, it must take a hard, frank look at the rights and wrongs it has committed.

Strengths and Weaknesses of
the Recovering Organization

As with the previous models, the strengths of the Recovering Organization are also its weaknesses. The biggest strength of the Recovering Organization is the clear recognition and emphasis that a slight or trivial modification of current business principles alone will not allow the organization to confront, let alone solve, its current problems. Nothing short of a radical break is required. A major strength of the Recovering Organization is thus the frank recognition of the extensive hard work that is needed to change an organization if it is to become more ethical and spiritual.

We are certainly aware that the language of addiction is one of the most limiting aspects of this model. We are also well aware that the whole concept of AA has received severe and repeated criticism.[13] Most managers and executives will undoubtedly resist characterizing their organization in terms of illness. It is difficult enough for an individual to accept finally that they are "sick," not to mention "insane." It is even more difficult for a whole organization to admit this. Yet without such a fundamental admission, no substantial or enduring change is possible. As we have noted continually throughout this book, for any of the models to work, a substantial investment of spiritual energy, will, and effort is required. Nothing can be accomplished without these elements.

In spite of the difficulty and resistance in characterizing organizations in terms of illness and dysfunction, some progress has been made. In recent years, evidence has been mounting that the terms *dysfunction* and *addiction* are applicable to organizations.[14] Indeed, behavior patterns such as extreme hostility, aggression, and workaholism are clear signs of addictive behavior in organizations.

If the problems of organizations were easy, or merely cognitive or intellectual, then surely humankind would have discovered by now what it takes to change organizations. But as society has had to learn over and over again, the resistance to change is deep and pervasive. As a result, deeper means for producing true and long-lasting change are required. One does not have to accept AA as the cure for an organization's ills in order to see that it is trying to deal with the fundamental elements that keep both individuals and large systems from changing.

Closing Reflections

AA functions according to an integrated set of principles—in effect, as noted earlier, it is a total ethical management system—that can be used for managing greed and power, not just alcohol or other addictive substances. Indeed, greed and power may be the most powerful addictive substances known to humans.

Greed and power are so central to the human condition that they have affected—or better yet, infected—our very concepts of God. Thus it is important to note that profound changes in conceptions of God have occurred in modern times.[15] These changes are relevant to the model discussed in this chapter, even though they are probably unknown and irrelevant to most persons in AA.

It is well-known to professional philosophers that one can neither prove nor disprove the existence of God, let alone any of God's particular attributes. It is also well known that although one cannot prove that God exists, every argument against God's existence can be met by powerful counterarguments. If such arguments demonstrate anything, they reveal how humans think about one of the most important concepts affecting their well-being.

In recent years, the concept of an *all powerful* god has been revised substantially.[16] Instead of claiming a god who is all powerful or who attains the maximum possible value on an infinity of dimensions, serious arguments have been advanced for a god who does not have to be maximum on all dimensions or who chooses to limit activity on certain dimensions. The notion is that of a god who exercises self-restraint and does not need to be supreme on any scale in order to be a loving, kind god. Any maxim that conflicts with the idea of this god being supremely good is thus ruled out.

Again, this notion does not prove that such a god exists. If it proves anything, it is that humans have a deep need for a particular kind of god to follow in designing and living ethical lives. This god is neither greedy nor all powerful. In short, without their knowing it, philosophers have in effect been designing a concept of god that is in perfect harmony with the Recovering Organization.

Chapter Seven

For the Betterment of Society

The Socially Responsible Organization

Instead of taking a finished product and trying
to figure out ways to add social value to it, the
development process represents a chance to
design a new product around its potential social
value. We learned that when we developed
Rain Forest Crunch around socially beneficial
ingredients. That's when you've established your
specs, and choosing and working closely with your
suppliers. That's when you have the most flexibility
to create a product that will benefit society on as
many levels as possible. Once you have a successful
product that doesn't have social benefit, it's much
more difficult to go back and retool or re-source it.

We've learned the importance of building
values into the development process the same
way we've learned a lot of other lessons: the
hard way. Rain Forest Crunch was the first time
we consciously decided to create a product that
served our social mission. Before that, there were
several times when we had to retrofit a successful
product to bring it into alignment with our values.

The thing to do is to start by designing
products for maximum social benefits, then work
back from there to a product that you can actually
produce and sell.

—Ben Cohen and Jerry Greenfield,
Ben & Jerry's Double-Dip

The Socially Responsible Organization is not known for going quietly, or traditionally, about its business. Certain of its leading exponents (such as The Body Shop and Ben & Jerry's) have become noticed, if not notorious, for their strong actions (giving away profits to social causes) and outspoken views (calling traditional business methods "the problem" and MBAs and professional managers "the competition").

Ben & Jerry's, the relatively small (by industry standards) Vermont-based ice-cream manufacturer, is as widely known for its many brands of social activism as it is for its numerous distinctive ice-cream flavors (such as Rain Forest Crunch, Chunky Monkey, and Cherry Garcia). Its entrepreneurs, Ben Cohen and Jerry Greenfield, are also well-known personalities, famous for starting their company with a mere $50, no management experience, and lots of energy, enthusiasm, and chutzpah.

Because the company has been written about so extensively, we do not spend time detailing its history, except where such details are helpful in understanding its underlying principles. We do, however, make use of the company's much vaunted strength and vocalism to extract the principles of the Socially Responsible Organization. As with the Religion-Based Organization, the advantage of a strong example is that it has strong principles, and strong principles are easier to extract than weaker ones.

A Common Language of Values

Before getting to the principles of Ben & Jerry's, we want to digress briefly on the use of the language and vocabulary of values. Both the Socially Responsible Organization and the Values-Based Organization (see Chapter Eight) employ a values-based language. Both speak and write in terms of "leading with values," of values being the basis of continuing success. Where the two types of organizations depart is in whether they also use the concepts of *spirituality* and *soul* in talking about their organizations. Leaders of the Socially Responsible Organization are comfortable speaking in terms of both values and soul, but leaders of the Values-Based Organization are not at all comfortable with the words *soul* and *spirituality*. As we show more clearly in the next chapter, this distinction is neither small nor trivial. The values language used by the Values-Based Organization is intentionally neutral.

Beyond language, the most serious and substantial difference between the Values-Based and the Socially Responsible Organization is the greater extent to which the various departments and functions of the Socially Responsible Organization (such as finance, manufacturing, marketing, and research) are "spiritualized," that is, infused with soul and spirituality. The word *infused* conveys the degree and depth to which traditional business departments and functions are reconceptualized and redesigned to reflect this principle.

Principles of the Socially Responsible Organization

As in our discussion of the Religion-Based Organization (see Chapter Four), in this chapter we extract the principles of the Socially Responsible Organization primarily from a single text, Cohen and Greenfield's book, *Ben & Jerry's Double-Dip: Lead with Your Values and Make Money, Too,*[1] although we supplement our analysis with other texts.

PRINCIPLE 1: Business has a binding contract with society; its values have to be realized through its infrastructure.

Socially Responsible Organizations are not founded on the Word of God; nor are they founded in response to crisis. If there is a precipitating element, it is intense dissatisfaction with the current models of business. Ben & Jerry's claims in effect that what is needed is the reconstitution of the social contract between organizations and society. Nothing less than this will work.

Ben & Jerry's speaks in terms of values (as noted earlier, Socially Responsible Organizations are comfortable speaking in terms of both values and spirituality) when it states that business has a fundamental ethical, moral, and spiritual responsibility to serve the whole of society. More precisely, business is responsible for making social values an integral part of its infrastructure:

> Values-Led business is based on the idea that business has a responsibility to the people and society that make its existence possible. More all-encompassing and therefore more effective than philanthropy alone, Values-Led business seeks to maximize its impact by integrating socially beneficial actions into as many of its day-to-day activities as possible. In order to do that, values must lead and be right up there in a company's mission statement, strategy, and operating plan.
>
> Let's say, for example, that we're looking at three possible new ice cream flavors. Being Values-Led means choosing the flavor that gives us the best opportunity to integrate our commitment to social change with the need to return reasonable profits to our shareholders.[2]

A vital point of this quote is that the enactment of the social contract cannot be left to chance. It needs to be built directly into a company's infrastructure (that is, its day-to-day functioning) if it is to have any meaning. In this sense, the principle is similar to AA's principle that implementation should be built directly into ongoing programs.

Although this principle states in no uncertain terms that a binding contract with society is required, it does not say where this requirement lies in the pecking order of all the other principles needed to run a socially responsible business. Is it the most important, the top priority? Elsewhere, Ben & Jerry's makes clear that concern for society is at the very center, not the periphery, of its organizational focus. Even so, there are hints that something beyond the magnitude of even a social contract is envisioned. The sense of soul that permeates all aspects of the Socially Responsible Organization implies the existence of a strong *spiritual contract* with the surrounding society.

PRINCIPLE 2: The main business texts should be rewritten to reflect social values.

With the social reinvention of business as the fundamental priority of the Socially Responsible Organization, it stands to reason that it sees itself as rewriting the texts of business, or even writing new ones. In this sense, Ben & Jerry's sees itself as authoring the new business text of the twenty-first century. Although there is not yet a specific text on hand—no AA Big Book, no Bible, no volumes of Kant—to serve as the repository of Ben & Jerry's thought, it is fair to describe what is going on as a "work in progress."

PRINCIPLE 3: The principle of hope is all about the good consequences of leading with good values.

The principle of hope in the Socially Responsible Organization is closer to being a statement of possibility than a principle: *Good things happen to companies that lead with good values.* This goes beyond a company's statement of faith in the quality of its products: the good that comes out of marketing from a deep sense of values is not just purchases but also customer loyalty—and not just loyalty but a deeper spiritual connection based on shared social values.

> Consumers are accustomed to buying products despite how they feel about the companies that sell them. But the Values-Led company earns the kind of customer loyalty that most corporations only dream of—because it appeals to its customer on the basis of more than a product. It offers them a way to connect with kindred spirits, to express their most deeply held values when they spend their money. Unlike most commercial transactions, buying a product from a company you believe in transcends the purchase. *It touches your soul* [emphasis added]. Our customers don't just like our ice cream— they like what our company stands for. They like how doing business with us makes them feel. And that's really what companies that spend huge amounts of money on advertising are trying to

do—making their customers feel good about them. But they do it on a superficial level, with sexy women and cool cars.[3]

In all fairness, the principle of hope is more complicated than the statement "lead with values and good things will follow" gives the impression of being. Its deeper intent is closer to the statement, "Make values the basis of attracting and motivating the work force and higher productivity will likely follow."

> More and more corporations are realizing that if they are going to attract the best employees and motivate the ones they have, they need to start dealing with [the] issues of values and social concerns. Just as consumers are loyal to companies whose values they share, when employees feel they are working for some higher purpose, as opposed to just maximizing the profits of the company they work for, they are more productive.[4]

Of all of the principles of the Socially Responsible Organization, the principle of hope is the one most open to empirical testing. One could certainly find a way to test whether "good things" (such as higher productivity and profits) do indeed follow from values-based marketing. But from the standpoint of the Socially Responsible Organization, empirical validation is almost beside the point. The more fundamental point is that important principles are indicative of a person's, organization's, or society's underlying beliefs, and instead of looking to validate them, to prove them "true" in the usual sense, one should determine whether they accurately reflect the organization's assumptions about the world. The place to look for confirmation of this is not in a company's statements of purpose and goals but in its day-to-day actions and activities.

PRINCIPLE 4: The real power of a business lies in its day-to-day actions and activities.

A clear goal of the Socially Responsible Organization is to have as little compartmentalization and fragmentation among as many aspects of the business, people's lives, and the outer world as possible. The Socially Responsible Organization acts out of the belief that true power lies in its ability to integrate its social values within its departments and day-to-day functions.

> Cause-related marketing is a positive step. But it doesn't challenge the basic paradigms of conventional business and conventional marketing. It acknowledges that business has a responsibility to give back to the community, but it doesn't take advantage of the fact that the real power of business lies in its day-to-day activities. So a company that's doing cause-related marketing operates from a traditional, exclusively profit-maximizing motivation—then adds a charitable component almost as an afterthought. Instead of giving products a boost using a half-naked woman in a multi-million dollar advertising campaign, cause-related marketing gives products a boost by associating them with compelling causes.
>
> The basic premise of Values-Led business is to integrate social values into day-to-day business activities—into the very fabric of the business and its products. By contrast, the basic premise of cause-related marketing is to tack social values onto the marketing campaigns of a business that does not take social values into account in its other business activities.[5]

The Socially Responsible Organization is extremely proactive in how it goes about attaining its goals. It tries to anticipate and create opportunities to tackle serious social problems rather than merely react to them. As noted earlier in the chapter, every one of its departments and functions has in principle been reconceptualized or redesigned as needed to fit the social mission and purpose of the organization.

PRINCIPLE 5: Business is necessary if we are to solve social problems.

> Business has now become the most powerful force in society. We cannot solve social problems unless business accepts a leadership role. This in turn requires business to act in the interest of the common

good. This is a very new role for business—one that it is not used to or prepared for. The norm has been for business to be a special interest, and adversarial to the rest of society.[6]

Although this principle says that business is necessary to solve social problems, it does not say that by itself business is sufficient. It does insist, however, that without the sincere and deep involvement of business in the common good, there is no hope of ever solving complex social problems.

We would go even further and contend that without taking business into account, the definition of important social problems is both faulty and incomplete.[7] For instance, there is an undeniable economic aspect of all important social problems.

PRINCIPLE 6: The values of a values-led business need to be made public.

Values-Led businesses need to be public about their social activities. How can people know which companies to "vote" for if companies are secret about their social stands and activities? When business acts covertly, it locks people out of the process. It deprives customers of the opportunity to use their purchasing power to support social goals they believe in.[8]

This principle reflects the Socially Responsible Organization's fundamental opposition to the ways in which traditional businesses are run. Much traditional business activity takes place behind closed doors and its operations are kept hidden. The Socially Responsible Organization subjects itself to a different modus operandus.

To be considered trustworthy and to be shown as living up to its ideals, the Socially Responsible Organization must opt for completely open, transparent operations. This is a matter of communicating its values not only to its outside stakeholders but also to its internal stakeholders.

The removal of secrecy does not mean, however, that everything about the organization is open to public scrutiny. It merely means that the goal is for everything to be as visible as possible. In principle there should be nothing that the Socially Responsible Organization would be ashamed of if it were to be widely publicized. To put it mildly, in an era of unparalleled media coverage and exposure, few individuals (President Clinton, for one!) and organizations can stand up to this principle. Very few, if any, organizations that purport to be socially responsible can live up to this principle.

Though this principle fails to apply in most cases, failure does not signal resignation or defeat. Once again, much like the principle of hope, this is an ideal for which to strive, not a testament to fact. That most organizations do not currently live up to the ideal is not reason to abandon it. If anything, the distance still remaining to its attainment should serve to spur our efforts on with greater energy.

PRINCIPLE 7: Start! Begin with any social issue.

If in some areas the ideal is purposefully set exceptionally high, in others it is intentionally lowered. The Socially Responsible Organization tries to make the threshold or barriers to taking responsible social action as low as possible.

> In the early days of Ben & Jerry's, when we first started taking public social and political stands, lots of different groups with lots of different progressive agendas came to us wanting Ben & Jerry's to take a stand on their issues. They were asking us to support causes we wanted to support, causes that were in keeping with our values. So we started doing that.
>
> . . . We were coming around to the idea of a Values-Led business. We came to believe that the best and highest use of the company was not just to take stands on social issues but to integrate the company's social mission into as many of its day-to-day operations as possible.

We found there was a conflict between focusing on a single issue in our public stands, on the one hand, and maximizing the integration of the social mission to the company's activities, on the other.[9]

... What level of our own needs should we meet before we start helping others? If we say that we'll devote all of our resources to meeting our own needs until we've reached a particular level, and *then* we'll devote ourselves to helping others, there is a good chance that we'll keep raising the level we're trying to reach. We'll never get there [italics in original].[10]

Of all of the principles of the Socially Responsible Organization, this one relates the most closely to those of the Recovering Organization. It corresponds to the repeated action steps of Alcoholics Anonymous.

Instead of endlessly debating which is the best or perfect social cause or program to adopt, the Socially Responsible Organization generally opts for action over words. Given that in today's highly interrelated world all issues are connected to all other issues, it doesn't really matter which issue one picks for becoming socially and spiritually involved in bettering the world. What matters is that one pick an important issue *with which to begin*.

This doesn't mean that the choice of cause in which to invest one's limited energies should be made at random. To the contrary, the selection should be given considerable thought. However, at some point deliberation must stop and action must begin.

In addition, this principle recognizes the need for social experimentation and learning. Having started with one particular issue does not mean that one is locked into that issue for all time. It is also important to recognize when the goal of finding the best issue is really a thinly disguised pretext for not acting at all. It is inaction, not qualified action, that is morally irresponsible and contractually unacceptable in the Socially Responsible Organization. In other words, the threshold for engaging in social action must be set as low as possible. To do otherwise is decidedly unethical.

PRINCIPLE 8: Recruit spiritually: engage the whole person.

> Companies are discovering that they are better able to attract and
> keep the best employees if they factor social concerns into how they
> run their business. Employees are more motivated—and productiv-
> ity is higher—when they bring their hearts and souls as well as their
> bodies and minds to work with them.[11]

In one form or another, an emphasis on making the person and
the organization whole is central to each of the models discussed in
this book. But it is especially central to the Socially Responsible Organization—indeed, so much so that it is made an explicit principle.
This principle derives from conscious realization of the consequences of compartmentalized workplaces described in Chapter
One: it is all but impossible to divide a person's or an organization's
soul. Organizations do so at their peril. Thus the Socially Responsible Organization weaves the fundamental—and spiritual—notion
of inseparability or wholeness into many of its principles.

PRINCIPLE 9: Soul and spirituality are real whether they can be quan-
tified or not.

> Most people would agree that there is a spiritual part of our lives as
> individuals. Yet when a group of individuals gets together in the
> form of a business, all of a sudden they throw out that whole idea.
> We all know as individuals that spirituality—the exchange of love,
> energy, kindness, caring—exists. Just because the idea that the good
> you do comes back to you is written in the Bible and not in some
> business textbook doesn't make it any less valid. We're all intercon-
> nected. As we give we receive. As we help others we are helped in
> return. As your business supports the community, the community
> will support your business.
> Most companies try to conduct their businesses in a spiritual vac-
> uum. But it is absurd to think that just because spiritual connection

is intangible or quantitatively immeasurable, it doesn't exist. When people are aware that there is a company that is trying to help their community, they want to support that company. They want to buy goods and services from that company. They want to be associated with that company. And that is what Values-Led business is all about.

But the reality is, we'll never actualize our spiritual concerns until we integrate them into business, which is where we spend most of our time, where our energy as human beings is organized in a synergistic way, and where the resources exist that allow us to be at our most powerful.[12]

Souls and spirituality are real. They have the same real, essential, and eternal status in the Socially Responsible Organization as they do in the Religious, Evolutionary, and Recovering Organizations. Indeed, as the preceding excerpt says, it is absurd to think that spirituality and soul do not exist, regardless of whether they can be measured.

If the social contract can be considered the "head" of the Socially Responsible Organization, this principle is the heart. It is absolutely critical. It expresses the vital notion that something can be important and meaningful whether or not it can be measured in numbers.

The language of ontology, the branch of philosophy concerned with the fundamental constitution of reality, is used by the Socially Responsible Organization to contrast itself with traditional business. In traditional organizations, the fundamental components of reality are economic units and measures, if not numbers themselves. The Socially Responsible Organization does not declare these components wrong, per se, but seriously incomplete and lacking. What is missing are measures of what it feels like to work in a particular organization or setting—measures of people's joys, hopes, anxieties and other basic existential concerns that they bring with them and also experience at work. Thus the Socially Responsible Organization is unwilling to give up on either the reality of existential concerns or the importance of dealing with them in the workplace just because they cannot be expressed in numbers alone.

PRINCIPLE 10: When dealing with stakeholders, it is more effective to set up a spiritual infrastructure than to transform an old one.

> Our experience has demonstrated how much more effective it is to help set up Values-Led suppliers than to try and change traditional suppliers' way of doing business. If you've got a market for a product, you can use their volume to help an alternative supplier grow and thrive.[13]

This principle recognizes that it is not always possible to transform old dogs—or stakeholders. Some stakeholders—like some addicts and alcoholics—cannot move beyond accustomed ways of doing things and must be let go. This principle injects a strong note of realism, as do certain principles of the Recovering Organization (see Chapter Six). One must accept that not all alcoholics can be saved. One must accept that not all stakeholders can grow spiritually and remain a part of the organization. All that is required is to do for stakeholders as much as is humanly possible to make mutual growth possible.

PRINCIPLE 11: A fundamental revolution must take place in our internal thinking.

> During the first several years of Ben & Jerry's existence, the common view of the social mission was that it took away from the company's profitability and caused extra work. Now there is a general understanding that what drives our financial success is being a different kind of company. People understand that the more kinds of Values-Led things we do, the more we contribute to that success.[14]

As noted in Chapter Six, in order for an addict to overcome his or her addiction, a major change in the person's thinking is required.

Basic beliefs about one's self and one's capabilities have to be radically transformed. In addition, an entire belief system has to be confronted and overturned. The preceding quote expresses one of the fundamental assumptions that Ben & Jerry's had to identify as wrongheaded and then jettison.

PRINCIPLE 12: Gradual, evolutionary change, not radical change, is needed, and size shouldn't matter.

> Size shouldn't be a barrier. Any company, small or large, can benefit from doing business with minority suppliers. What's difficult about opening your business to minority suppliers is the same thing that is hard about changing any supplier.
>
> Each supplier is represented by sales people. Those sales people have done their jobs very well. They have built relationships with your buyers. They have stroked, and schmoozed, and sent chocolates at Christmas, and made whatever accommodations they needed to stay in your buyers' good graces. So your buyers have to be very dedicated to the social mission if they are going to abandon those relationships. And the move needs to be made gradually, while the new relationships are being established.[15]
>
> . . . At the time we believed that business was a machine for making money. Therefore, we thought the best way to make Ben & Jerry's a force for progressive social change was to grow bigger so we could make more profits and give more money away. We decided to give away 10 percent of our profits every year. Ten percent of a $100 million company could do a lot more good than 10 percent of the $3 or $4 million we were currently doing.[16]

There is no mistaking what this principle says. It asserts strongly that size shouldn't be a barrier to the social mission of the organization. The underlying message is that the Socially Responsible Organization is not, or need not be, subject to the constraints that hamper traditional businesses.

If we had to pick any single principle of the Socially Responsible Organization about which we have serious doubts and reservations, it would have to be this one. Size and its accompanying power are extremely addictive "substances" for organizations. Indeed, they are as addictive as anything known to humans. Without proper management, upward notches in size can defeat the very purpose of organizations. The recent chapter in the history of America on Line (AOL) comes to mind. To the public's way of thinking, AOL's surge in growth was unprincipled, even unethical. As a result of uncontrolled growth, it was unable to serve its customers properly. It found that it could not increase without limit and still provide social benefits.

It is understandable that a company like Ben & Jerry's would wish to continue to grow so as to be able to give away even more money to social causes. It is also understandable that the market in which a company is situated exerts continual pressure for a company to grow. Indeed, it is often difficult, if not impossible, to maintain existence without growing in a particular market segment. Nonetheless, the fallacy in this reasoning is that as one continues to grow, the spirit of the original company will remain the same, that it will hold to the true course of the company's original purpose and mission. Again, we have serious doubts about this proposition. It seems that the Socially Responsible Organization may have to focus its intensity and creativity on discovering ways of developing rather than growing. As Russell Ackoff pungently observed, "Cemeteries grow, but they don't develop."[17]

PRINCIPLE 13: Good things follow from soul and spiritual interconnectedness.

> It's all the things we've done, including the social-action campaigns in the stores, that have built the spiritual connection customers feel with Ben & Jerry's—which, along with great ice cream, is what makes people more likely to visit our scoop shops.[18]

> . . . If your company has values, and an essence, you need to
> capitalize on that strategic advantage and make sure your marketing
> expresses your values and your essence. A company with values is a
> company with soul. When you've got soul, you can market from
> your values.[19]

This principle expresses the notion that spirituality is the very
basis on which a successful business rests. It is what creates and
keeps alive the important connection between the company and
consumers. In addition, this principle reinforces two earlier ones:
the principle of hope (that good things happen to companies that
lead with good values) and the real status of spirituality and soul
(that spirituality and soul are real even if they cannot be quanti-
fied). An added reason for citing this principle is that it is, by itself,
enough to differentiate the Socially Responsible Organization from
the Values-Based Organization. The belief that good things follow
from spirituality and soul, and not from values alone, is the belief
that separates the two types of organizations.

What Kind of Business Is the Socially Responsible Organization?

> *Ben:* No one would expect the non-profit that works with the
> homeless to hire people who believe homeless people de-
> serve to be on the street. Greenpeace doesn't hire people
> who don't care about the environment to go door-to-door
> trying to get donations.
>
> *Jerry:* But we're not a non-profit, Ben. I'm sure there are peo-
> ple at Ben & Jerry's who disagree wholeheartedly with
> what we believe and what we do. And that's OK, as long
> as they are doing their jobs.[20]

It is fair to ask whether the Socially Responsible Organization
in general and Ben & Jerry's in particular is a for-profit organization in service of not-for-profit goals or a not-for-profit organization

supported by for-profit means. As soul-searching as Ben & Jerry's is, it has not answered this question among its principles.

We would argue that the Socially Responsible Organization is a true hybrid, if not a new type of organization altogether. The extent to which its for-profit and not-for-profit motives interact and influence one another is not simply a tension to be resolved. It is beyond even being a dilemma. It is something to be approached with new concepts and terms altogether.

This is not to say that a company's for-profit and not-for-profit concerns are to be given equal footing. If anything, the Socially Responsible Organization's not-for-profit (that is, spiritual) goals not only will but by all rights should dominate. In one form or another, this has been the expectation of all the models we have explored thus far: the fundamental purpose of business is *not* to make money but to serve the moral and spiritual needs of individuals and the common good of society. Nevertheless, the manner of balancing its goals will inevitably give rise to deep conflicts.

For instance, should the Socially Responsible Organization hire people as traditional organizations do, because they possess the necessary business and technical skills? Or should they hire people because their values are in close alignment with the social and ethical concerns of the organization? With the models in this book still in their infancy, we should not expect definitive answers at this stage in their development.

Ultimately, each type of organization will have to decide for itself which way it leans in response to these questions. Undoubtedly a mix of people with various skills and orientations is needed for managing any business in an increasingly complex world. But this means that whether people are hired initially for their business and technical skills or for their values alignment with an organization, they will need to undergo extensive additional training. In an ideal world one would hire people who are already equally developed socially and technically. But presently neither our educational system nor society in general produces such people in great abundance. Once again, the relevance of interconnectedness as a principle of all spiritually based organizations comes forth. Businesses are fundamentally dependent on society to produce the kinds of people it requires to do its work, and society in turn is dependent on businesses and other institutions to develop these persons into good and moral citizens.

Closing Reflections

The strengths of the Socially Responsible Organization are considerable. Working for the common good and to realize social values throughout its infrastructure are foremost goals. Equally challenging, it strives to close the gap between its ideals and its actions, to live up to the values it supports. There is also little doubt about its appeal to individuals. Many people experience working in such organizations as spiritually uplifting. Its customers, too, are held in highest regard. They are meant to derive satisfaction from buying products from a company whose values they share.

The weaknesses of the Socially Responsible Organization are also considerable. In the case of Ben & Jerry's, the organization was started by "two ordinary guys" who were not only unschooled in but also disdainful of professional management. In addition, they were extremely proud of their attitudes. In the early days especially, but even now, their mistrust of professional management created considerable problems for their staff. A persistent complaint of Ben & Jerry's employees is that they have not been given the training and professional development necessary to move up in the organization. Indeed, because of the lack of training, outsiders are often considered for openings ahead of the company's own employees. In this and other respects, the organization suffers from what we call the Missionary Paradox: while the missionary parents are out saving the world, the children at home often suffer from benign neglect.

The management style of Ben & Jerry's has also been subjected to scrutiny. In tune with today's "no secrets" policy, it is not surprising that alternate, behind-the-scenes accounts of its inside operations have appeared. Fred "Chico" Lager, former CEO of Ben & Jerry's, has authored a somewhat controversial and less than complimentary picture of the company's two founder-leaders.[21] Ben Cohen in particular is portrayed as a dictator—a benevolent one perhaps, but a dictator nonetheless. Cohen is shown as stressing, on the surface, the importance of a fully participatory organization in which everyone is free to air their views and values. In Lager's account, however, in the end all important decisions are made by Cohen himself.

From all that we've observed and from what we've heard in our interviews with other organizations that we would label socially responsible even though they are not as articulated as Ben & Jerry's, Socially Responsible Organizations are prone to falling into a "holier than thou" attitude. If they are not careful, some are extremely prone to becoming closed off and dogmatic, almost akin to a cult. For this reason alone they would do well to adopt more thoroughly the Recovering Organization's insistence on regular spiritual audits. In this manner of admitting defects and taking corrective action, they could better live up to their ideals.

In spite of its unrealized goals and its signs of weakness, the Socially Responsible Organization is an extremely valuable model. In spite of its newness, it identifies and attempts to introduce new principles not found in previous models. It has enormous potential as an alternative to traditional business values and practices. It leads the way in its quest for spiritual interconnectedness.

Chapter Eight

We Are Family!

The Values-Based Organization

From its distribution channels to its management
principles, Kingston's philosophy in conducting
business has been unique. The concept of a family
is central to Kingston's philosophy. Every Kingston
employee is treated as a member of the family. No
one person is more important than the other and
egos are left at the door.

—Kingston Technology Company

Kingston Technology Company, located in Orange County, California, is a designer and manufacturer of memory, processor, networking, and storage products for personal computers, workstations, and laser printers. The company was founded in 1987 by John Tu and David Sun, who have stayed on as its executives over the course of two doublings in size and the sale of the organization to a larger conglomerate.

Like many companies affiliated with the burgeoning computer industry, Kingston has grown from being the manufacturer of a single product, an in-line memory module, into an international company with more than 1,900 products and more than a billion dollars in annual sales. Kingston's internal publications as well as reports in the popular business press offer a glimpse into its unique philosophy and style of management.

Courtesy, honesty, modesty, trust, respect, and compassion for others are at the heart of Kingston's philosophy. Kingston's founders believe that by creating an environment free of politics and mistrust, employees will enjoy their jobs more and reach their individual potential. As a result, those employees will work harder and produce higher quality work. This feeling of respect and values also extends outside the company, as Kingston treats each vendor and customer as a valued family member.[1]

Kingston pays its employees salaries that are 20 percent to 30 percent above industry norms. It pays no commissions to its salespeople, believing that their success would not be possible without the group's efforts. Its bonuses are paid out in equal shares, not pegged to salary level, because Sun reasons that the bonus is a reflection of "how the company is doing," whereas salary is "what you know."[2]

In family-style management, says Sun, "You start from the basics and let everybody understand what you're thinking. When the employees become more mature in the company they become the management, and they will carry the same philosophy. That's why we never hire managers from outside. There is no common background. You put somebody from outside in a management position, and all these people you've been working with for four or five years say 'Who should I listen to?'"

Sun says it's hard for him to understand why a company would want growth as its goal. "How can you keep on saying, 'More, more, more'? I don't think that's realistic. There is nothing forever, right?" Kingston's leaders turn the growth question around: how fast can the company expand without compromising its integrity?

"When you're obligated to the employee, you are very conservative," says Sun. "You say, 'Let's make the base work first.' What's the base? It's whatever you do today—it's making sure that what we do today is better than what we did yesterday. Revenue is nothing. Let's make sure the base is right. So in a certain way we are very relaxed. We're patient. We say 'Let's just do it the right way, build ethical, honest products, don't brag about our success. Just do it.'"[3]

Instead of falling apart . . . Kingston somehow keeps on keeping it together. How? With an unyielding principle. As Tu, Kingston's 53-year-old President, describes it, "Never do anything you don't want to do to your own family." Sun and Tu owe their management philosophy to values handed down by their Taiwanese parents. "When I was a boy my mother always told me to put my friends in front of money," Sun says. That's why Sun, the 43-year-old V.P. of Engineering, so readily assumed responsibility for making an employee's house payments. It's also why both are making sure they can offer each of their employees at least one year's pay if, for some reason, Kingston fails. "They don't owe us," Tu says in all sincerity. "We owe them." Kingston's love-thy-neighbor philosophy even extends to competitors. It has re-sold DRAM to some of them during shortages—on the bet it would be able to recall the favor someday.[4]

The theme that ties together all of these excerpts about Kingston is the company's allegiance to an unyielding principle: The company is family—a *healthy, caring,* and *extended* family—and family values reign supreme within the company. In most organizations, to say that company is family is to speak metaphorically, and very loosely, of an idealized family-like atmosphere. But in the Values-Based Organization, the idea of family is taken as real. It is primary, governing, and reflected, as one quote says, in everything from distribution channels to management principles.

It can be fairly said of most organizations that they date their inception and operating principles from the actual time of their founding. But in Values-Based Organizations, the genesis and underlying principles can be traced back to the earliest experiences of and indelible influences on those who grew up to be their founders.

Precipitating Values, Not Events

The Values-Based Organization is the exception among the models we have seen in that it has no connection with a key or critical precipitating event. The organization as a whole has not necessarily been faced with a crucial crisis or series of crises; the founder or head has not been called to pursue a new direction. Instead, the Values-Based Organization derives from the fundamental personal values of its founders and leaders, values that these people believe in intensely and wish to carry forward. These fundamental values in turn derive from the personal histories and earliest experiences of those who go on to found companies guided by general philosophical principles or values.

As children, most founders and heads of Values-Based Organizations identified strongly with a parent or other close adult relative whose standards and values were unwaveringly strong. As the opening picture of Kingston Technology suggests, this identification was so strong that it continues into the present day in how the Values-Based Organization is structured and managed.

The heads of Values-Based Organizations we interviewed mentioned over and over again that the adult role models who influenced them were highly critical of organized religion. Although those role models believed strongly in family values and general virtues, religious and even spiritual values were greatly downplayed or rejected outright. At the same time, thinking for oneself and taking on the role of a maverick were highly encouraged from an early age. Apparently, too, parents and other role models are remembered not merely for stating their strong values but for showing them by ethical acts. In this way, the ethical examples were clearly modeled and constantly reinforced, and in time became the basis of both a personal philosophy and a management philosophy designed to produce ethical organizations.

Personal Values Produce Ethical Organizations

In Values-Based Organizations, the same values that guide individual behavior are used to produce ethical organizations. Values-Based Organizations operate according to a strong set of nonreligious, nonspiritual values—or to put it more accurately, virtues. These include but are not limited to awareness, consciousness, dignity, honesty, openness, respect, integrity, and above all, trust. Like the heads of Socially Responsible Organizations, the leaders of Values-Based Organizations take steps to incorporate these virtues systematically into the everyday actions of their businesses. Furthermore, they mean for these virtues to be taken as concrete, not abstract, guides and adopted into the daily conduct and behavior of individuals. If, however, there is an abstract principle of any kind involved, it is the belief that one should do what is right regardless of whether or not it leads to profits. But even this is too abstract a principle, because doing what is inherently right means acting directly on concrete values or virtues.

The leaders of Values-Based Organizations believe in doing the internal work necessary to build companywide trust, openness, and integrity and to cultivate an environment in which it is not only easy but natural to act on the right values. Though these leaders may from time to time call in outside consultants to help them build more ethical cultures and train employees in ethical talking and listening, they mostly lead by strong example alone. They mean to lead others as they were once led. They are now role models to an organization whose nature is best captured by the single governing metaphor of extended family.

More Than a Metaphor

The Values-Based Organization's principle of hope is like the assumption made by the Socially Responsible Organization: if one runs a company with good family values—that is, as a caring, healthy extended family—one can expect customers and employees to respond in kind and that good economic consequences will follow. In addition, the Values-Based Organization works to preserve traditional business functions. It maintains a highly professional profile, but still within the context of a family atmosphere.

The Values-Based Organization makes trust the cornerstone or touchstone of all of its so-called family values, and breaches of trust are intolerable because they are seen as betrayals of both the organization and the extended family.

Sourcebooks for the Values-Based Organization

When it comes to finding books that illuminate the more deeply embedded principles of Value-Based Organizations, the choice is much greater than for any of the previous models. The academic and professional literature, not to mention popular business books, contain plentiful examples of how to build Values-Based Organizations. Faced with a more arbitrary choice here than with the other models, we have been guided in our efforts by two books in particular, Dorothy Marcic's *Managing with the Wisdom of Love: Uncovering Virtue in People and Organizations* and Robert Shaw's *Trust in the Balance: Building Successful Organizations on Results, Integrity, and Concern.*[5] Both books are superior to others in their clear articulation of specific underlying principles and in being generally illustrative of Values-Based Organizations. Notably, each proceeds from a markedly different orientation.

Beyond its clear and forceful presentation, the striking feature of Marcic's book is that it proceeds from a strong spiritual base or platform. It would seem to be a good example of the Spiritually Based Organization, and it is. However, although it starts from a spiritual base, it ends by demonstrating an even stronger values base. As the book proceeds, the values voice becomes dominant.

Whereas Marcic's book tries to span the spiritual-values-based spectrum, and succeeds, Shaw's book is squarely embedded in the values-based tradition. Whereas Marcic feels free to draw heavily on spiritual concepts, Shaw keeps firmly within values-based bounds.

In our uncovering of the deep principles of the Values-Based Organization, we drew on both books, although not equally or for the same reasons. Marcic is interested in illuminating a universal set of values. Shaw, by contrast, looks at a few particular values in depth. Accordingly, we use Marcic to help identify the general types of principles, and Shaw to fill in some of the more substantive details.

The differences in the books' two treatments of values are profound. In Shaw's explicitly values-based approach, values are concretized. In other words, they are operationalized as measurable, attainable variables, or even stronger, as objectives. Conversely, in Marcic's blended approach, spirituality and soul are definitely not variables or objectives. Even to cast them in such terms is a profound denial of what they really are. However, in fairness to Shaw, even Marcic resorts to using various explicit rating scales to "evaluate" the spiritual state of an organization—a form of commentary on our times and a sign of their "measuring tendencies."

Leading Principles of the Values-Based Organization

From Marcic's book we can draw the two basic and foremost principles of the Values-Based Organization, as well as commentary on their origins:

PRINCIPLE 1: The Golden Rule is universal; it underlies all of the world's great religions and philosophies.

PRINCIPLE 2: The Golden Rule in turn derives from love, the most basic underlying value or virtue.

> The spiritual laws that govern human behavior have been articulated for thousands of years by all the world's religions and schools of philosophy, with remarkable consistency. . . . We have been given this ancient wisdom, these precepts for right living and for creating healthy societies, by all of the great religious leaders. The phrasing may be different, but the message is essentially the same: Love your neighbor, be honest, live in justice, control your impulses, avoid corruption, let your intentions be pure, and serve your fellow humans.
> . . . At the core of all these guiding principles is one fundamental law from which all others spring: Love your neighbor and treat your neighbor as you would wish to be treated. Although not all religious texts use the word *love* to portray this principle, in fact love is

the common thread underlying all spiritual laws. From this precept, which we can call 'the Wisdom of Love,' derive all the laws of honorable living.

By following these spiritual laws, we develop our spiritual natures and acquire virtues, such as trustworthiness, respect, patience, and so on. Virtues become, then, the outward manifestation of our inward spirituality, which is rooted in love.

When asked what was the most important commandment, Jesus replied that it was to love God with all your heart and soul, and the second was to 'love your neighbor as yourself. There is no commandment greater than these' (Mark 12:29–13). This commandment has been so important that it has been termed 'The Golden Rule.' In fact, though many people in Western societies associate this principle with Jesus, the concept itself actually preceded him and has been an integral part of all the major religions. It goes as far back as early Judaism, Hinduism, and Buddhism, and ancient Zoroastrianism. . . ."[6]

Like many "basic" principles, those that underlie the Values-Based Organization sound more familiar than new, more derivative than original. Although the Values-Based Organization strongly eschews any identification with religion or spirituality, its basic principles are inarguably drawn from the world's great religions. But take note: *Values-Based Organizations are able to separate their guiding beliefs and day-to-day practices from religion and spirituality because they have borrowed the most universal and least controversial of all religious values.* Having at an earlier point in their personal lives severed the connection with formal religion, the founders of these organizations allow themselves to believe that they owe no debt to religion whatsoever. They believe that people can come upon the Golden Rule independently of religion or spirituality. Not surprisingly, questions having to do with the possible origins and deeper meaning of the Golden Rule—questions that are fundamentally religious (at a minimum, metaphysical), such as, What implanted the notion of the Golden Rule in humans? and What makes love so compelling?—

are considered irrelevant or even nonsensical from the explicitly values-based point of view.

PRINCIPLE 3: The alternate text is an oral tradition of common, universal values.

In the minds of the founders and leaders of Values-Based Organizations, the underlying business texts are the moral lessons and ethical examples implanted early on by their parents or other influential role models. Thus the texts are more in the form of an oral tradition, as well as a form of inheritance. This is another reason that values-oriented leaders can readily separate "golden virtues" from the Golden Rule of religion or spirituality.

Paradoxically, however, the oral tradition they claim as their own can be traced back to the most spiritual, or as some would consider it, the most religious of sources: the common principles embedded in all of the world's great religions. Thus, not only does the Values-Based Organization borrow from texts it does not acknowledge, but it also often borrows from sources it strongly repudiates.

PRINCIPLE 4: Values alone are sufficient to produce and run ethical organizations.

The leaders of Values-Based Organizations believe not only that good values are necessary to the operation of an ethical business, but also that good values are very often sufficient by themselves to obtain ethical results. The same sort of reasoning that was used to support the unacknowledged "borrowing" of the Golden Rule is also used in support of this principle. People can come to good values independently of religion and spirituality. Consequently, religion and spirituality are not necessary to evoke ethical principles and actions.

There is, in addition, a hidden agenda of caution or warning in the insistence that values be strictly separate from religion and spirituality. The underlying thinking is that appeals to spirituality can lead people down wrong and potentially dangerous paths. To strongly values-minded individuals, spirituality is associated with either "New Age" mushiness or, worse, fundamentalism, with its autocratic, some say even totalitarian, overtones. Obviously there is no allowing for shades of gray in this principle or the next two principles of the Values-Based Organization.

PRINCIPLE 5: Values are more real than spiritual notions such as faith.

The thinking behind this principle is as follows: not only can the "right" values (such as honesty and openness) build important qualities such as trust (without which no organization could function), but trust and other qualities are a direct and positive outcome of the right values. In other words, values are proved real by the positive effects (such as greater trust and increased output) they produce. Furthermore, though trust can certainly be linked to spiritual notions such as faith, trust that is the outcome of positive values is more real and tangible, and in some fundamental sense superior, to faith alone. We quote from Shaw on the critical difference between trust and faith:

> Trust . . . is not absolute faith. In its most extreme forms, faith can be seen as a belief that is largely immune to contradictory information or events. Pure faith is beyond reason: those with such faith can justify any event or view, even if it conflicts with their world view; this is what we mean by "blind faith." Faith is resistant to change even when the price of having faith, of being a "believer," is detrimental to the faithful. But trust is commonly understood as being more fragile than faith. Trust can be broken more readily—and by events of considerably less significance—than faith. The possibility of withdrawing the trust we place in others—and of others withdrawing their trust in us—is very real.[7]

Notice that it was necessary for Shaw to equate faith with "blind" faith, which is faith "beyond reason." It seems not to have occurred to Shaw that he has put an extreme slant on faith by contrasting it with trust. Faith and reason are not necessarily fundamentally opposed to one another. (Indeed, some who espouse a values position take it "on faith" that reason is in direct opposition to faith.) An added point worth heeding here is that in assessing each model—indeed, in assessing *any* model—one must guard against picking extreme or worst-possible forms as representative. As we have stressed repeatedly throughout this book, although extreme examples may be useful in illuminating a model's underlying principles, they may lead to the unnecessary rejection of that model.

PRINCIPLE 6: Not only are values alone sufficient, but there are also only a few basic simple values.

Again we quote from Shaw, who quotes Jack Welch, CEO of General Electric, on the appeal of a few basic, simple values:

> The success of our company lies in the fact that a lot of people understand these values. They have joined the company knowing these were the values, and they worked to implement them. This is our life. This is how we behave. If someone cheats in our company, they are thrown out the first time. If somebody's boundary or turf-oriented [sic], they get a second chance, but they don't get a third. If they're not open, if they don't share ideas, that's bad behavior. We're translating values into operational behavior.[8]

This principle pares down the field of potentially numerous right values to the notion of just a few basic and simple ones. It does not spell out what these values are or should be; it only states that they are sufficient in themselves to produce desirable ethical behavior. This principle also hints at something tacit but exceedingly important about the choice of the few basic and simple values: they undoubtedly depend on the particular values of the founders or leaders of the Values-Based Organization, and they set the threshold for future actions.

From a long-term perspective, the perennial search for a common core of fundamental values by which to guide all human behavior is a persistent theme throughout history. It is especially persistent in the history of Western civilization. If one thing has been learned, albeit painfully and reluctantly, from this long and persistent search, there is no small set of basic values sufficient for ethical behavior in all situations. This does not mean that there are no values at all by which to guide human behavior. It merely means that no universal, fixed, and (especially) simple set of principles applies for all time and for all situations. The general rules and principles are matters to be debated over and over by succeeding generations.

The absence of a common core of simple values also suggests that all potential "best" principles—be they general virtues or spiritual values—are complex and by no means intuitively obvious. If they were, they would have been adopted long ago and left unchanged by the vast majority of businesses. Instead, history, including recent organizational history, constantly shows that the supposedly intuitively obvious principles of one period are rejected by succeeding ones.

PRINCIPLE 7: Employees who are ethical and who work in ethical organizations will outproduce unethical workers in unethical organizations.

The meaning behind this particular principle is stronger than it overtly conveys. That is, in addition to ethical workers in ethical organizations outproducing unethical workers in unethical organizations, ethical workers in ethical organizations will also outproduce unethical workers in ethical organizations as well as ethical workers in unethical organizations. It is fair to assume from this principle that unethical workers—and more pointedly, unethical organizations—are viewed as the competition of Values-Based Organizations.

In some Values-Based Organizations, this principle comes across as even more uncompromising than stated here. The belief in such organizations is not merely that ethical workers and ethical organizations will outperform other types of workers and organizations, but that over the long run *only* ethical workers in ethical organizations will *survive*. In effect, the argument is that all other organizations will collapse according to their own unethical principles, which will not be robust enough to get them through tough times. In this sense, being ethical is the toughest management principle of all.

PRINCIPLE 8: The values-based organization insists on a neutral vocabulary.

As noted in Chapter Seven, words having to do with spirituality and soul are off limits for the Values-Based Organization. Although terms such as *love, respect, trust,* and *wisdom* are used freely and the concepts they represent are readily accepted, words having any hint of a religious or spiritual connotation are rejected outright.

This attitude derives from an underlying and strongly held belief that certain words possess the power to do more harm than good. Certain words are thought to be outright turnoffs, capable of turning people away from the universal virtues espoused by the Values-Based Organization. Certain words are also declared as "too hot," "too emotionally laden," or "carrying too much emotional baggage." Thus this distancing principle also hints at another underlying belief of the Values-Based Organization: that religion and spirituality and the words used to express them compete negatively with universal values. In much the same way that traditional business practices are antithetical to the Socially Responsible Organization, and that addictive substances "bedevil" the Recovering Organization, a nonneutral, spiritually infused language of values is inimical and threatening to the Values-Based Organization.

PRINCIPLE 9: Actions not only mean more than words but are also the ultimate test.

Values-Based Organizations have no use for preaching good values, only for living them. In our interviews with the heads of such organizations, a strong sense of identification with this principle emerged again and again. There was even a strong undertone of condemnation toward preaching of any kind.

This does not mean that the leaders of Values-Based Organizations considered themselves exempt from ever stating their values or making them known throughout the organization. But such statements were extremely few and the times and situations were carefully chosen. At the same time, there was no doubt whatsoever that everyone in the organization knew the principles and values guiding those at the helm (as the example of Kingston at the beginning of the chapter shows so well). There was also little doubt that departures from these values and anything less than ethical behavior would not be tolerated, and would even be grounds for instant dismissal. Thus it should not be inferred in the slightest that the Values-Based Organization takes a soft or easy touch toward human relations. If anything, it prides itself on being clear about its values and tough about enforcing them. Although a great deal of latitude is given to people to express themselves, none is given to behavior seen as unethical. The importance placed on trust and on the governing vision of the organization as family makes unethical behavior by employees a two-way expression of betrayal: betrayal of family as well as organization. To quote from Shaw:

> Trust requires more than a soft-headed approach to human relations. Trust requires more than creating a supportive environment. It requires a tough set of actions and procedures that may even appear ruthless or cold-hearted to some people. For example, trust in a business setting requires, in part, that we feel confident that others will deliver on their commitments. Trust is impossible when a large percentage of the firm's employees cannot meet their business commitments. Building a trust-based organization requires that firms move or remove those who fail to perform despite sufficient feedback and coaching. This is necessary even if those impacted are wonderful, hardworking people with the best of intentions. Similarly, building a trust-based organization requires that those who violate

principles of integrity be removed immediately in order to reinforce the importance of conducting business by a set of accepted practices. Otherwise, the viability of the entire enterprise is at risk. Few organizations, however, have the capacity or conviction required to make these difficult decisions.[9]

PRINCIPLE 10: Treat people as whole persons and each person with deep respect.

A strong principle of *inseparability* operates in the Values-Based Organization, very much as it does in the Socially Responsible Organization. This similarity is another indication of the thin line that exists between these two types of organizations. It is recognized and acknowledged that the whole person comes to work, even though this "wholeness" is unlikely to be expressed in any sort of spiritual terms. People are expected to bring their code of values, outside concerns, and daily worries to work with them. Values-Based Organizations are thus, in general, extremely well tuned to the emotional needs of their employees. It is not uncommon to find workers sharing problems and being overt with their emotions. This does not mean that everything "hangs out." It does mean, however, that such organizations feel neither embarrassment nor reluctance at allowing the expression of deeply felt emotions. It also means that such organizations are much more likely than other organizations to call in special counselors when occasions demand it, such as in response to the death of an employee or an employee's child. (Indeed, we know of more than one example where organizations have had all-day grieving and mourning services in response to the untimely death of an employee or a member of an employee's family. In such cases, grief counselors were called in to be of service to those who needed them.) In this regard, it is interesting that Values-Based Organizations do not believe in preaching values at the top, but they also do not hesitate to have employees attend programs promoting higher consciousness in service of higher, ethical ends.

PRINCIPLE 11: The Values-Based Organization's "extended family" includes all of its stakeholders—internal and external, current and future, human and environmental.

This is the "Stakeholder Principle" of the Values-Based Organization. External stakeholders are as much a part of the organization as internal stakeholders and are accorded as much respect. In fact, Values-Based Organizations often treat their internal stakeholders better than Socially Responsible Organizations treat theirs. There is also a broad array of current and future stakeholders, as is the case for both Evolutionary Organizations and Socially Responsible Organizations. The families of employees, their relatives, the surrounding community, and the environment, if not the entire planet, are all considered stakeholders. By extension, so too are future generations, who are to inherit the consequences of the actions of Values-Based Organizations.

The broadening of the concept of stakeholders to include the environment and its preservation for future generations is further illustration of the thinning of the line between spiritually based organizations—especially Socially Responsible Organizations—and Values-Based Organizations, even though the latter go out of their way to deny this. In both types of organizations, concern for the environment is in many ways a "substitute religion." The environment is revered and people are likely to think and talk about the environment in spiritual-sounding terms. Such talk is a far cry from how traditional businesspeople are likely to think of and talk about the environment: in terms of economic costs and benefits, or literally, as a "thing."

From a strictly economic or utilitarian perspective, it makes no sense at all to talk of the entire Earth as a stakeholder. For traditional businesspeople and economists, a stakeholder is only a human being, a group, an organization, or an institution. Not even the economy as a whole is regarded as a stakeholder, although there are times when economists come close to concretizing it as a literal being.

The greater difference in thinking lies between utilitarian-based and environmentally reverent organizations, not between Religion- and Values-Based Organizations.

PRINCIPLE 12: Being profitable is an important value, but not necessarily the most important.

There is a wide range of variation among Values-Based Organizations with respect to this principle. For some, making money is one of the most important considerations, because profits allow the organization to continue, and hence to continue executing its values. For others, being profitable and making money is on par with building the core values of employees and communities. For still others, making money is only a means to the end of according dignity to all stakeholders.

As evident in this chapter's opening quote, the founder-leaders of Kingston Technology have had to face the question of size, and the skepticism of critics in regard to size, more than a few times in the company's recent history. They noted that when they were a one-hundred-person organization, they were warned that their special company-as-family feeling would be lost when the organization doubled in size and then doubled again. In every case, they have confounded the critics. As a result, they have continued to believe in their ability to preserve the spirit of the organization, even when a few years ago they finally sold the organization to a much larger conglomerate. Because they stayed on as the leaders of Kingston Technology, the founders still believe they can withstand rapid expansion without loss of integrity. Whether Kingston Technology can preserve its values while continuing to grow and to be part of a larger organization remains to be seen. It especially remains to be seen how it will work out for Kingston to be part of a larger organization that does not necessarily abide by Kingston's special values or see reason to preserve them.

The attenuated reasoning on size and growth found in this principle gives rise to and support for the following and final principle.

PRINCIPLE 13: The Values-Based Organization relies heavily on various assessments and measurements.

This principle is both a consequence and a characteristic of the unyielding nature of the Values-Based Organization. The elements assessed and measured include, for example, employees' morale, their satisfaction with their jobs, their general health, their relationships with their families, and so on. Although the assessments and measurements used by the Values-Based Organization may not be as narrow as those used in traditional economics-based organizations, there is no less of an emphasis on numerical evaluation and measurements. In the Values-Based Organization, the emphasis is on assessing people's values, attachments, and feelings toward the organization, especially when gaps are noticed in the organization's allegiance to its basic ideals, that is, between what the organization says it stands for and its actions. When the gaps become too great or too significant, special organization development programs or exercises are undertaken to narrow the gaps, that is, to bring the organization's actions in line with its values. The reliance on programs and training is in tune with the secular emphasis of Values-Based Organizations. Paradoxically, this extreme overemphasis on values and their measurement is often the starting point for spirituality.

If assessment devices, measurements, programs, and training exercises were enough and the right thing for motivating people and producing ethical results, there would not be the widespread skepticism about such devices that exists in so many organizations. In far too many organizations, most programs and exercises are merely seen as the latest fad or gimmick. This does not mean that all organizational development programs and ethical training sessions are worthless. However, they are better seen as part of a repertoire of management tools that an organization should have at its disposal.

Closing Reflections

Founded on a firm and stable base of universal and family values by which it strives constantly to live, the Values-Based Organization has much to recommend itself. For the most part, its founders remain as its leaders. Their style is not to preach but rather to lead by exemplary actions. In reaction to other models of spirituality in the workplace, the Values-Based Organization continually goes out of its way not to offend people in its use of concepts and words. All in all, with its regard for the whole person, its insistence on a neutral vocabulary, and its maintenance of a high degree of professionalism within an atmosphere of family values, it manages to appeal to a wide body of people. If anything, the values-based approach would seem to be the most acceptable of the various models we have encountered, precisely because its appeal is the most widespread and universal.

Nevertheless, we are highly critical of the values-based approach. This is not because we do not believe in good values or virtues. Rather, it is because we do not believe that values and virtues alone are sufficient to produce organizations that can sustain a high sense of ethics. Good values or virtues alone are not sufficient to stop alcoholics from drinking and dysfunctional organizations from achieving further dysfunction, or its converse, greater health.

In our view, both to produce and to sustain ethical organizations requires deep and extensive changes in the organizations' values and operating structures. Indeed, on the basis of our interviews, we believe that a great many—though by no means all—people are searching for deeper, more meaningful, timeless, and more universal ideas in which to invest their energies, rather than operate only according to mere values. In fact, many of our respondents were skeptical of the notion that good values alone were sufficient to keep organizations from making destructive or harmful products or engaging in harmful practices.

At the same time, we are well aware that many people are attracted to Values-Based Organizations because values are, or seem to be, much more neutral terms than *soul* or *spirituality*. Unfortunately, we have to accept the fact that, at least currently, many people strongly resist the notions of *spirituality* and *soul*, let alone actually use these words. For such people, there is no way of sanitizing these words to make them more acceptable.

Finally, we also question the extreme confidence that values-based approaches place in trust, especially in the notion that trust can replace loyalty. Many of the arguments that have been advanced in defense of this thesis do not stand up under scrutiny. For instance, isn't loyalty of some kind required as an essential precursor of trust? Furthermore, is it necessary to construe loyalty in the most extreme manner (as Shaw did with respect to faith), that is, as all or nothing, so that it is thereby easy to reject? Finally, are loyalty and trust really separable from, or completely independent of, one another?

> *Trust is replacing loyalty as a way of bonding people into collective enterprises.* Trust grows with effective collaboration in meeting the competitive challenges facing a firm. In contrast, loyalty, at its most extreme, is based on obligations independent of market realities. Several year ago, I worked with a firm that defined loyalty as guaranteed lifetime employment regardless of market forces or the performance of people within the firm. In other words, you were assured of a job and a pay increase as long as you followed the directions set out by leadership. Loyalty, in this case, prevented the firm from tackling the tough issues it faced and, over time, made it less competitive. *Trust is thus a more realistic and ultimately more beneficial way of building the human bonds needed in any organization* [italics added].[10]

In the end, our doubts and reservations with regard to the Values-Based Organization and the approach that underlies it are based on a certain naiveté that we believe is associated with the model. This naiveté is often revealed in the basic premises that undergird the model. For instance, many people, including those we have interviewed, believe that greater consciousness or awareness will lead to better actions on the part of organizations and individuals. It is thus only a matter of time until humans realize the insufferable amount of harm they have caused to the planet through their actions. When they come to this realization and thereby attain greater consciousness, a radical change in human evolution will result.

We are neither so sure nor so sanguine. Although we believe that humans are certainly capable of and in need of greater consciousness, we also believe that humans need different and better institutions, or models, to help them develop greater consciousness.

In complex systems, everything is simultaneously cause and effect. Thus, greater consciousness plays a necessary role in helping to make better institutions possible, and vice versa. But greater consciousness alone is not sufficient. For this reason, we are unwilling to put all our trust in greater human consciousness alone. If anything, we are willing to place our bet on the design of new institutions that will allow greater and renewed hope to emerge. This is the subject of Chapter Nine.

Part Four

A Plan for Spiritual Development

Chapter Nine

A Best-Practice Model

Religion is not a discrete category within human
experience; it is rather a quality that pervades all
of experience [emphasis added]. Accustomed as we
are to distinguishing between "the sacred" and
"the profane," we fail to remember that such a
dividing up of reality is itself a religious idea. It is
often an awkward idea, rather like someone trying
to carry himself over his frame in his own arms—
a confusion of part and whole, form and function.
There are no inherently religious objects, thoughts,
or events; in contemporary culture so much of our
world has been "contaminated" with the *mundane*
we hardly recognize the quality of the sacred [italics
in original]. This has been called the process of
secularization or of modernization, but it may be
something else, it may be a nearly inevitable
consequence of a dualistic paradigm, a religious
point of view that divides reality into two.
                                        —Lynda Sexson

To call management one of the most fundamental, if not the most
fundamental, of all human activities is not an exaggeration. All
people are managers of the events of their lives. Daily, each of us has
to manage hundreds of immediate and long-range activities if we

are to survive, let alone prosper: what to eat, when, and with whom; where to live and how much to spend on housing; how much money to save; with whom to communicate and become friends; whom to marry; if and when to have children; which career or careers to pursue; which schools to attend; which god or gods to worship; and so forth. Each and every one of these activities, large and small, is an act of management. Each involves the creation and selection of various means and ends, along with ways of evaluating whether the means employed are effective in securing the desired ends.

We have stressed the obvious—call them *truisms*—about management because we are afraid that the vast body of business academics, as well as practitioners, do not realize how critical management is, as both a field of inquiry and an essential human activity. Strangely enough, management scholars may have greater tunnel vision than most because of their inordinate desire to be as scientific and legitimate as the so-called hard sciences.

Of all the acts of management, the management of spirituality is one of the most important, mysterious, and frightening. And because of the nature of spirituality, ambivalence and fear are integral parts of this management. They are not tangential to it in the slightest.

Humankind has rightly learned both to fear and to revere spirituality. Fear is a proper response because humankind has repeatedly been reminded that spirituality (under the guise of religion) is capable of being abused, that is, mismanaged, in the worst possible ways. Nonetheless, the passion for spirituality will not go away. It is an enduring and permanent part of the human condition. Responding to it with ambivalence and fear are merely two ways of managing it. We say "managing it" because unless all of us learn to manage our fear and ambivalence, we will be prone to wall off spirituality from our everyday lives.

We believe that the choice confronting humanity at this critical point in history is not *whether* organizations should become more spiritual but rather *how* they can. If organizations are to survive, let alone prosper, then frankly we see no alternative to their becoming spiritual. For this reason, this chapter concentrates more on how than on whether.

The preceding chapters have identified five distinct models for fostering spirituality in the workplace. These models capture the different approaches to the extent to which they are currently known. The purpose of this chapter is to compare the various models so that we can recommend the best currently available model for fostering spirituality in the workplace.

Comparative Spirituality in the Workplace

In the previous chapters, we highlighted various dimensions of the models we have discussed. A set of thirty dimensions that underlie the five models (including many not covered in the chapters) is listed in Appendix C. For our purposes here, it is not necessary to discuss all thirty dimensions—a Herculean task. Ten suffice. The fact that the field of organization studies has not come to grips with these ten dimensions, let alone with the full set of thirty, or has given a superficial response to many of them, is precisely why traditional approaches to studying and changing organizations have failed in so many cases.

Table 9.1 presents the ten dimensions discussed in this chapter. (The numbers and interpretations of these ten dimensions match the numbers and interpretations in Appendix C.) In most cases, there is not a single or definitive interpretation of each dimension. This does not render them invalid. We are dealing with inordinately complex phenomena, many of whose features are still not known at the present time or are open to diverse, multiple, and even divergent interpretations. In addition, there are countless variations within each of the models.

Dimension 1: Precipitating Events

A variety of precipitating events are necessary, but not in themselves sufficient, to start an organization on the path to spirituality

Table 9.1. Ten Dimensions of the Five Models.

			The Models		
Dimensions of the Models	Religion-Based Organization	Evolutionary Organization	Recovering Organization	Socially Responsible Organization	Values-Based Organization
(1) Precipitating Events	Divine Illumination/Inspiration; Religious Revelation; Epiphanies; Active Participation in the Mystery of God	Social Injustice; A Long and Repeated History of Social Crises; Personal Angst; The Paradox of Success; Moderate Dysfunctions	Severe Dysfunctions; Repeated Failures; Repeated Severe Life-Threatening Crises; Pronounced Inability to Learn from Failures	Intense Desire for Personal Self-Realization; Deeply Felt Personal Ethical Ideals; Inspiration Due to World Leaders; Life-Long Commitment to Social Causes; Intense Dissatisfaction with the Current Models of Business	Personal History; Parents/Strong Role Models; Ethical Examples
(2) Alternate Business Texts	The Word of God Interpreted Literally, i.e., in Strict Fundamentalist Terms	Social History; Strong Rejection of Utilitarianism as the "Accepted Philosophy" of Business; Acceptance of Different Ethical Philosophers, e.g., Buber, Kant, etc., as Fundamental Sources for Running Ethical Businesses	Oral Stories; Twelve Steps; Traditions	Founders/Leaders as the Writers of the New Texts of Business; The Social Reinvention of Business; Social Ecology	Common, Universal Values, Virtues; Personal Values/Family Values

(3) Hierarchy, i.e., Owner of Work, Ultimate Authority	God in the Person of Jesus Christ is the CEO and President	Social Justice; Higher Purpose; Social Philosophers	Spiritual Well-Being as Manifested and Realized Through Societal Well-Being; Higher Power/God as Each Conceives of It	Spiritual Well-Being; Community/Social Well-Being; The Disadvantaged; Communities and Societies Themselves	The Community; Company Is Family; Humankind; Liberal Values
(4) Competition, Enemies	The Devil Construed in Fundamentalist, i.e., Literal, Terms	Racists; Sexists; MBA's; Traditional Economists; Accountants	Alcohol; Insanity; Harmful, Addictive Substances; Unethical Behavior	Traditional Business Values and Practices; MBA's; Accountants; Defense Industries; Cigarettes	Religion; Spirituality; Unethical Organizations
(5) Ontology, i.e., Basic Building Blocks of Reality; The Status of Spirit and Soul	The Spirit and Soul Are Real; The Soul and Spirit Are the Essence of What It Is to Be Human and to Have a Relationship With the Transcendent, Essential, and Eternal	Real; Essential, Eternal	Real; Essential, Eternal	Real; Essential, Eternal?	Spirit and Soul Are Meaningless Concepts; Or, They Are Intensely Personal and Private; In Either Case They Are Irrelevant to the Ethical Operation of Business

Table 9.1. Ten Dimensions of the Five Models, cont'd.

The Models

Dimensions of the Models	Religion-Based Organization	Evolutionary Organization	Recovering Organization	Socially-Responsible Organization	Values-Based Organization
(6) The Principle of Hope	Everything Is Possible Through God	Evolution Is Possible; Profits Will Take Care of Themselves if One Runs an Environmental-Friendly Business	Recovery Is Possible if One Works the Program; Miracles Will Happen	If One Markets Out of a Deep Sense of Values, Then One Will Gain Incredible Customer Loyalty; Customers Are Hungry to Identify With Ethical and Socially-Responsible Organizations	If One Runs a Company With Good Family Values, Then One's Employees and Customers Will Respond in Kind; Economic Success Will Follow
(7) Time Required to Bring to About/Enact the Model	Conversion Is Possible at Any Time Through Instantaneous Illumination and the Reception of Christ Into One's Heart	Slow; Long; Moderate	Never Finished; Lifetime; Continual Maintenance; Reinforcement	Moderate/Lifetime	Long; Requires Early Immersion, Maintenance, and Continual Reinforcement

(11) Size and the Management of Size	Small to Large; Privately Held/Church Held	Small to Moderate?; Social Service; Private	Small; Social Service; Private	Unclear?; Private? Tension Between the Desire to Grow and the Commitment to the Development/Maintenance of an Ethical Organizational Climate	Small to Large? Private?
(16) Ontological Status of Future Generations	Present in God's Plan; Real	No Discounting of Future Generations; Broad Stakeholders	Carry the Message to All, Where "All" Includes Future Generations; Real	No Discounting of Future Generations; Broad Array of Stakeholders; Real	No Discounting of Future Generations; Broad Array of Stakeholders; Real
(17) Management Style	Autocratic	Change Oriented; Democratic?; Mixed	True Democracy; Mixed	Autocratic?; Resistant; Mixed	Autocratic? Professional

or the search for deeper meaning and purpose in work. The Religion-Based Organization starts from an initial state of divine illumination or inspiration. In this model, the initial precipitating event is not a single or isolated instance but part of a life-long experience with a particular religion.

In the remaining models, the precipitating event is a more explicit and specific underlying cause. With the exception of the Values-Based Organization, the remaining models depend on recent events, crises, or specific turning points in a person's life. There are considerable overlaps among the models, however. For example, one can trace an individual's desire to seek recovery from alcoholism to his or her most recent and worst cases of alcoholic blackout, but if one takes a much longer perspective, one can say that the most recent crises are merely part of a history of repeated tragedies.

Dimension 2: Alternate Business Texts

Each of the models draws on its own texts for inculcating business wisdom. In most cases, these texts differ strongly from those that are used in most conventional business programs. Although these alternate texts differ considerably from one another, they all share a search for higher, deeper, philosophical truth. Every one of them is grappling seriously with the sincere desire to move beyond strict economic principles, or blatant economic gain, in operating a business. We cannot overemphasize that all of the models we have discussed are actively seeking a source of wisdom different from that of the traditional organization. We would consider the search for wisdom both a necessary and a vital condition for the initial decision to embark on a spiritual path.

Every organization that wishes to foster spirituality in the workplace has to give serious consideration not only to an alternate set of texts but also, more fundamentally, to alternate programs of education. The spiritual development of individuals and organizations cannot be attained through traditional educational programs alone. It also cannot be left to chance. It must be the result of an explicitly designed, systematic, and sustained effort.

Dimension 3: Hierarchy, Owner of Work, Ultimate Authority

The "ultimate authority" or "owner of work" is not a literal or even metaphorical "person." Rather, it is a higher authority. This dimension points to a higher ethical plane, or higher set of ethical management principles, according to which organizations can be run.

Dimension 4: Competition, Enemies

In contrast to the previous dimension, Dimension 4 represents the "lower principles" that are in opposition to the higher plane. *Competition* should be conceived of as the set of counterprinciples that lead to the destruction of the soul of an organization.

Dimension 5: Ontology

The fundamental building blocks of the spiritually based organization are not necessarily economic transactions alone. To be sure, economic considerations are not trivial, as we have emphasized repeatedly. However, in light of the higher values by which the spiritually based organization is run, the basic building blocks, or ontology, of such an organization are signs that it rests on a very different foundation. Whereas traditional businesses (and the Values-Based Organization) are extremely loath to use the "S-words," the spiritually based organization is not. It recognizes that it is governed by a higher set of principles, including the principles of its founders.

Dimension 6: The Principle of Hope

This dimension has been discussed extensively throughout this book; we have nothing to add here.

Dimension 7: Time Required to Enact the Model

The time line on which the spiritually based organization operates is much, much greater than the time line used by today's traditional organizations, the great many of which are preoccupied with next week, or next quarter at best. Thus this dimension recognizes explicitly that spirituality is not something to be accomplished in the next week or quarter, but rather is a task that extends over the entire course of a person's—and organization's—life. If one grants that the soul is immortal, then the task extends even beyond one's physical life.

Dimension 11: Size and Management of Size

The same tension, or at least lack of clarity, is reflected in the size of organizations. Some of the models recognize explicitly that it is difficult at best to foster or maintain spirituality in large organizations. Other organizations believe that they can continue to grow and still maintain spirituality. This ambivalence goes back to the underlying tension between making money and doing good. Some organizations not only believe that they can continue to be spiritual as they grow in size, but also, as in the case of Ben & Jerry's, that the more money they make, the more they can give to good causes.

Dimension 16: Ontological Status of Future Generations

None of the models believe in the traditional economic concept of discounting future generations. All of the models stress the importance of future generations as stakeholders in the organization. Future generations are a potent factor that must be included in the organization's current decisions. It is unethical not only to ignore future generations, but also to undertake present-day actions that will affect future generations negatively.

Dimension 17: Management Style

There is a complex mixture of ideals as well as current realities among the management styles of the various models. Unfortunately, the leaders of a number of the models govern according to autocratic styles of management. Obviously this is not a desirable feature. To say the least, it is highly contradictory to have an organization claim that it is pursuing spirituality while its leaders are autocratic. This tension is responsible for much of the skepticism regarding spiritually based organizations as they currently exist. It is probably one of their biggest internal contradictions and doubtless a source of great external mistrust.

This is where the model of the Recovering Organization is especially helpful. The notion of constantly taking audits, admitting one's errors, and making direct amends should be a vitally important design feature of spiritually based organizations. Of course, nothing currently guarantees that such organizations will confront their unsavory sides. Denial is present not only in individuals but also in organizations, large scale institutions, and unfortunately even whole societies.

The Best-Practice Model

Choice is all but impossible in the absence of clear and recognizable alternatives. One of the most important things that the five models make possible is the basic ability to make choices, let alone more intelligent ones. For some organizations, one or more of the various models as they currently exist will be appropriate for their particular circumstances. For most organizations, we expect that none of the pure models will be appropriate. Some combination, or a hybrid model, will undoubtedly be more fitting.

In this section we outline what in our judgment is the best alternative at this time. By *best* we mean a strategy that is least likely to incur an intense counterreaction by stakeholders. As a result, such a strategy is inherently conservative. Also, given the present state of knowledge, we discuss this alternative model in very general terms. We cannot discuss its detailed operation in terms of any specific organization.

We present our recommendation in terms of the general business principles of the five models. Organizations are run fundamentally by principles, no matter how implicit they are. When things are running smoothly, the underlying rules of the game are rarely questioned, and perhaps do not need to be questioned. However, when an organization is contemplating a fundamental shift, or when such a shift is required, then it behooves the organization to examine as systematically and as critically as possible its underlying principles. Indeed, it is absolutely essential that these underlying principles be brought to the surface so they can be explicitly examined. The principles outlined here are those that we believe will lead to the spiritually based organizations of tomorrow.

The hybrid we recommend is composed of two main strands. First, it evolves from the Values-Based model; second, it incorporates some of the most desirable features, or business principles, of each of the remaining designs.

The Evolutionary Organization was first discussed in relation to the Religion-Based Organization, from which, we pointed out, it had originally evolved. However, now that all five models have been presented, new possibilities arise. In creating a hybrid model, we can now use any of the design models as a *starting point* and any of the others as an *ending point*. We can thereby evolve backwards, forwards, or sideways as the situation demands.

Even though we are highly critical of the Values-Based Organization, we nonetheless believe that it is the best and most appropriate starting point. The fact that we start there does not mean we should end there, *whereas once the supreme challenge was to evolve beyond the Religion-Based Organization, the supreme challenge today is to evolve beyond the Values-Based Organization.*

The Values-Based Organization is a proper starting point precisely because it is the least controversial, and consequently the least threatening, of all of the various models. It clearly and succinctly expresses the philosophy that an organization is not to be aligned with any particular religion. In addition, it also states clearly and strongly that no expressions of religion are to be tolerated in the workplace. Individual employees may form lunchtime religious study groups if they so desire, but any actions whatsoever directed toward proselytizing their fellow employees, as well as toward expressing religious ideas in the workplace, are to be discouraged in the strongest possible terms.

This is not necessarily in conflict with the First Amendment. Indeed, a great deal of confusion exists with regard to the meaning and interpretation of the First Amendment,[1] which merely says that *no government unit* may pass laws that are in conflict with or that interfere with the expression of free speech. The First Amendment does not say that nongovernmental organizations may not set their own management policies. For example, no recording company is forced by law to produce or distribute every and all artistic expressions. If they were, they would in effect be forced to publish everything. Thus, if a company did not like rap music or sexist and violent lyrics, it would not be obligated to publish the music of a particular artist. For such an artist to charge censorship would be disingenuous.

At this particular time in the history of the design and management of organizations, most organizations are well advised to begin their pursuit of spirituality in the workplace in terms of the most neutral and least offensive language possible. There is nothing wrong per se with the leaders of an organization declaring the values by which they wish to live. The neutral vocabulary of the Values-Based Organization and its underlying metaphor of a family are probably the most inclusive elements with which to proceed. Thus, the Best-Practice Model not only borrows the notion of inclusiveness from the Values-Based Organization, but it also adopts its neutral vocabulary.

The Best-Practice Model borrows from each of the other models as well. For instance, from the Religion-Based Organization it incorporates the fundamental notion that spirituality adds a vital dimension to life that is not supplied by any other human agency or activity. In the language of the great American philosopher William James,[2] religion—or in our age, spirituality—adds a "vital zest" for life that is not derived from any other sphere of human activity. The Religion-Based Organization also adds the vital dimension of hope and optimism. One may not like the particular and limited form that this principle assumes in the Religion-Based Organization, but it speaks to the necessity of developing and preserving the "soul" of an organization as a manifestation of hope. In this same context, the Religion-Based Organization also vitally appreciates the need for deepening one's relationship with God, or one's higher power, if that is preferred.

The notion of a higher power is one of the many important components that comes from the model of the Recovering Organization. Premised on the ideal that God or spirit is not to be construed literally, this notion sets the concept of a higher power free from the moorings and trappings of traditional religion. A further qualification is also made clear: most if not all humans are unable to solve their deepest problems solely on their own or merely by reference to human values.

We realize and appreciate the many criticisms that have been leveled against Alcoholics Anonymous in particular and Twelve Step groups in general. We also understand that many people construe the steps of AA as calling for abandoning personal responsibility by giving it up to a higher power. This is not AA's intention. This is also not what the chapter on the Recovering Organization intended. By participating in AA or the Recovering Organization, one is not abandoning personal responsibility. Rather, one is expanding it through enlisting the help of a power greater than oneself.

The Recovering Organization also adds another valuable component to the Best-Practice Model: the necessity of constantly taking moral audits of the organization to ascertain whether it is living up to its proclaimed ideals of managing in a more spiritual manner without forcing ideas down people's throats. The audit is not meant to be a version of the "thought police." It merely means that organizations must be constantly on guard against spirituality spilling over into full-fledged religion, that is, against becoming a religious cult. It also means that as many of the organization's stakeholders as possible must be involved in its continual assessment and design.

In this sense, the Best-Practice Model borrows from the Evolutionary Organization the element of "circles for listening." The purpose of such circles is not only to hear the anxieties and concerns of the members of an organization, but also to ensure that their participation is taken seriously.

From the Evolutionary Organization the Best-Practice Model also borrows the notion of incorporating broader philosophical texts, such as those of Martin Buber, Immanuel Kant, and so on. The Best-Practice Model also acknowledges the necessity of bringing in outside speakers who are knowledgeable about philosophy and spirituality in nonsectarian, nondenominational terms. It also borrows the concept of running regular workshops for the development of everyone connected with the organization. In addition, it attempts to institute as many daily "acts of kindness" as possible.

The Best-Practice Model borrows from the Recovering Organization the important realization that even with the best of intentions, religion, spirituality, and even recovery itself are similarly prone to addiction. That is, the process of treating addictions can itself become addictive. Humans are such complex creatures that the very means they use to control various diseases are entirely capable of engendering more subtle diseases in turn.

From the Socially Responsible Organization the Best-Practice Model borrows the important notion that when it comes to performing ethical acts, the threshold ought to be kept as low as possible. If one sets a particular relatively high threshold (such as a certain amount of profit), once this threshold is reached the temptation is to raise it higher and higher. As the case of Ben & Jerry's demonstrates, one is well advised to set the threshold low and to start acting responsibly from day one of an organization's existence.

From the Recovering Organization comes another important operating principle: organizational responsibility must be broadened to include all stakeholders. Contrary to the experience of the Socially Responsible Organization, as illustrated in the example of Ben & Jerry's, an organization is well advised to focus as much attention on its internal stakeholders as it focuses on its external stakeholders. To neglect internal stakeholders under the guise of serving external ones is to court problems and contradict the very meaning of spirituality.

From the Values-Based Organization comes the advisement to recognize and treat people as "whole persons." People are not fragmented beings whose souls can be cut up and bartered.

The leaders of a would-be spiritually based organization are well advised to emphasize and reinforce their ideals through a consistent set of acts. In addition, they should be forthcoming and forthright in admitting their shortcomings. This does not mean that they necessarily need to respond to every criticism. They do need to make clear that what they are attempting to achieve is an ideal, and further, that it is better to fall short of one's ideals than not to have them at all. In many ways, everyone in an organization needs to understand that they are engaged in an incredible experiment. Indeed, the word *experiment* cannot be emphasized enough.

If an organization is to become spiritual, then clearly it must put as much energy toward achieving this goal as it has put toward anything else it has ever tried to accomplish. If anything, the spiritually based organization demands a higher degree of commitment than any program tried so far, such as Total Quality Management or reengineering. Along the way to becoming spiritual, there will be as many failures and setbacks as there are successes. One of the main purposes of the principle of hope is to maintain a spirit of optimism so that the organization is not crippled by such failures but instead continually learns from them.

Closing Reflections

Our study of spirituality in the workplace reaches the unfortunate conclusion that none of the models, at least to the extent that they are currently known, are very advanced. This conclusion is made all the more painfully apparent by Ken Wilber's important work.[3]

In Wilber's terms, each of the various models is still at an elementary stage of development. At best, each model merely taps into one or two of the four general orientations to spirituality that Wilber has identified (see Chapter Two). None of the models is particularly well integrated or developed across all of the four orientations. For instance, the Recovering Organization is not especially well developed in the outer-communal orientation, because AA's principles are still too restrictive to be applied to the redesign and transformation of whole societies. Also, its organization at the national level is still minimal. Similarly, Ben & Jerry's, a prime example of the Socially Responsible Organization, is more well developed in its outer-communal facets than in its inner-communal aspects.

This painful conclusion should not be taken as final proof of the futility of attempting to foster greater spirituality in the workplace—to the contrary! If anything, it should be taken as a supreme challenge to spur organizations on to further action.

In the end, spirituality is its own fuel. It provides the abiding hope, boundless energy, and enthusiasm needed to surmount all the obstacles that always lie in its path.

To emphasize an earlier point, whereas early in the twentieth century the challenge was to learn how to evolve from the Religious to the Values-Based Organization, the challenge today is to learn how to evolve from the Values-Based to the Spiritually Based Organization. For organizations to become more spiritual, they will have to learn to incorporate a deeper set of texts and practices from both Eastern and Western traditions.

A far deeper transformation of organizations than has even been dreamed of is required. Unless this happens, neither organizations nor the individuals who work in them will prosper materially as well as spiritually. Spirituality gives us the constant hope necessary to embark on the path of transformation and to endure the constant setbacks in its way.

The following are discussion points for individuals and organizations that are contemplating introducing and promoting greater spirituality in the workplace. They are for all the members of an organization, not just top management.

1. Spirituality is best attained through gentleness and softness. Organizations are advised to choose the softest and the most gentle path. They are not to cram spirituality down the throats of individuals or the organization as a whole. This does not mean that the leaders of organizations should be either covert or deceptive, let alone, Machiavellian. It means that they are extremely well-advised to put actions over words. Because Western societies are extremely wary of false religions in disguise, and rightly so, the leaders of organizations are forewarned not to promote anything that smacks of religion. This does not mean that they should not declare their values or their spiritual feelings. Instead, they are advised to let their sentiments emerge naturally, as part of the natural evolution and development of their organization. Thus, the first questions for discussion are, *What is the appropriate gentle and soft path for the organization? What do people consider offensive? What is their "comfort zone" regarding spirituality? How can an organization promote spirituality without sanctioning religion?* These questions should be discussed by all the members of an organization.

2. The path to spirituality more often than not is initiated as the result of a repeated series of individual or organizational crises. Thus, the questions are, *What crises or near crises has our organization had that indicate that we need to move to a higher ethical plane if we are to avoid future crises? What forms of denial have prevented our organization from recognizing the crises that have befallen us?*

3. *What new sources of knowledge and wisdom does our organization need to draw on in order to move it to a higher ethical and spiritual plane? What new forms of education are required to develop our organization and members, especially in non-coercive ways?*

4. *What are the previous principles by which the organization has been run that have led it to the brink of crisis and prevented it from being more ethical? How can such principles be countered?*

5. *What forms of greed has our organization been subject to in the past? How has our organization been unable to limit greed and growth?*

What new mechanisms does our organization propose in order to confront and limit greed and growth?

6. Organizations that are spiritual do not discount future generations. Thus, other crucial questions are, *How does our organization intend to honor the existence and well-being of future generations? What kinds of actions will we undertake that will show our commitment to the longest time span possible?*

These are only a few of the many questions that an organization needs to ask itself repeatedly. They are the essence of what it means to be spiritual.

Spirituality is not a final state. It is an ongoing process—a process that leads to itself. Above all, spirituality is not a simple-minded how-to list or checklist. It is a perpetual process of becoming, a continual unfolding of the human spirit.

Questionnaire on Meaning and Purpose in the Workplace

All responses to this questionnaire will be held and
treated in strict confidence. In no case will the
names of individuals or organizations be disclosed.

Please give us some background information about yourself:

Questionnaire on Meaning and Purpose in the Workplace

1. Sex: Male ___   Female ___   2. Race: _____

3. Marital
   Status: Single ____   Married ____   Divorced ____   Widowed ____

4. Number of Children: ____

5. Current Position/Title: ____   6. Industry _____

7. Number of Years   8. Number of Employees
   in the Industry: ____   You Supervise: ____

9. Undergraduate   10. Undergraduate
   Major: _____   School: _____

11. Highest   12. Graduate
    Graduate Degree: _____   School: _____

13. Field in which you received your highest degree: _____

14. Birthplace: _____   15. Age: ____

16. What gives you the *most meaning and purpose* in your *JOB?* (Check only
    the *TOP THREE*)

    a. Being associated with   h. Being associated with
       a good organization ____   an ethical organization ____

    b. Service to others ____   i. Service to my immediate
                                          community ____
    c. Service to my country ____
                                      j. Service to humankind ____
    d. Service to future
       generations ____   k. Making money ____

    e. Having good colleagues ____   l. Interesting work ____

    f. Realize my full   m. Being innovative ____
       potential as a person ____
                                      n. Nothing ____
    g. Producing good
       products/services ____

17. How much does your work contribute to the general meaning in your life?

    Not   Contributes
    at All   1   2   3   4   5   6   7   Very Much

18. How fearful are you of losing your job?

    Not   Extremely
    at All   1   2   3   4   5   6   7   Fearful

Questionnaire on Meaning and
Purpose in the Workplace, Cont'd.

19. Please circle the approximate percentage of downsizing which your organization has undergone in the last 3 to 5 years.

0%	25%	50%	75%	100%

20. a. Please list briefly some of the basic values which guide your life:

_____

_____

_____

_____

_____

b. How often do you feel you are forced to compromise your basic values in making important decisions *AT WORK*?

Never Forced to Compromise	1	2	3	4	5	6	7	Often Forced to Compromise

21. On each of the dimensions below, please circle the number that best describes your organization. For instance, if your organization is more "warm" than "cold," then circle one of the numbers 1, 2, or 3 depending upon how "warm" your organization is.

Warm	1	2	3	4	5	6	7	Cold
Rigid	1	2	3	4	5	6	7	Flexible
Autocratic	1	2	3	4	5	6	7	Democratic
Caring	1	2	3	4	5	6	7	Uncaring
Spiritual	1	2	3	4	5	6	7	Worldly
Happy	1	2	3	4	5	6	7	Sad
Unprofitable	1	2	3	4	5	6	7	Profitable
Turbulent	1	2	3	4	5	6	7	Calm
Profits-first	1	2	3	4	5	6	7	People-first
Ethical	1	2	3	4	5	6	7	Unethical
Insane	1	2	3	4	5	6	7	Sane
Tolerant of minorities	1	2	3	4	5	6	7	Intolerant of minorities
High anxiety	1	2	3	4	5	6	7	Low anxiety
Tolerant of gays	1	2	3	4	5	6	7	Intolerant of gays

Questionnaire on Meaning and Purpose in the Workplace, Cont'd.

22. Please write in the current religious affiliations, if any, of your parents, yourself, and your spouse.

    Mother: _____

    Father: _____

    You: _____

    Your spouse: _____

23. How often did your parents attend religious services?

Never	Very Rarely	Once or Twice a Year	3 to 6 Times a Year	Once a Month	1 to 3 Times a Week	Every Day
1	2	3	4	5	6	7

24. How often do you and your spouse attend religious services?

Never	Very Rarely	Once or Twice a Year	3 to 6 Times a Year	Once a Month	1 to 3 Times a Week	Every Day
1	2	3	4	5	6	7

25. How often do you pray or meditate?

Never	Very Rarely	Once or Twice a Year	3 to 6 Times a Year	Once a Month	1 to 3 Times a Week	Every Day
1	2	3	4	5	6	7

26. What meaning does the term *religious* have for you? (Please write in.)

    _____

    _____

    _____

    _____

    _____

27. What meaning does the term *spiritual* have for you? (Please write in.)

    _____

    _____

    _____

    _____

    _____

Questionnaire on Meaning and Purpose in the Workplace, Cont'd.

28. How important is *religion* in your life?

    Not   Very
    important at all   1   2   3   4   5   6   7   important

29. How important is *spirituality* in your life?

    Not   Very
    important at all   1   2   3   4   5   6   7   important

30. Very briefly, what are the *main differences* between religion and spirituality for you?

    _____

    _____

    _____

31. Please rate the term "religious" on the following dimensions.

    Tolerant   1   2   3   4   5   6   7   Intolerant
    Close-minded   1   2   3   4   5   6   7   Open-minded
    Inclusive   1   2   3   4   5   6   7   Exclusive

32. Please rate the term "spiritual" on the following dimensions.

    Tolerant   1   2   3   4   5   6   7   Intolerant
    Close-minded   1   2   3   4   5   6   7   Open-minded
    Inclusive   1   2   3   4   5   6   7   Exclusive

33. What is the role of *spirituality* in the workplace?

    Irrelevant   1   2   3   4   5   6   7   Relevant

    An   An
    inappropriate   appropriate
    topic for   topic for
    discussion   discussion
    at work   1   2   3   4   5   6   7   at work

    Should be   Should be
    dealt with   dealt with
    outside of work 1   2   3   4   5   6   7   at work

    Why? _____

    _____

Questionnaire on Meaning and
Purpose in the Workplace, Cont'd.

---

34. What is the role of *general philosophical values* in the workplace?

Irrelevant	1	2	3	4	5	6	7	Relevant
An inappropriate topic for discussion at work	1	2	3	4	5	6	7	An appropriate topic for discussion at work
Should be dealt with outside of work	1	2	3	4	5	6	7	Should be dealt with at work

Why? _____

_____

35. What *processes*, if any, would you recommend that organizations could use to foster *fruitful* discussions of the role of spirituality in the workplace (e.g., the use of a trained outside facilitator, special team building exercises, etc.)? (Please write in.)

_____

_____

_____

_____

36. Do you believe in a Deity or Higher Power?

Disbelieve Strongly	1	2	3	4	5	6	7	Believe Strongly

37. Have you ever felt the *presence* of a Deity or Higher Power at work?

Never	1	2	3	4	5	6	7	Often

Describe the situations when you *experienced a* Deity or Higher Power *at work*:

_____

_____

_____

_____

_____

_____

Questionnaire on Meaning and
Purpose in the Workplace, Cont'd.

---

38. Have you ever discussed issues of *spirituality* with your co-workers?

Never   1   2   3   4   5   6   7   Often

What topics have you discussed?_____

_____

_____

_____

39. Have you ever discussed issues of *general philosophical values* with your co-workers?

Never   1   2   3   4   5   6   7   Often

What topics have you discussed?_____

_____

_____

_____

40. How often have you felt *joy* and/or bliss at work?

Never   1   2   3   4   5   6   7   Often

Why? Over what? _____

_____

_____

41. How often have you had an *epiphany*, or a strong spiritual experience, at work?

Never   1   2   3   4   5   6   7   Often

Why? Over what? _____

_____

_____

42. How often have you felt depressed at work because of the nature of your *job* and/or *organization*?

Never   1   2   3   4   5   6   7   Often

Why? Over what? _____

_____

_____

Questionnaire on Meaning and Purpose in the Workplace, Cont'd.

43. How often have you felt like crying at work?

    Never   1   2   3   4   5   6   7   Often

    Why? Over what? _____

    _____

    _____

    _____

44. What gets you through hard times at work? _____

    _____

    _____

    _____

45. a. How much of your *total self* are you able to express at work?

    Very little
    of me   1   2   3   4   5   6   7   All of me

    b. How much of your *complete creativity* are you able to express at work?

    None   1   2   3   4   5   6   7   Completely

    c. How much of your *total feelings* are you able to express at work?

    None   1   2   3   4   5   6   7   Completely

    d. How much of your *complete soul* are you able to express at work?

    None   1   2   3   4   5   6   7   Completely

    e. How much of your *total intelligence* are you able to express at work?

    None   1   2   3   4   5   6   7   Completely

    f. How much of your *full humor* are you able to express at work?

    None   1   2   3   4   5   6   7   Completely

46. How often do you *pray* and/or *meditate AT WORK*?

Never	Very Rarely	Once or Twice a Year	3 to 6 Times a Year	Once a Month	1 to 3 Times a Week	Every Day
1	2	3	4	5	6	7

For what, if anything, do you pray? (List *all* that apply.)

a. To get me through the day _____

b. To renew myself _____

c. To overcome boredom _____

d. To exist in a dysfunctional society _____

e. To prepare myself for difficult situations _____

f. For co-workers who are going through difficult times _____

g. For general guidance in making tough decisions _____

Questionnaire on Meaning and
Purpose in the Workplace, Cont'd.

h. To help with feelings of loneliness ____

i. To fight off attacks to my esteem ____

j. To cope with an angry boss ____

k. To cope with angry co-workers ____

l. To give thanks for something good that has happened ____

m. To cope with a difficult personal loss ____

n. Other (Please write in.)

_____

_____

_____

47. What things has your organization done that you are *most proud* of?

_____

_____

48. What things has your organization done that you are *most ashamed* of?

_____

_____

49. Please give the name, if any, of an organization which you would regard as a *role model* in fostering *spiritual values* at work: _____

50. How many of the following programs does your organization have? (Check all that apply.)

a. Twelve Step programs ____

b. Wellness groups ____

c. Health programs ____

d. Consciousness raising programs ____

e. Family counseling ____

f. Community service at company expense and time ____

g. Flex-time ____

h. Meditation groups ____

i. Stress management programs ____

j. Psychological counseling ____

k. Psychotherapy ____

l. Mandatory drug testing ____

m. Diversity programs ____

n. Prayer groups ____

o. Other:_____

If you wish to receive a summary report, please give us your name and address.

Name: _____

Name of Your Organization: _____

Address: _____

If you would be willing to be interviewed over the phone, please give us your telephone number: _____

Appendix B

Selected Quantitative Results

Our sample consisted of the following groups:

G 1: Mailed Questionnaires	N = 131
G 2: Mitroff West-Coast Utility	N = 13
G 3: Mitroff Partial Interviews	N = 39
G 4: Denton Partial Interviews	N = 18
G 5: Denton East-Coast Manufacturer	N = 14
Total	N = 215

Figure B.1. Demographics

Mailed Questionnaires: N = 131

Gender	N
Male	48
Female	83
Total	131

Race	N
Caucasian	96
Hispanic	17
Asian	6
African-American	6
Other	3
Unspecified	3
Total	131

Marital Status	
Single	21
Married	90
Divorced	18
Widowed	2
Total	131

Number of Children	
Mean	1.3

Age	
Youngest	20
Oldest	68
Mean	38

Number Years in Industry	
Minimum	1
Maximum	40
Mean	5

Industry	
For-Profit	121
Not-for-Profit	10
Total	131

Figure B.2. Positions

Mailed Questionnaires: N = 131

Positions	N
Human Resource Manager	40
Director of Human Resources	29
VP Human Resources	25
Personnel Manager	7
Administrator HR	6
HR Representative	2
Owner	2
Unknown	2
Other	18
Total	131

Figure B.3. Education

Mailed Questionnaires: N = 131

Undergraduate Degrees	N
Business	40
Psychology	24
None	9
Sociology	8
Accounting	6
English Literature	6
Liberal Arts	6
Anthropology	4
Behavioral Sciences	3
Economics	3
Unknown	2
Education	2
Mathematics	2
Engineering	2
Social Sciences	2
Biology	1
Chemistry	1
Speech & Hearing Pathology	1
Education	1
Speech Communication	1
Fine Arts	1
Lighting Design for Theatre	1
Legal Administration	1
Government	1
Industrial	1
Journalism	1
Public Relations	1

Graduate Degrees	N
MS/MA	30
MBA	18
PhD	1
JD	1

Figure B.4. Demographics

West Coast Utility: N = 13

Gender	N
Male	12
Female	1
Total	13

Number of Children	
Mean	2.2

Age	
Mean	51

Race	N
Caucasian	10
Hispanic	0
Asian	0
African-American	2
Other	0
Unspecified	1
Total	13

Number Years in Industry	
Mean	21

Marital Status	
Single	0
Married	13
Divorced	0
Widowed	0
Total	13

Figure B.5. Positions

West-Coast Utility: N = 13

Positions	N
District Operations Mgr	2
Director Finance	1
Director HR	1
Director Operations & Planning	1
Director Personnel	1
Director Region	1
VP	1
VP & Chief Information Officer	1
VP Business Development	1
VP Controller	1
VP Government Affairs	1
Unspecified	1
Total	13

Figure B.6. Education

West-Coast Utility: N = 13

Undergraduate Degrees	N
Business	5
Accounting	2
Economics	1
Political Science	1
Chemical Engineering	1
Unspecified	3

Graduate Degrees	N
MBA	4
MS	2

Figure B.7. Demographics

Mitroff Partial Interviews: N = 23 to 39

Gender	N
Male	29
Female	7
Total	36

Number of Children	
Mean	2.2

Number Years in Industry	
Mean	18

Race	N
Caucasian	17
Hispanic	–
Asian	–
African-American	2
Other	–
Unspecified	18
Total	27

Marital Status	
Single	2
Married	28
Divorced	4
Widowed	1
Total	35

Note: The number of participants in this group varies from 23 to 39 depending on the particular question and the stage of the questionnaire or interview. In addition, another 8 persons were interviewed informally as part of the development of the questionnaires and interviews.

Figure B.8. Positions

Mitroff Partial Interviews: N = 23 to 39

Positions	N
President/CEO	12
Executive Director	6
Senior Manager	4
Chief Financial Officer	2
Head of HR	2
Partner	2
Senior Admin Assistant	1
Director Marketing Research	1
Director of Planning	1
General Counsel	1
Team Leader	1
Unspecified	4
Total	37

Note: The number of participants in this group varies from 23 to 39 depending on the particular question and the stage of the questionnaire or interview. In addition, another 8 persons were interviewed informally as part of the development of the questionnaires and interviews.

Figure B.9. Industries

Mitroff Partial Interviews: N = 23 to 39

Industries	N
Not-For-Profit	14
Outdoor	4
Utility	4
Consulting	3
High-Tech	3
Entertainment	1
Food Manufacturing	1
Government	1
Holding Company	1
Legal	1
Total	33

Note: The number of participants in this group varies from 23 to 39 depending on the particular question and the stage of the questionnaire or interview. In addition, another 8 persons were interviewed informally as part of the development of the questionnaires and interviews.

Figure B.10. Education

Mitroff Partial Interviews: N = 23 to 39

Undergraduate Degrees	N		Graduate Degrees	N
Political Science	6		MBA	6
Sociology	3		MS	4
History	3		PhD/DBA	2
Engineering	3		LLB	1
Economics	3		JD	1
Accounting	3			
Business	2			
Math	1			
Public Relations	1			
Theatre	1			
Mass Communications	1			
Literature	1			
Journalism	1			
Navigation	1			
Theology	1			
Social Work	1			
No Degree	4			
Total	36			

Note: The number of participants in this group varies from 23 to 39 depending on the particular question and the stage of the questionnaire or interview. In addition, another 8 persons were interviewed informally as part of the development of the questionnaires and interviews.

Figure B.11. Demographics

East-Coast Manufacturer: N = 14

Gender	N
Male	13
Female	1
Total	14

Number of Children	
Mean	2.3

Age	
Mean	49

Race	N
Caucasian	14
Hispanic	0
Asian	0
African-American	0
Other	0
Unspecified	0
Total	14

Number Years in Industry	
Mean	21

Marital Status	
Single	0
Married	13
Divorced	0
Widowed	1
Total	14

Figure B.12. Positions

East-Coast Manufacturer: N = 14

Positions	N
President	4
President/CEO	4
President/COO	1
Senior VP/CFO Finance	1
Senior VP	2
VP	1
Unspecified	1

Figure B.13. Education

East-Coast Manufacturer: N = 14

Undergraduate Degrees	N
Accounting	1
Business	1
Chemistry	1
Economics & Politics	1
Financial Management	1
Industrial Engineering	1
Industrial Management	1
Marketing	1
Marketing & Economics	1
Math	1
Political Science	1
Textile Technology	1
None	1
Unspecified	1

Graduate Degrees	N
MBA	3
MS	1
PhD	1
JD	1

Figure B.14. Demographics

Denton Partial Interviews: N = 18

Gender	N
Male	11
Female	7
Total	18

Number of Children	
Mean	2.2

Age	
Mean	45

Race	N
Caucasian	17
Hispanic	0
Asian	0
African-American	1
Other	0
Unspecified	1
Total	18

Number Years in Industry	
Mean	14

Marital Status	
Single	2
Married	9
Divorced	7
Widowed	0
Total	18

Figure B.15. Positions

Denton Partial Interviews: N = 18

Positions	N
President	3
CFO	1
Consultant/Owner	1
Consultant	1
Consultant/Director	1
Consultant HR	1
Consultant/Trainer	1
Executive Director	1
Executive Editor	1
Manager	1
Partner	1
Principal	1
Senior Librarian	1
Senior Research Associate	1
Special Asst to EEOC Commission	1
Organizational Specialist	1

Figure B.16. Industries

Denton Partial Interviews: N = 18

Industries	N
Consulting	7
Commercial Food Equipment	1
Electric Utility	1
Government	2
Health Care	1
Insurance/Financial Services	1
New Media	1
Non-Profit	1
Public Library	1
Public Transit	1
Security	1

Figure B.17. Education

Denton Partial Interviews: N = 18

Undergraduate Degrees	N
Business	3
Communications	3
History	2
Psychology	2
Art History	1
Education	1
English	1
Home Economics	1
Labor Relations	1
Sociology	1
Unspecified	1

Graduate Degrees	N
MBA	4
MA/MS	1
MLS	1
PhD	1

Data Analyses

The following tables and figures illustrate our analyses of the data obtained from the questionnaires and interviews.

Figure B.18. Top Three Items That Gave Participants the Most Meaning and Purpose in Their Jobs

Mailed Questionnaires: N = 131

The Top 3 Items That Give You Most Meaning & Purpose In Your Job			
Rank	*Item*	N	%
1.	Interesting Work	67	17
2.	Realize My Full Potential as a Person	60	15
3.	Being Associated with a Good Organization	52	13
4.	Being Associated with an Ethical Organization	47	12
5.	Making Money	40	10
6.	Service to Others	33	8
7.	Good Colleagues	27	7
8.	Being Innovative	26	7
9.	Producing Good Products/Services	21	5
10.	Service to Humankind	7	2
11.	Service to Future Generations	5	1
12.	Service to My Immediate Community	3	1
13.	Nothing	1	0
14.	Service to My Country	0	0
	Total	389[a]	98[b]

[a] The total number of responses do not add up to 393 (3 x 131) because not all respondents checked three items.

[b] Percentages do not add up to 100 percent because of rounding.

Figure B.19 shows that work is an important contributing factor to the meaning that people find in their lives, and that work contributes significantly more to this meaning than fear of losing their job or how often they are forced to compromise their basic values at work. These conclusions are based on participants' responses to the following questions (see Appendix A):

(17) How much does your work contribute to the general meaning in your life?

(18) How fearful are you of losing your job?

(20b) How often do you feel you are forced to compromise your basic values in making important decisions at work?

Figure B.19. Contributions of Work, Fear of Job Loss, and Compromise to Meaning in Life

Mailed Questionnaires: N = 131

Q #17: How Much Does Your Work Contribute to the Meaning in Your Life?
Q #18: How Fearful Are You of Losing Your Job?

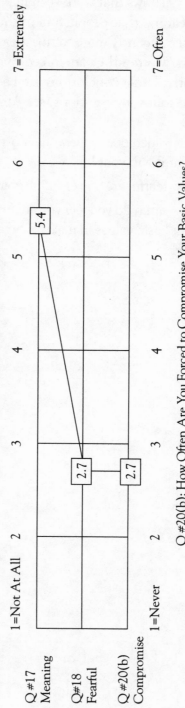

Q #20(b): How Often Are You Forced to Compromise Your Basic Values?

Note: There is a significant statistical difference between the means at *p* = 0.000.

Factor analyses reveal that five factors are sufficient to explain the structure underlying Figure 3.1. The *eigenvalues* associated with the factors in Figures B.20 and B.21 are particularly strong. The first factor in Figure B.20, the *emotional support* an organization offers its members, shows that the respondents grouped together four emotional scales into a single cluster or factor. The second factor shows clearly that the scales that contribute to *organizational distress* also cluster strongly together. The third factor, a propensity for *tolerance*, is also clear and strong. The fourth factor, *control*, shows that a worldly orientation and a rigid and autocratic structure associate strongly in the minds of the respondents. The final factor, *alignment*, shows clearly that it is not contradictory or incompatible for an organization to be both profitable and ethical.

Figure B.20. Maximum Likelihood, Varimax Factor Analysis of Question 21 (Organization Profile)

Q #21: Organization Profile, Mailed Questionnaires: N = 131

	Factor 1	Factor 2	Factor 3	Factor 4	Factor 5	Communality
Eigenvalue	4.069	1.525	1.382	1.223	1.021	
Proportion	0.291	0.109	0.099	0.087	0.073	
Cumulative	0.291	0.400	0.498	0.586	0.659	0.505
	Emotional Support	Distress	Tolerance	Controlling	+Alignment	

Item	Factor 1	Factor 2	Factor 3	Factor 4	Factor 5
Caring	+0.685				
Warm	+0.680				
Happy	+0.606				
People-First	−0.511				
High Anxiety		+0.844			
Turbulent		+0.615			
Insane		+0.463			
Tolerant Gays			+0.969		
Tolerant Minorities			+0.492		
Autocratic				+0.823	
Rigid				+0.440	
Worldly				−0.242	
Profitable					−0.568
Ethical					+0.449

	Factor 1	Factor 2	Factor 3	Factor 4	Factor 5	Communality
Variance	2.0068	1.6369	1.3461	1.1171	0.9565	7.0634
% Variance	0.143	0.117	0.096	0.080	0.068	0.505

Figure B.21. Principal Component, Varimax Factor Analysis of Question 21

Q #21: *Organization Profile, Mailed Questionnaires: N = 131*

	Factor 1	Factor 2	Factor 3	Factor 4	Factor 5	Communality
Eigenvalue	4.069	1.525	1.382	1.223	1.021	
Proportion	0.291	0.109	0.099	0.087	0.073	
Cumulative	0.291	0.400	0.498	0.586	0.659	0.659
	Emotional Support	**Ease**	**Controlling**	**Tolerance**	**−Alignment**	
Caring	+0.798					
Happy	+0.749					
Warm	+0.710					
People-First	−0.537					
Calm		−0.800				
Low Anxiety		−0.796				
Sane		−0.537				
Autocratic			+0.802			
Rigid			+0.702			
Worldly			−0.540			
Tolerant Gays				+0.845		
Tolerant Minorities				+0.824		
Unprofitable					+0.859	
Unethical					−0.467	
Variance	2.4116	2.1353	1.6504	1.5878	1.4365	9.2216
% Variance	0.172	0.153	0.118	0.113	0.103	0.659

Figures B.22 and B.23 are factor analyses of Figure 3.2. They show that there is a sharp separation between the parts of themselves that participants felt they could bring to work. They felt that it was much more acceptable to bring their brains, or *cognition*, to work than to bring their feelings, or *affect*.

Figure B.22. Maximum Likelihood, Varimax Factor Analysis of Questions 45a–45f

Q #45(a)–(f): How Much of Yourself Can You Bring to Work?
Mailed Questionnaires: N = 131

	Factor 1	Factor 2	Communality
Eigenvalue	3.0844	0.9404	
Proportion	0.514	0.157	
Cumulative	0.514	0.671	

Affect

Soul	+0.864
Feeling	+0.805
Self	+0.668

Cognition

Intelligence	+0.870
Humor	+0.726
Creative	+0.662

Variance	2.2200	1.9895	4.2095
% Variance	0.370	0.332	0.702

Figure B.23. Maximum Likelihood, Varimax Factor Analysis of Questions 45a–45f

Q #45(a)–(f): How Much of Yourself Can You Bring to Work?
Mailed Questionnaires: N = 131

	Factor 1	Factor 2	Communality
Eigenvalue	3.0844	0.9404	
Proportion	0.514	0.157	
Cumulative	0.514	0.671	

Right Brain

Feeling	+0.773
Self	+0.692
Soul	+0.564
Creative	+0.524

Left Brain

| Intelligence | +0.915 |
| Humor | +0.531 |

	Factor 1	Factor 2
Variance	1.8965	1.5703	3.4668
% Variance	0.316	0.262	0.578

Figure B.24 shows that the participants in those organizations with a greater perceived spiritual identification, G2 and G3, are significantly less fearful of losing their jobs. The remaining figures are largely self-explanatory, or they are referred to in Chapter Three.

Figure B.24. Question 18—How Fearful Are Participants of Losing Their Jobs?

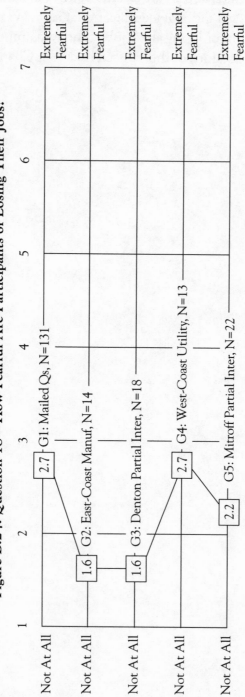

G1: mailed questionnaires (N = 131); G2: East Coast manufacturer (N = 14); G3: Denton partial interviews (N = 14); G4: West Coast utility (N = 13); G5: Mitroff partial interviews (N = 24)

Note: The differences between groups are statistically significant at *p* = 0.004.

Figure B.25. Importance of Religion and Spirituality (Questions 28 and 29)

Mailed Questionnaires: N = 131

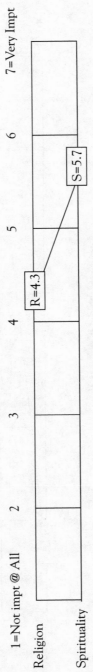

How Important Is *Religion* in Your Life?

How Important Is *Spirituality* in Your Life?

Note: The difference between the means is statistically significant at $p = 0.0000$.

Figure B.26. Scaled Comparisons Between Views on Religion and Views on Spirituality

Mailed Questionnaires: N = 131

R = View of Religion

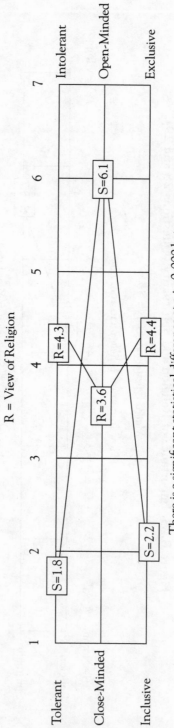

There is a significant statistical difference at a *p=0.000* between Religion and Spiritual on *all three scales.*

R = view of religion, S = view of spirituality

Figure B.27. Stance Toward Religion and
Spirituality Based on Scaled Evaluations

Mailed Questionnaires: N = 131

	Spirituality +	Spirituality –	Totals	Rounded %s	Approximate Ratio
Religion +	28 (36)	2 (2)	30 (38)	30	1 to 2.3
Religion –	63 (80)	7 (9)	70 (89)	70	
Totals	91 (116)	9 (11)	100 (127)		

Rounded %s

90	10

Approximate Ratio

9 to 1

Note: Large numbers = percentages, small numbers = number of respondents; midpoints (4) of the scales were used to determine the cutoff points of the distributions.

Figure B.28. Spirituality Versus General Philosophical Values

Mailed Questionnaires: N = 131

S = Role of Spirituality   GPV = Role of General Philosophical Values

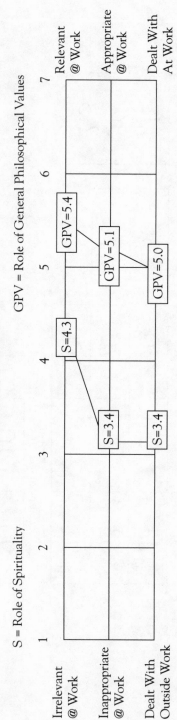

Note: There is a significant statistical difference at *p = 0.0000* between spirituality and general philosophical values on all three scales.

S = role of spirituality, GPV = role of general philosophical values

Figure B.29. Parts of Self That Participants Feel They Can Bring to Work (Question 45a–45f)

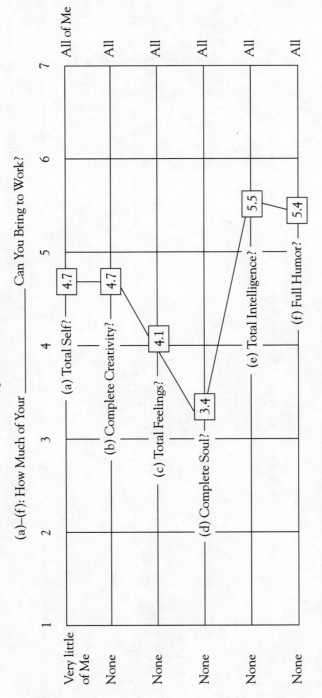

Mailed Questionnaires: N = 131

(a)–(f): How Much of Your _____ Can You Bring to Work?

Note: The differences between the means are statistically significant at p = 0.000.

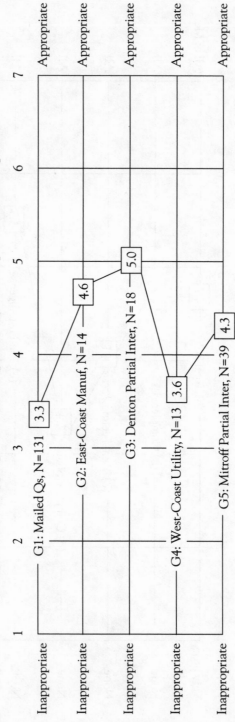

Figure B.30. Appropriateness of Spirituality as a Topic in the Workplace

G1: mailed questionnaires (N = 131); G2: East Coast manufacturer (N = 14); G3: Denton partial interviews (N = 14); G4: West Coast utility (N = 13); G5: Mitroff partial interviews (N = 24)

Detailed Dimensions
of the Five Models

Appendix C

	The Models				
Dimensions of the Models	Religion-Based Organization	Evolutionary Organization	Recovering Organization	Socially Responsible Organization	Values-Based Organization
(1) Precipitating Events	Divine Illumination/ Inspiration; Religious Revelation; Epiphanies; Active Participation in the Mystery of God	Social Injustice; A Long and Repeated History of Social Crises; Personal Angst; The Paradox of Success; Moderate Dysfunctions	Severe Dysfunctions; Repeated Failures; Repeated Severe Life-Threatening Crises; Pronounced Inability to Learn from Failures	Intense Desire for Personal Self-Realization; Deeply Felt Personal Ethical Ideals; Inspiration Due to World Leaders; Life-Long Commitment to Social Causes; Intense Dissatisfaction with the Current Models of Business	Personal History; Parents/Strong Role Models; Ethical Examples
(2) Alternate Business Texts	The Word of God Interpreted Literally, i.e., in Strict Fundamentalist Terms	Social History; Strong Rejection of Utilitarianism as the "Accepted Philosophy" of Business; Acceptance of Different Ethical Philosophers, e.g., Buber, Kant, etc., as Fundamental Sources for Running Ethical Businesses	Oral Stories; Twelve Steps; Traditions	Founders/Leaders as the Writers of the New Texts of Business; The Social Reinvention of Business; Social Ecology	Common, Universal Values, Virtues; Personal Values/Family Values

(3) Hierarchy, Owner of Work, Ultimate Authority	God in the Person of Jesus Christ is the CEO and President	Social Justice; Higher Purpose; Social Philosophers	Spiritual Well-Being as Manifested and Realized Through Societal Well-Being; Higher Power/God as Each Conceives of It	Spiritual Well-Being; Community/Social Well-Being; The Disadvantaged; Communities and Societies Themselves	The Community; Company Is Family; Humankind; Liberal Values
(4) Competition, Enemies	The Devil Construed in Fundamentalist, i.e., Literal, Terms	Racists; Sexists; Traditional Economists; Accountants	Alcohol; Insanity; Harmful, Addictive Substances; Unethical Behavior	Traditional Business Values and Practices; MBA's; Accountants; Defense Industries; Cigarettes	Religion; Spirituality; Unethical Organizations
(5) Ontology, i.e., Basic Building Blocks of Reality; The Status of Spirit and Soul	The Spirit and Soul Are Real; The Soul and Spirit Are the Essence of What It Is to Be Human and to Have a Relationship With the Transcendent, Essential, and Eternal	Real; Essential, Eternal	Real; Essential, Eternal	Real; Essential, Eternal?	Spirit and Soul Are Meaningless Concepts; Or, They Are Intensely Personal and Private; In Either Case They Are Irrelevant to the Ethical Operation of Business

Appendix C, Cont'd.

The Models

Dimensions of the Models	Religion-Based Organization	Evolutionary Organization	Recovering Organization	Socially Responsible Organization	Values-Based Organization
(6) The Principle of Hope	Everything Is Possible Through God	Evolution Is Possible; Profits Will Take Care of Themselves if One Runs an Environmental-Friendly Business	Recovery Is Possible if One Works the Program; Miracles Will Happen	If One Markets Out of a Deep Sense of Values, Then One Will Gain Incredible Customer Loyalty; Customers Are Hungry to Identify With Ethical and Socially-Responsible Organizations	If One Runs a Company With Good Family Values, Then One's Employees and Customers Will Respond in Kind; Economic Success Will Follow
(7) Time Required to Bring About/Enact the Model	Conversion Is Possible at Any Time Through Instantaneous Illumination and the Reception of Christ Into One's Heart	Slow; Long; Moderate	Never Finished; Lifetime; Continual Maintenance; Reinforcement	Moderate/Lifetime	Long; Requires Early Immersion, Maintenance, and Continual Reinforcement

(8) Duration of Changes Affected by the Model	Eternity	? Unclear	? Unclear	? Unclear	? Unclear
(9) Management of Greed	Tension Between Severe Constraints Placed by The Word of God Versus the Realization of Enormous Profits by Fundamentalist Businesses	Unclear; Tension Between Making Money and Managing for the Common Good	Explicit/Severe; Clear and Strong Constraints Are Put on Greed Through the Twelve Steps	Unclear; Trapped/Seduced by Growth	Personal Restraint; Unclear; Conflict Between Personal Values and Larger Acquiring Organizations
(10) Guides for Spiritual (Ethical) Talking and Listening	Bible Study/Reflection; "Trace"; Touched by the Spirit	Religious Traditions; Seminars; Personal Study/Reflection/Development; Explicit Circles for Listening	Explicit Rules and Training for Spiritual Speaking/Listening	Organizational Development?; Seminars?; Outside Facilitators?; Personal Values	Organizational Development?; Seminars?; Outside Facilitators?; Personal Values

Appendix C, Cont'd.

Dimensions of the Models	Religion-Based Organization	The Models			Values-Based Organization
		Evolutionary Organization	Recovering Organization	Socially Responsible Organization	
(11) Size and the Management of Size	Small to Large; Privately Held/Church Held	Small to Moderate?; Social Service; Private	Small; Social Service; Private	Unclear; Private? Tension Between the Desire to Grow and the Commitment to the Development/Maintenance of an Ethical Organizational Climate	Small to Large? Private?
(12) Voice; Active/Passive; Background Vs. Foreground	Active and Passive; Intrusive?; Both in the Background and the Foreground	Active; Ecumenical; Background and Foreground	Active; Ecumenical; Background and Foreground	Active; Ecumenical; Background and Foreground	Active; Ecumenical; Background and Foreground
(13) Values Alignment	Severe/Tight	Open?	Severe; Demanding	Demanding	Open Yet Demanding(?)

(14) Degree to Which Lives Up to Its Own Ideals; Contradictions	Strong; No Contradiction in Terms of Its Own Standards	???	???	???	???
(15) Prime Virtues	Obedience; Submission; Strength	Ethical Knowledge; Service to Others; Lifelong Learning; Commitment to Growth	Humility; Deep Introspection; Commitment to Change; Continual Development/Growth	Social Service to Community/Nation/World	Knowledge; Integrity; Trust
(16) Ontological Status of Future Generations	Present in God's Plan; Real	No Discounting of Future Generations; Broad Stakeholders	Carry the Message to All, Where "All" Includes Future Generations; Real	No Discounting of Future Generations; Broad Array of Stakeholders; Real	No Discounting of Future Generations; Broad Array of Stakeholders; Real
(17) Management Style	Autocratic	Change Oriented; Democratic?; Mixed	True Democracy; Mixed	Autocratic?; Resistant; Mixed	Autocratic? Professional
(18) Language/Talk/Vocabulary	Biblical; Old/New Testament; Requirement for Salvation	Philosophical; Love, etc.	Spiritual; Earthy; Frank; Unafraid; Raw	Integrative; Global; Ecological; Spirit/Soul; Business	Values × Business; Love; Trust; Integrity; General Virtues

Appendix C, Cont'd.

		The Models			
Dimensions of the Models	Religion-Based Organization	Evolutionary Organization	Recovering Organization	Socially Responsible Organization	Values-Based Organization
(19) Definition of Spirituality	Deeply Felt and Experienced Participation in the Universal Mystery of Christ	The Ultimate Purpose of a Business; Business Has a Soul	There is a Higher Power; There is a Force Greater than Ourselves That Manages Recovery	Business is a Spiritual Enterprise	Greater/Higher Consciousness in Service of Higher Ethical Ends
(20) Self/Spiritual Audits	Individual Stock/Soul Taking; Personal Communion	Social Philosophical	Constant; Explicit Part of the Program	Timely	???; Employee Surveys
(21) Explicit Interventions Justified? Warranted? Degree of Fit Between Employees and Organization/Test	A Religious Requirement; Necessary for the Salvation of the Souls of Oneself and Others; Tight	Mutual Negotiation?	Warranted; Justified + Voluntary	???; Conflicted	???; Not Permitted?; Tight?

(22) Religious Advisor? Teachers/Spiritual Guides?	Yes; Jesus Christ	Yes; Philosophical Advisors/Teachers	Explicit Confrontation of the Individual One on One and in Groups; Mentors	Yes; Social Activist/Business × Social Entrepreneurs	Parents/Role Models; Guides/Consultants?
(23) Depth of Commitment to Beliefs	100%; One's Entire Soul for All Eternity	Deep But Conflicted; Mixed	100%; One's Entire Will; Life Dependency	Deep, Ethical Commitment; Conflict?	Strong; 100%; Value Dependent
(24) Extent to Which Business Functions Are Spiritualized; New Business Functions Added	Functions Are Not Necessarily Spiritualized, But Infused With Strong Religious Values; Traditional Business Functions Preserved; Somewhat Independent	Somewhat Separable; Partial, Moderate	Preserves Traditional Business Functions but Attempts to Transform Them	Whole New Design; Holistic; Extensive; Systemically Proactive	Traditional Business Functions Preserved; Highly Professional; Exists Within a "Family" Atmosphere
(25) Primary Governing Metaphor	Everything Is a Fundamental Part of God's Plan	The Hero's Journey/Quest	Organizations as Dysfunctional Families	Business as One of the Primary Forces for Social Change/Justice	Company as a Caring/Healthy Family

Appendix C, Cont'd.

The Models

Dimensions of the Models	Religion-Based Organization	Evolutionary Organization	Recovering Organization	Socially Responsible Organization	Values-Based Organization
(26) Primary Focus	Internal Stakeholders/External Community/Economic Markets	Internal Stakeholders/Community/External Markets	Internal Stakeholder Development/Recovery	Conflict and Tension Between External Stakeholder/World Development and Industry Markets	Equal Focus on Internal Stakeholder Satisfaction *and* External Markets
(27) Reliance on Professional Management	Mixed	Unclear/Tension	???	Weak/Tension	Strong
(28) Commitment to the Environment	Weak	Strong	???	Strong	Strong?
(29) Systems Interconnectedness	Limited; Whole Person?	Strong/Tight?; Whole Person	Strong/Tight?; Whole Person	Strong/Tight?; Whole Person?	Strong/Tight?; Whole Person?
(30) Threshold For Social Action	Part of Religious Mission; Tends to Be Focused Exclusively on Religious Community	High to Low	???	Make as Low as Possible; Pick Any Social Issue With Which to Begin; Just Start!	???; Dependent Upon the Particular Values of the Founders/Leaders

Notes

Chapter One

1. Capps, D., *Agents of Hope: A Pastoral Psychology* (Minneapolis, Minn.: Fortress Press, 1995).
2. Wilber, K., *A Brief History of Everything* (Boston, Mass.: Shambhala, 1996).
3. Mitroff, I. I., and Linstone, H. A., *The Unbounded Mind: Breaking the Chains of Traditional Business Thinking* (New York: Oxford University Press, 1993); see also Mitroff, I. I., *Smart Thinking for Crazy Times: The Art of Solving the Right Problems* (San Francisco: Berrett-Koehler, 1998).

Chapter Two

1. See, for instance, Hillman, J., *The Soul's Code: In Search of Character and Calling* (New York: Random House, 1996); Moore, T., *Care of the Soul: A Guide for Cultivating Depth and Sacredness in Everyday Life* (New York: HarperPerennial, 1994); Moore, T. (ed.), *The Education of the Heart: Reading and Sources for* Care of the Soul, Soul Mates, *and* The Re-enchantment of Everyday Life (New York: HarperCollins, 1996).
2. See Bolman, L. G., and Deal, T. E., *Leading with Soul: An Uncommon Journey of Spirit* (San Francisco: Jossey-Bass, 1995); Briskin, A., *The Stirring of Soul in the Workplace* (San Francisco: Jossey-Bass, 1996); Chappell, T., *The Soul of a Business: Managing for Profit and the Common Good* (New York: Bantam Books, 1994); Cohen, B., and Greenfield, J., *Ben & Jerry's Double-Dip:*

Lead with Your Values and Make Money, Too (New York: Simon & Schuster, 1997); Conger, J. A., and Associates, *Spirit at Work: Discovering the Spirituality in Leadership* (San Francisco: Jossey-Bass, 1994); DeFoore, B., and Renesch, J., *Rediscovering the Soul of Business: A Renaissance of Values* (San Francisco: NewLeaders Press, 1995); Novak, M., *Business as a Calling: Work and the Examined Life* (New York: Free Press, 1996); Salkin, J. K., *Being God's Partner: How to Find the Hidden Link Between Spirituality and Your Work* (Woodstock, Vt.: Jewish Lights, 1994).

3. Even the few studies that do appear are quantitative and pertain more to the study of religion in the workplace than to spirituality; for instance, see Chusmir, L. H., and Koberg, C. S., "Religion and Attitudes Toward Work: A New Look at an Old Question," *Journal of Organizational Behavior,* 1988, 9, 251–262.

4. Borysenko, J. *Fire in the Soul: A New Psychology of Spiritual Optimism* (New York: Warner Books, 1993), pp. 111, 116.

5. Whyte, D., *The Heart Aroused: Poetry and the Preservation of the Soul in Corporate America* (New York: Currency-Doubleday, 1994).

6. For in-depth serious discussion of the philosophical meanings of spirituality and soul, not to mention other important topics, see Senor, T. D. (ed.), *The Rationality of Belief and the Plurality of Faith: Essays in Honor of William P. Alston* (Ithaca, New York: Cornell University Press, 1995); and Taliferro, C., *Contemporary Philosophy of Religion* (Malden, Mass.: Blackwell, 1998).

7. Hadot, P., *Philosophy as a Way of Life: Spiritual Exercises from Socrates to Foucault* (Cambridge, Mass.: Blackwell, 1995).

8. For one of the most powerful expositions of this point, see Sexson, L., *Ordinarily Sacred* (Charlottesville: University of Virginia, 1992).

9. Wilber, 1996.

Chapter Three

1. See Fineman, S. (ed.), *Emotion in Organizations* (Thousand Oaks, Calif.: Sage, 1993).

2. See Marcic, D. *Managing with the Wisdom of Love: Uncovering Virtue in People and Organizations* (San Francisco: Jossey-Bass, 1997), which claims that such systematic links exist between the actual profitability of organizations and their spiritual beliefs; it is probably too early, however, to say that such linkages are definitive.

Chapter Four

1. Van Biema, D., "Mormons, Inc.: The Secrets of America's Most Prosperous Religion," *Time*, 1997, *150*(5), p. 53.
2. Nix, W. H., *Transforming Your Workplace for Christ* (Nashville, Tenn.: Broadman and Holman, 1997); for a similar as well as complementary portrait of an organization governed by Christian values, see Farnsworth, K. E., *Wounded Workers: Recovering from Heartache in the Workplace and the Church* (Mukilteo, Wash.: Wine Press, 1998).
3. Nix, 1997, p. 13.
4. Bawer, B., *Stealing Jesus: How Fundamentalism Betrays Christianity* (New York: Crown, 1997).
5. Nix, 1997, p. 63
6. Nix, 1997, pp. 195–196.
7. Nix, 1997, p. 74.
8. Bawer, 1997, pp. 213–214.
9. Nix, 1997, p. 27.
10. Nix, 1997, p. 157.
11. Nix, 1997, p. 47.
12. Nix, 1997, pp. 202–203.
13. Nix, 1997, p. 69.
14. Nix, 1997, p. 171.
15. Nix, *Op. Cit.*, p. 171.
16. Fowler, J. W., *Stages of Faith: The Psychology of Human Development and the Quest for Meaning* (San Francisco: Harper San Francisco, 1995).
17. Fowler, 1995, p. 149.

18. Fowler, 1995, p. 149.
19. Fowler, 1995, p. 149.

Chapter Five

1. Chappell, T., 1994.
2. Mjagkij, N., and Spratt, M., *Men and Women Adrift: The YMCA and the YWCA in the City* (New York: New York University Press, 1997), p. 4.
3. Mjagkij and Spratt, 1997, p. 237.
4. Nix, 1997.
5. Chappell, 1994.
6. Campbell, J., *The Hero with a Thousand Faces* (Princeton, N.J.: Princeton University Press, 1949).
7. Mitroff, I. I., Pearson, C. M., and Harrington, L. K., *The Essential Guide to Managing Corporate Crises: A Step-by-Step Handbook for Surviving Major Catastrophes* (New York: Oxford University Press, 1996).
8. Bentham, J., *The Principles of Morals and Legislation* (Amherst, N.Y.: Prometheus Books, 1988); Kant, I. (M. Gregor, ed.), *Critique of Practical Reason* (Cambridge: Cambridge University Press, 1997); Niebuhr, R. *Love and Justice: Selections from the Shorter Writings of Reinhold Niebuhr* (Westminster John Knox Press, 1992); Buber, M. (W. Kaufman, trans.), *I and Thou* (Old Tappan, N.J.: Macmillian, 1974).
9. Chappell, 1994, pp. 202–203.
10. Ackoff, R. L., *Creating the Corporate Future* (New York: Wiley, 1981).
11. Chappell, 1994, p. 62.

Chapter Six

1. See Robbins, L., "Designing More Functional Organizations: The Twelve-Step Model," *Journal of Organizational Change Management*, 1992, 5(4), 41–58; Schaef, A. W., and Fassel, D.,

The Addictive Organization: Why We Overwork, Cover Up, Pick Up the Pieces, Please the Boss, and Perpetuate Sick Organizations (New York: HarperCollins, 1988).

2. See, for instance, Alcoholics Anonymous World Services, *Alcoholics Anonymous Comes of Age: A Brief History of AA* (New York: Alcoholics Anonymous World Services, Inc., 1985); Dick B., *The Books Early AAs Read for Spiritual Growth* (San Rafael, Calif.: Paradise Research, 1997); Kurtz, E., *Not God: A History of Alcoholics Anonymous* (Center City, Minn.: Hazelten, 1979); Makela, K. (ed.), *Alcoholics Anonymous as a Mutual-Help Movement* (Madison: University of Wisconsin Press, 1996); Morreim, D. C., *The Road to Recovery: Bridges Between the Bible and the Twelve Steps* (Minneapolis: Augsburg Fortress, 1990).

3. Morreim, 1990, p. 35.

4. Alcoholics Anonymous World Services, *Alcoholics Anonymous: The Story of How Many Thousands of Men and Women Have Recovered from Alcoholism* (3rd. ed.) (New York: Alcoholics Anonymous World Services, 1976).

5. Descartes, R. (F. E. Sutcliffe, trans.), *Discourse on Method and the Meditations* (New York: Penguin Books, 1968).

6. Mäkelä, 1996.

7. Morreim, 1990, p. 45.

8. *Alcoholics Anonymous*, 1976.

9. *Alcoholics Anonymous*, 1976.

10. *Alcoholics Anonymous*, 1976, pp. 58–59.

11. Makela, 1996, pp. 140–144.

12. Robbins, L. P., "Learning in Organizations: The Effects of Interactive Planning and Twelve Step Methodologies," unpublished Ph.D. dissertation, University of Pennsylvania, Philadelphia, 1987.

13. See Bufe, C., *Alcoholics Anonymous: Cult or Cure?* (Tucson, AZ: See Sharp Press, 1998); Peele, S., *Diseasing of America: Addiction Treatment Out of Control* (Boston: Houghton Mifflin, 1989); Sykes, C. J., *A Nation of Victims: The Decay of the American Character* (New York: St. Martin's Press, 1992).

14. LaBier, D., *Modern Madness: The Emotional Fallout of Success* (Redding, Mass.: Addison-Wesley, 1986); see also Reason, J., "The Contribution of Latent Human Failures to the Breakdown of Complex Systems," *Philosophical Translations of the Royal Society of London, 327,* 1990, 475–484.
15. See Taliferro, 1998.
16. Taliferro, 1998.

Chapter Seven

1. Cohen and Greenfield, 1997.
2. Cohen and Greenfield, 1997, p. 30.
3. Cohen and Greenfield, 1997, pp. 30–31.
4. Cohen and Greenfield, 1997, p. 49
5. Cohen and Greenfield, 1997, pp. 32–33.
6. Cohen and Greenfield, 1997, p. 33.
7. Mitroff, I. I., 1998.
8. Cohen and Greenfield, 1997, p. 35.
9. Cohen and Greenfield, 1997, pp. 39–40.
10. Cohen and Greenfield, 1997, p. 178.
11. Cohen and Greenfield, 1997, p. 48.
12. Cohen and Greenfield, 1997, pp. 51–52.
13. Cohen and Greenfield, 1997, p. 70.
14. Cohen and Greenfield, 1997, p. 72.
15. Cohen and Greenfield, 1997, p. 82.
16. Cohen and Greenfield, 1997, p. 94.
17. Ackoff, 1981.
18. Cohen and Greenfield, 1997, p. 118.
19. Cohen and Greenfield, 1997, p. 148.
20. Cohen and Greenfield, 1997, p. 187.
21. Lager, F. C., *Ben & Jerry's: The Inside Scoop* (New York: Crown, 1994).

Chapter Eight

1. Kingston Technology Company, "Background Information on Kingston," (Orange County, Calif.: Kingston Technology, pp. 1–3.
2. Welles, E. O., "Built on Speed," *INC.*, Oct. 1992, p. 3.
3. Burck, C., "The Real World of the Entrepreneur," *Fortune*, 1993, *127*(7), 62–81.
4. Aragon, L., "Family Values," *PC Week*, Sept. 19, 1994, pp. A1–A2.
5. Marcic, 1997; Shaw, R., *Trust in the Balance: Building Successful Organizations on Results, Integrity, and Concern* (San Francisco: Jossey-Bass, 1997).
6. Marcic, 1997, pp. 3–5.
7. Shaw, 1997, p. 21.
8. Shaw, 1997, pp. 144–146.
9. Shaw, 1997, pp. xiv–xv.
10. Shaw, 1997, p. 208.

Chapter Nine

1. See Barron, J. A., and Dienes, C. T., *First Amendment Law in a Nutshell* (St. Paul, Minn.: West, 1993).
2. James, W., *The Varieties of Religious Experience* (New York: Collier Books, 1961).
3. Wilber, 1996.

The Authors

IAN I. MITROFF is Harold Quinton Distinguished Professor of Business Policy and founder of the Center for Crisis Management, which he directed for ten years, at the Graduate School of Business, University of Southern California, Los Angeles. He is also president of Comprehensive Crisis Management, a private consulting firm in Manhattan Beach, California.

Mitroff received a B.S. degree in engineering physics, an M.S. degree in structural engineering, and a Ph.D. in engineering science and the philosophy of social science, all from the University of California at Berkeley. He has been a professor of business administration, information science, and sociology, and a research associate in the Philosophy of Science Center at the University of Pittsburgh. He has been a visiting professor in the departments of management and social systems sciences at the Wharton School, University of Pennsylvania. He also consults widely on crisis management, critical thinking, organizational and strategic change, and strategic planning for a wide array of public and private organizations.

Mitroff is a Fellow of the American Psychological Association and the Academy of Management. He has published more than 270 articles and 20 books, of which his most recent is *Smart Thinking for Crazy Times: The Art and Science of Solving the Right Problems* (1997). He writes frequent op-ed pieces for leading newspapers, and is a frequent guest on *Marketplace* on National Public Radio.

ELIZABETH A. DENTON is a management and organizational consultant based in New York City. She works with senior executives and executive-level teams in both Fortune 100 and entrepreneurial companies, primarily in vision and values, leadership, and performance effectiveness.

An active promoter of values-based, conscious business practices, Denton is frequently invited to speak to business and professional groups on management and organizational development issues, and has been quoted in publications such as *Fortune* and *The New York Times*. She is a past president of the Metropolitan New York Association for Applied Psychology and has taught master's and doctoral degree students at Baruch College, City University of New York, and at the University of Tennessee, Knoxville. Denton received her Ph.D. in counseling psychology from the University of Tennessee, Knoxville, and was given the title "Transformation Midwife" by some of her corporate clients.

Index

A

Academia, lack of spirituality studies by, 16, 17

Ackoff, Russell, 92, 93, 137

Action steps. *See* Alcoholics Anonymous Twelve Steps

Actions: alignment between ideals and, 155, 157, 160, 182; the test of values, 155, 157, 184; threshold for social, 131, 132, 153, 154, 181, 182, 238

Active listening, principle of, 11, 93. *See also* Talking and listening, spiritual

Addiction: addiction to controlling, 181; admitting to delusion and, 103, 104, 120; and the recovery goal, 104, 109; as a spiritual disease, 106, 107

Advisors, teachers, and guides (spiritual) in the five models (table), 237

Age, of study respondents, 198, 201, 203, 207, 209

Alcohol as the enemy, 110, 111, 113

Alcoholics Anonymous (AA): extension to organizations, 115, 119; as a model for spirituality in the workplace, 100, 102; the principles of, 102, 115

Alcoholics Anonymous Twelve Steps: application to business firms, 117; and personal responsibility, 180; and program, 110, 113, 115; table, 100

Alignment between being ethical and profitable, 39, 48, 49, 50, 215, 217; and hiring employees, 139; and profit status, 46, 47, 138, 139

Alignment between ideals and actions, 155, 157, 160, 182

Alternate business texts: the Bible, 10, 109, 150; the Big Book of AA, 109, 110; of ethical business models, 10; in

Evolutionary Organizations, 83, 84, 89, 90; of the five models (table), 170, 230; oral tradition of universal values, 151; philosophical works as, 90, 181; in Recovering Organizations, 105, 109, 110; reflections on, 174; in Religion-Based Organizations, 62, 63, 83, 84; in Socially Responsible Organizations, 127; in Values-Based Organizations, 148, 149, 151. *See also* Language and vocabulary; Literature

Ambivalence about spirituality at work, xix, 6, 44, 168

Amends, making, 100, 114

Analyses of publications on spirituality, xvii, 53, 174

"Anything-is-possible" principle, 66

Arts, the, 20

Assessment and training, employee, 160

Audits, self and spiritual: in AA, 113, 114, 119; in business organizations, 119, 141, 178, 181; or denial of errors, 100, 113, 177; in the five models (table), 236

Authority, the ultimate, 171, 175, 231; and autocratic managers, 140, 177; God as, 61, 63, 64, 74, 84, 108, 230

Autonomy principle, spiritual, 96, 97

Awe and reverence for creation, 14

B

Barriers to study. *See* Studying spirituality, barriers to

Bawer, B., 62, 64, 65

Behavior based on simple values, 153, 154

Belief in a higher power or god: in AA, 107, 108, 113, 114, 180; in the five models (table), 171, 231; and its presence at work, 42, 43, 118, 119, 175; in Recovering Organizations, 104, 107, 118, 119, 180

Beliefs, depth of commitment to: in AA, 108; in the five models (table), 237; reversal of prior, 112, 113, 120, 135, 184, 185; in a spirituality based organization, 182; and stages of religious development, 74, 75

Beliefs and practices, management. *See* Management policies

Ben & Jerry's, 182; and making money, 176; as nonprofit-profit hybrid, 138, 139; principles of, 125, 138; social activism of, 123, 124; strengths of, 139, 140; weaknesses of, 140

Ben & Jerry's Double-Dip (Cohen and Greenfield), 123, 126, 127–128, 129, 130, 131, 132, 133–134, 135, 136, 137, 138, 182

Benefits versus costs, 86

Best for an organization, doing what is, 86

Best-practice model of a spiritual organizations, 177, 182

Betrayal of trust, 156, 157

Bible, the, 150; as a fundamental text, 10, 109

"Big Book of AA," 105, 109, 110

Black leadership and the YMCA, 81

"Blind faith," 152, 153

Bonuses, employee, 144

Buber, M., 90, 181

Business education: hiring for employee values or, 139; lack of study of spirituality in, 16, 17

Business functions: and the industries studied, 205, 211; preserving traditional, 80, 147

Business functions, spiritualization of, 11, 12; in a best practice model, 178, 182; and company infrastructure, 125, 126; and day-to-day activities, 128, 129, 131, 132; extent in the five models (table), 237; sustained effort to maintain, 94, 97, 98; and traditional ways, 80, 134, 135, 147; transparent operations and, 130, 131; and Twelve Step fellowship methodologies, 119

Business texts. *See* Alternate business texts; Literature

Businesses studied. *See specific organization names*

C

Campbell, J., 86, 89

Caring or healthy family as governing metaphor, 143, 145, 237

CEO: of another faith, 77; God as owner and, 63, 64

CEOs: precipitating values of, 143, 146; stories from, 45, 49, 77. *See also* Positions of respondents, professional; *specific organization names*

Change catalysts. *See* Precipitating events (crisis principle)

Change, organizational: gentleness of, 184; reactive versus proactive responses to, 78, 79; from religious bases to ecumenical outlooks, 77, 79; resistance to, 87, 120, 121; spiritual openness to, 89, 116; time invested in, 78, 79; and traditional practices, 134, 135; YMCA and long-term, 79, 85. *See also* Evolutionary Organization, the

Chappell, T., 78, 79, 85, 88, 89, 90, 92, 94, 104

Charity and philanthropy, 57, 66, 92, 126; and marketing, 129

"Charles," story of, 45, 47

"Chinese wall" between public and private issues, 6, 168

Christ, discussion of at work, 63, 64

Christianity: and AA, 107; Fundamentalist, 62, 63, 64, 75, 84; and the YMCA, 77, 79, 80, 81, 83, 84

Circles for listening, 87, 93, 181

Classes, YMCA aid to social, 81, 83

Cohen, B., 123, 126, 127–128, 129, 130, 131, 132, 133–134, 135, 136, 137, 138, 140, 182

Commitment. *See* Beliefs, depth of commitment to

Common good, business involvement in, 126, 127, 129, 130

Communal orientations toward spirituality, 26, 27

Communication channel, prayer as the, 66, 67

Community focus, in the five models (table), 238

Comparative spirituality in the workplace, 169, 177

Competition, enemies, or counterprinciples: alcohol as the, 110, 111, 113; Devil as the, 84, 110, 111; of the five models (table), 171, 231; organization attitudes toward, 12; overview, 175; Satan as the, 64, 65; standing up to, 87; unethical organizations and workers as, 154, 155

Conformity, expectation of, 72, 73

Consciousness and spirituality, 41, 42

Contract, the social, 125, 126

Control factor, organizational, 50, 60, 140, 215, 217

Conversation, spiritual: in Evolutionary Organizations, 96, 97, 98; and prayer, 66, 67; in Recovering Organizations, 101; in Religion-Based Organizations, 63, 64; rules in AA meetings, 111, 112. See also Talking and listening, Spiritual

Crisis principle. See Precipitating events (crisis principle)

Cults, organizations seen as, 72, 141

Customers, spiritual connection with, 127, 128, 137

D

Data analyses tables and figures: meaning in life factors, 213, 214; top three meaning and purpose factors, 212. See also Spirituality in the workplace (study)

Decision making, autocratic, 140, 177

Decision steps. See Alcoholics Anonymous (AA)

Definitions of spirituality: agreement on, xv, 22; attitudes toward, 20, 21; by respondents, 22, 25. See also Spirituality

Degrees held by respondents, 200, 202, 206, 208, 211

Demographics of respondents, 198, 201, 203, 207, 209

Denominations, spirituality above and beyond, 23, 97, 107, 108

Depression or crying at work, 34, 193, 194

Descartes, R., 105, 106

Development, business growth or, 91, 93, 136, 137, 144, 185

Devil as chief competitor, 84, 110, 111

Discrimination, racial, 81, 82

Discussion at work: about Christ, 63, 64; for promoting spirituality there, 184, 185. See also Talking and listening, spiritual

Distress, organizational, 50, 215, 217. See also Recovering Organization, the

Drucker, P. F., 31

Duration of organization changes: in the five models (table), 233

Dysfunctional families as governing metaphor, 118, 120, 237

E

Ecumenicalism, 75, 82, 84, 85

Education: alternate, 174; business, 16, 17, 139

Educational degrees held by respondents, 200, 202, 206, 208, 211

Emotional support by organizations, 50, 215, 217; in Evolutionary Organizations, 94, 95; or "holier than thou" attitude, 140, 141; in Socially Responsible Organizations, 132, 134; in Values-Based Organizations, 157. See also Wholeness of persons in the workplace

Employees: employment for unemployable, 65; in Evolutionary Organizations, 95, 96; expectations and performance of, 62, 96, 154, 155, 160; the Faustian dilemma of, 6, 7; as God's servants, 63, 64; homogeneity of, 72, 73; productivity of ethical, 154, 155; promotion and professional development of, 140, 144; recruiting, 132, 133; recruiting and the values of, 139; religion and motivating, 62, 71, 72; religious pressure on, 59, 60, 71, 72; resistance to change, 87, 120, 121; salaries and bonuses for, 144; shared values motivating, 128, 132, 133, 154; spirituality and motivating, 52, 87; training and assessment of, 160; YMCA aid to business, 79, 80. See also Family, the organization; Stakeholders

Employees interviewed. See Positions of respondents, professional

Enemies. See Competition, enemies, or counterprinciples

Enthusiasm, a spiritual concept, 6

Environmental preservation values, 45, 46; commitment to, 238; of Values-Based Organizations, 158, 159

Epiphany. *See* Precipitating events (crisis principle)

Errors, confrontation or denial of, 100, 113, 177

Ethical organizations. *See* Values-Based Organization, the

Ethical values. *See* Values of interviewees

Events, precipitating. *See* Precipitating events (crisis principle)

Evolution beyond Values-Based Organizations, 179, 183, 185

Evolutionary Organization, the, 8, 9, 77, 98; business principles change in, 84, 85; components in a best-practice model, 181; dimensions of (tables), 170, 173, 230, 238; principles of, 88, 96; reflections on, 97, 98; series of essential crises in, 88, 89; spiritual autonomy principle in, 96, 97; subsidiary principles of, 95, 96; Tom's of Maine, 85, 88; the YMCA, 79, 85

Existential concerns, 134

Experiences, spiritual, 111, 112; and spirituality, 25, 26

Experiment, the spiritually based organization, 182

Extreme cases, benefits of studying, 58, 153

F

Fads and buzzwords, management, 65

Failure and humbling, repeated, 104

Faith: definition of, 31; developmental theory of, 74; difference between trust and, 152, 153

Faith and spirituality, 106; inseparableness of, 25

Family, the organization: actions and commitment to the, 155, 157; as caring or healthy, 95, 143, 145, 237; as dysfunctional, 118, 120, 237; in Values-Based Organizations, 158, 159, 179, 180. *See also* Employees; Stakeholders

Faustian dilemma of employees, 6, 7

Fear: associated with spirituality, xix, 6, 168; of losing jobs, 221, 222

Feelings of employees, 37, 219; frustrated, 4; joy or bliss expressions, 95; tolerance for expressing, 93, 94, 95; and wholeness, 42, 45; wholeness or split, 32. *See also* Wholeness of persons in the workplace

Fellowship, twelve step. *See* Alcoholics Anonymous (AA)

First Amendment, 19, 20, 179

Five models of spiritual organizations, 8, 13; benefits of studying extreme cases and, 58, 153; a best-practice model based on, 177, 182; common dimensions of, 9, 12; comparative discussion of, 169, 177; core principles of, 9, 12; detailed dimensions of, 229, 238; incomplete nature of, 183. *See also* Spirituality in the workplace (study); *specific organization names*

Fowler, J., 74

Free speech, 19, 20, 179

Freeman, M., 69

Fundamental texts. *See* Alternate business texts

Fundamentalism, Protestant Christian, 62, 64, 75

Future generations: ontological status of, 173, 176, 177; as stakeholders, 90, 91, 158, 159, 185

G

Gentleness, the path of, 17, 184

Goal of the organization: commitment to, 182; the common good as, 91; development not growth as, 91, 93, 93–94, 136, 137; not-for-profit and for-profit, 138, 139; proactive social, 129, 130; recovery of the addict as, 109; religious takeover and transformation as, 58, 60, 71. *See also* Purpose-of-business principle

God: as all powerful or restrained, 121, 122; as nondenominational, in AA, 107, 108; as supreme leader and business owner, 63, 64, 84, 108

God's Plan, as governing metaphor, 237

God's Word, as business text, 61, 62, 63, 74, 230

Golden Rule principles, 149, 151

Greed: corporate, 38; limitation of, 11, 71, 185; management in the five models (table), 233; and power, 121

Greenfield, J., 123, 126, 127–128, 129,

130, 131, 132, 133–134, 135, 136, 137, 138, 182
Group orientations to spirituality, 26, 27
Groups, respondent. *See* Respondents, study
Growth, business: or development, 91, 93, 136, 137, 144, 185; and greed, 11, 38, 71, 185, 233; and integrity, 144, 159; spiritually managed, 70, 71. *See also* Profits, business

H

Harvard Divinity School, 86, 87, 88
The Heart Aroused: Poetry and the Preservation of the Soul in Corporate America (Whyte), 20
Hero's Journey/Quest metaphor, 86, 88, 237
Hierarchy, owner of work, ultimate authority dimension: and autocratic managers, 140, 177; of the five models (table), 171, 231; overview, 175; in Religion-Based Organizations, 63, 64
Higher power. *See* Belief in a higher power or god; God
Histories of interviewees, personal, 32, 33
"Holier than thou" attitude, 140, 141
Hope and love as foundations of spiritual experience, 3, 4
Hope, the principle of, 9, 10, 180, 182; in AA, 108, 109; and anything-is-possible principle, 66; in the five models (table), 172, 232; and purpose of business, 93, 94; in Recovering Organizations, 109; in Religion-Based Organizations, 65, 66; in Socially Responsible Organizations, 127, 128, 137, 138; in Values-Based Organizations, 147, 148
Human resource (HR) managers: positions, 199, 202, 204, 208, 210; reason for studying, 34, 35. *See also* Respondents, study
Human spirit, spirituality in terms of the, 41
Huntsman Chemical Corp., 57, 58
Huntsman, J., 57, 58

I

Ice cream manufacturer. *See* Ben & Jerry's
Ideals, living up to, 182; in the five models (table), 235; of the YMCA, 79, 80

Illness. *See* Recovering Organization, the
Inclusiveness: best-practice model, 179, 180; of spirituality, 23
Individual orientations toward spirituality, 26
Industry types in the study, 205, 211
Infinite and finite, the, 105, 106
Inner life, as subjective and meaningless, 27
Insanity in humans, 110, 111
Inseparability. *See* Wholeness of persons in the workplace
Integrity: and growth, 144, 159; violations of, 156, 157
Interconnectedness, systems: in AA, 116, 121; in Evolutionary Organizations, 95, 96; in Socially Responsible Organizations, 133, 134, 138, 139; of spirituality, xvi, 22, 24, 48, 71, 238. *See also* Stakeholders
Intervention and counseling programs, organization-sponsored, 34, 195; in the five models (table), 236; in Religion-Based Organizations, 68, 71, 72; in Values-Based Organizations, 157. *See also* Recovering Organization, the
Interview Guide (Appendix A), 187, 195
Interviews, in-depth, xv; of AA members, 101; composite stories based on, 45, 49; job positions of respondents to, 34, 35, 199, 202, 204, 208, 210; and partial (background) interviews, 36; qualitative results of, 36, 45; response rates, 35, 36; sample group sizes, 35, 36, 197; selected quantitative results, 49, 52
"I-Thou" relationships, 90

J

James, W., 180
"John," story of, 47, 49
Joy or bliss in the workplace, 33, 42, 193
Jung, C., xiii

K

Kant, I., 90, 181
Kingston Technology Company, 143, 145
Kohlberg, L., 74

L

Labor, organized, 80
Lager, F. C., 140

Language and vocabulary: about the environment, 158, 159; alternate texts and business, 10; of common values, 124, 125, 155, 161; in Evolutionary Organizations, 84, 96; fear of using spiritual, xvi, xvii, 125, 155, 161; in the five models (table), 235; preference for neutral, 155, 161, 179, 180; in Recovering Organizations, 101; of spirituality or business, 19, 20. *See also* Talking and listening, spiritual

Leadership, organizational: autocratic, 140, 177; black, 81; ecumenical, 77; personal crises and, 68, 69, 85, 87; precipitating values of, 146; problem of succession in, 176, 238; and threshold for social action, 238. *See also* Management style; *specific organization names*

Limitation, size. *See* Size and management of size

Listening. *See* Talking and listening, spiritual

Literature: interpretation of TYWFC, 61; philosophical texts, 90, 181; on spirituality and business, 16, 53, 184. *See also* Alternate business texts

Love and the Golden Rule, 149, 151

Loyalty: customer, 127, 128; and trust, 162

M

Maintenance steps. *See* Alcoholics Anonymous (AA)

Majors of respondents, undergraduate, 200, 202, 206, 208, 211

Mäkelä, K., 111, 112

Management: importance of, 167, 168; reliance on professional, 238; of spirituality, 168, 169

Management policies: best-practice model principles and, 177, 182; of integration of spirituality, 13, 14; in Religion-Based Organizations, 62, 63, 71, 72; of separation of spirituality, 13; and Twelve Step principles, 115, 119; in Values-Based Organizations, 156, 157

Management style: in the five models (table), 173, 235; overview, 177; and subsidiary tactics, 59, 71, 72. *See also* Leadership, organizational

Managing with the Wisdom of Love: Uncovering Virtue in People and Organizations (Marcic), 148, 149

Marcic, D., 148, 149

Marketing: add-on cause-related, 129; from your values, 137, 138

Markets of the five models, economic (table), 238

Maslow, A., 37

Meaning in people's work, 213, 214; and inner life, 27; interview questions on, 32, 33; qualitative results on, 36, 37; questionnaire on, 187, 195; the spiritual vacuum and, 133; and spirituality, 24; top three factors, 212

Measurement and quantification: of spirituality and organizational performance, xviii; spirituality as problematic to, 17, 133, 134; tendency toward scientific, 16, 17, 149; in Values-Based Organizations, 160

Metaphors: acorn and oak tree, 112; Devil, 110, 111; God's Plan, 237; hero's journey, 86, 88, 237; primary governing, of the five models (table), 237; social change or justice, 131, 132, 237. *See also* Family, the organization

Migrations: European immigrant, 81; farm to city, 79, 80

Ministry, in the organization, 59

Minorities and women, representation of, 81, 83

Minority suppliers, 136

Mission, corporate. *See* Goal of the organization; Profits, business

Models, the five. *See* Five models of spiritual organizations

Models of practicing spirituality: best-practice model based on the five, 177, 182; common dimensions of, 9, 12; comparative discussion of, 169, 177; extreme cases, 58, 153; lack of, xvii; need for, xvi, 52, 53; presenting the full range of, xvii, xviii. *See also specific organization names*

Money, making: for redistribution to causes, 57, 66, 92, 125, 126; for the religious mission, 65, 66; tensions about, 233; tensions between doing good and, 176. *See also* Profits, business

Moore, T., 2, 3, 15

Morale. *See* Wholeness of persons in the workplace

Mormons, religious-based organizations owned by, 60, 72

Morreim, D., 107, 108

N

Naiveté of Values-Based Organizations, 162, 163

Narratives. *See* Stories, personal

New Age philosophy, 47; and standards of inquiry, 17, 18

Nix, W., 61, 68

Nondenominational religious organizations, 97, 107, 108

Not-for-profit organizations, 39, 205; and worker exploitation, 46, 47

O

Ontological status of future generations: in the five models (table), 173, 235; overview, 176, 177

Ontology (building blocks): of the five models (table), 171, 231; overview, 175; in Socially Responsible Organizations, 134

Openness: or covert beliefs and tactics, 71, 72; to organizational change, 89, 116; of values and business goals, 130, 131, 140, 182

Oral tradition of universal values, 151

Organizational studies, xv

Organizations: as ecosystems, 95; ethicality and profitability of, 39, 48, 49, 50, 215, 217; extension of AA to, 115, 119; interview questions on, 33, 34; not-for-profit, 39, 46, 47, 205; profiles of, quantitative, 50, 215, 217; social contract between society and, 126, 127; social problem solving by business, 129, 130, 131–132; types of, 205

Organizations fostering spirituality: AA as a unique, 101, 102; role models of, 34, 195; unawareness of, 44. *See also specific organization names*

Organizations studied, the industries of, 205, 211

Orientations to spirituality, individual versus group, 26, 27

Ownership, business. *See* Hierarchy, owner of work, ultimate authority dimension

P

Parts of themselves people bring to work. *See* Wholeness of persons in the workplace

Peace and calm, inner, 24

Personal feelings. *See* Feelings of employees

Philosophers, texts from the, 89, 90, 181

Poetry, 20

Political correctness, 19

Positions of respondents, professional, 34, 35, 199, 202, 204, 208, 210; CEO stories, 45, 49, 77, 143, 146

Power: of God, 121, 122; limitation of, 11; and size and social mission, 136, 137

Praying or meditation at work, 11, 43, 48; questions on, 34, 190, 194, 195; in Religion-Based Organizations, 66, 67

Preaching: condemnation of, 155, 156; and ministry, 59

Precipitating events (crisis principle): discussing, 184; epiphany, 193; in Evolutionary Organizations, 88, 89; in the five models, 170, 230; intensity of, 9; overview, 169, 174; in Recovering Organizations, 104; in Religion-Based Organizations, 67, 69; as stimulus toward spirituality, 46, 47, 85, 86

Precipitating values, of organization founders and heads, 146

Pride or shame toward organizations, 34, 195

Principles: AA's Twelve Steps and, 100, 110, 113, 115; adaptation to business firms of AA, 115, 117; in Evolutionary Organizations, 88, 97; purpose-of-business, 11, 93, 94, 125, 126; of the Religion-Based Organization, 61, 72; unintended consequences of organization, 83

Principles common to the five models: business, 178; comparative discussion of, 169, 177; the core, 9, 12; examination of, 12, 13; tables of dimensions and, 170, 173, 229, 238. *See also* Precipitating events (crisis principle)

Private and public issues: the wall between, 6, 168

Problem solving: business and social, 129, 130, 131–132; counterintuitive, 116, 118

Product design based on social value, 123

Productivity and ethical employees, 154, 155

Professional management use, in the five models (table), 238

Professional positions, of study respondents, 34, 35, 199, 202, 204, 208, 210

Profits, business: following from being ethical, 10, 94, 127, 128, 137, 138, 154, 155; and future generations, 90, 91; limiting growth and, 11, 70, 71, 185; and non-profit goals, 138, 139; purpose of, 11, 94; redistribution of, 57, 66, 92, 125, 126; spirituality and greater, xviii; in Values-Based Organizations, 159. *See also* Money, making

Purpose-of-business principle, 11; and hope, 93, 94; and the social contract, 125, 126. *See also* Goal of the organization

Q

Qualitative data: from interviews, 36, 45; personal stories, 45, 49, 110, 112

Quantitative results: detailed *(figures)*, 198, 228; discussion, 49, 52; organization profile, 50; personal wholeness profile, 51; sample groups, 197; traditional acceptability of, 16, 17. *See also* Measurement and quantification

Questionnaire on meaning and purpose in the workplace, 187, 195; sample size and response rates, 35. *See also* Spirituality in the workplace (study)

Questions, in-person interviews, 32, 34. *See also* Studying spirituality

R

Race, of study respondents, 198, 201, 203, 207, 209

Racism, 81, 82

Reality: dualistic religious paradigm of, 167; and inner life, 27; of spirit and soul, 133, 134; Western science focus on objective, 27

Recovering Organization, the, 9, 99, 122; AA as a model of, 100, 102; and AA's principles, 102, 115; AA's Twelve Steps for, 100, 110, 113, 115; components in a best-practice model, 180, 181, 182; dimensions of (tables), 170, 173, 230, 238; extension of AA to,

115, 119; reflections on, 121, 122; strengths and weaknesses of, 120, 121

Religion and government, separation of, 19, 20, 179

Religion and spirituality: difference between, xiv, xvi, 23, 40, 41, 46; interview questions on, 33, 190, 191; positive and negative views of, 39, 42, 225; relative importance of, 223; separation of, 184; and tolerance levels, 224; universal values independent from, 149, 154; as unnecessary to ethical actions, 151, 152

Religion in the workplace: and free speech, 19, 20, 179; reflections on, 72, 75; views of, xvi, 39, 48, 225

Religion-Based Organization, the, 8, 57, 75; AA's principles compared to, 103; benefits of studying, 58; benefits of working in, 73, 74; components in a best-practice model, 180; dimensions of (tables), 170, 173, 230, 238; method of analyzing the, 60, 61; principles of, 61, 72; reflections on, 72, 75; religious takeover goal in, 58, 60; stakeholders of, 69, 70; the YMCA change from, 79, 85

Religions, organized: affiliation with, 8, 46, 190; fundamentalist, 59, 60; and nondenominational attitudes, 23, 97, 107, 108; skepticism toward, 48, 49, 59, 60, 146, 184

Religious faith, developmental theory of, 74

Research findings: on definitions of concepts, 21; summary of the ten, xv, xix. *See also* Principles common to the five models; Qualitative data; Quantitative results

Research topics and methods, tradition of quantifiable, 16, 17

Resistance to change, 120, 121; and the unknown, 87

Respondents, study: AA members, 100, 101; demographics, 198, 201, 203, 207, 209; education and degrees of, 200, 202, 206, 208, 211; groups of, 35, 36, 197; human resources professionals as, 34, 35, 199, 202, 204, 208, 210; response rates by, 34, 36. *See also* Spirituality in the workplace (study)

Robbins, L., 115, 116

Role models and parents, 146, 237
"Rolodex, a spiritual," 71, 72
Rosen, L. R., 77

S

"S-words," the, 175
Sacredness, spirituality is, 24
Salaries, 144
Sales people and buyers, 136, 144
Satan: the major competitor, 64, 65, 84, 110, 111; as stakeholder, 70
Science and spirituality, Western, 27
Secrecy, ideal of avoiding business, 130, 131
Secularization, 84, 167
Self-actualization, desire for, 36, 37
Separation: and compartmentalization at work, 38, 133; between religion and government, 19, 20, 179; between religion and spirituality, 184; of spiritual concerns from the workplace, 7, 13
Servants, God's, 63, 64
Service: obligation of religious, 65, 66; obligation of social, 125, 126
Sexson, L., 167
Sexual policies, YMCA, 83
Shah, B., 99
Shaw, R., 148, 152, 153, 156, 157
Size and management of size: in Evolutionary Organizations, 91, 93; in the five models (table), 173, 234; and organizational purpose, 11; overview, 176; in Recovering Organizations, 116, 119; in Socially Responsible Organizations, 135, 137; in Values-Based Organizations, 144, 159
Size of research sample, 35, 197
Social action threshold: in the five models (table), 238; in Socially Responsible Organizations, 131, 132, 181, 182
Social change or justice: as governing metaphor, 131, 132, 237; and the YMCA, 81, 83
Social contract of business with society, 125, 126; and social problems, 129, 130
Socially Responsible Organization, the, 9, 123, 141; compared to Values-Based Organization, 124, 125, 138; components in a best-practice model, 181, 182; dimensions of (tables), 170, 173,

230, 238; as hybrid profit and nonprofit, 138, 139; management style of, 140, 141; principles of, 125, 138; strengths of, 139, 140; weaknesses of, 140, 141
Soft phenomenon, spirituality viewed as a, xviii, 17
Soul, the: acknowledgement of, xvi; definitions of, 5, 15; the power and potential inherent in, 5, 6; reality of, 133, 134; selling one's, 6, 7; status of Spirit and, 95, 96, 125, 133, 134, 161, 171, 175, 231; work and wounding of the, 45, 47. *See also* Wholeness of persons in the workplace
Spirit, the status of Soul and, 95, 96, 125, 133, 134, 161, 171, 175, 231
Spiritual organizations: a best-practice model for, 177, 182; comparative discussion of, 169, 177; discussion points for evolution into, 184, 185
Spirituality: addiction to, 182; agreement on definition of, xv, 22, 23; ambivalence associated with workplace, xix, 6, 44, 168; attitudes toward defining, 20, 21, 39, 42; as basis of business success, 137, 138; comfort zone regarding, 184; comparing ten dimensions of, 169, 177; discussion points for promoting, 184, 185; "evaluating," 149; four inner/outer orientations toward, 26, 27, 183; four positive/negative orientations toward, 39, 42; as an individual phenomenon, xviii; and interconnectedness, xvi, 22, 24, 48, 127, 128, 137, 238; neglect of by organizations, 3, 5; outer structural dimensions of, xviii; the perpetual process of, 185; reality of, 133, 134; as a topic at work, 43, 44, 228; versus general philosophical values, 226; and Western science, 27; "You go first" attitude toward, 44, 45. *See also* Definitions of spirituality
Spirituality definitions: elements common to, 22, 25; in the five models (table), 236
Spirituality in the workplace (study): closing reflections on, 183, 185; comparative discussion based on, 169, 177; design of research, 32; discussion points, six, 184, 185; qualitative results, selected, 36, 45; quantitative

results, selected, 49, 52; questions as probes on, 32, 34; reflections on findings of, 52, 53; stories on, composite, 45, 49; ten dimensions discussion, 169, 177. *See also* Data analyses tables and figures; Respondents, study

Stability and simplicity, organizational: the price of, 72; in Religion-Based Organizations, 64, 68, 70

Stages of Faith (Fowler), 74

Stakeholders: in AA, 115, 117, 118; a best model for acceptance by, 177, 182; customers as, 127, 128, 130, 131, 137; Earth and its environment as, 158, 159; employees as, 158, 182; in Evolutionary Organizations, 90, 91; in the five models (table), 238; future generations as, 90, 91, 158, 235; number and variety of, 69, 182; organizational attitudes toward, 11, 238; in Recovering Organizations, 117; in Religion-Based Organizations, 69, 70; in Socially Responsible Organizations, 127, 128, 134, 135; suppliers as, 134, 135; in Values-Based Organizations, 158, 159. *See also* Employees; Family, the organization

Steps, the Twelve. *See* Alcoholics Anonymous (AA)

Stories, personal: based on the interviews (composite), 45, 49; self-narratives of AA members, 110, 112

Study, the research. *See* Spirituality in the workplace (study)

Studying spirituality: initial goal of, 31; research purpose and development, 32; worldwide, 26, 27. *See also* Questions, research

Studying spirituality, barriers to, 15, 16; from academe, 16, 17; language, 19, 20; from New Age proponents, 17, 18; philosophical definition, 20, 26; political correctness, 19; U.S. history and culture, 18, 19

Sun, D., 143, 145

Suppliers and vendors, 144; minority, 136; Values-Led or traditional, 134, 135

Survey, research. *See* Spirituality in the workplace (study)

T

Takeovers, business, 97, 143

Talking and listening, spiritual: in AA meetings, 111, 112; circles for listening, 87, 93, 181; discussion points for, 184, 185; in Evolutionary Organizations, 93; guides in the five models (table), 233; and prayer, 11, 66, 67; in Religion-Based Organizations, 66, 67, 71, 72; religious expression and, 73. *See also* Language and vocabulary

Taylor, C., 2

Teaching: employees, 140, 160; religion in the workplace, 68; spirituality missing from academic, 17

Time required to enact model: and business self-evaluation, 12, 185; in Evolutionary Organizations, 78, 79; of the five models (table), 172, 232; overview, 176; in Religion-Based Organizations, 63. *See also* Evolutionary Organization, the

Timelessness of spirituality, 23, 24

Tolerance, propensity for: of expressing deep emotions, 93, 94, 95; of minorities, 50, 215, 217; of spirituality or religions, 73, 224; or tough enforcement, 156, 157

Tom's of Maine, 94, 95; evolutionary history of, 85, 88; YMCA compared with, 77, 79, 97, 98

Training of employees, 140, 160

Transforming Your Workplace for Christ, TYWFC (Nix), 61

Trust: compared to faith, 152, 153; and loyalty, 162; unethical behavior as betrayal of, 156, 157; in Values-Based Organizations, 147, 148

Trust in the Balance (Shaw), 148

Tu, J., 143, 145

Twelve Steps. *See* Alcoholics Anonymous Twelve Steps

U

U.S. Constitution, 19, 179

Universality of spirituality, 23, 24

University of Utah, 57

Urbanization, and the YMCA, 79, 80

Utilitarianism, 86, 90

V

Vacuum, spiritual, 133

Values of interviewees: questions on, 33; and spirituality, 41, 42; work and compromises of, 33, 38

Values of leaders: acting on concrete virtues or, 146, 147; personal crises and, 68, 69; precipitating, 145, 146; publicizing the, 130, 131; simplicity and number of, 153, 154; and social action threshold, 153, 154, 238

Values, philosophical: commitment to living, 42, 155, 157, 182; historic search for common core of, 154, 161; independent of religion and spirituality, 149, 154; language and vocabulary of, 124, 125; nonreligious and nonspiritual virtues and, 146, 147; texts on, 90, 181; versus spirituality, 226

Values-Based Organization, the, 9, 143, 163; best-practice model based on, 178, 180, 182; compared to Socially Responsible Organization, 138; dimensions of (tables), 170, 173, 230, 238; leading principles of, 149, 160; reflections on, 160, 163; Socially Responsible Organization compared to, 124, 125; strengths of, 161; weaknesses of, 161, 163; widespread appeal of, 161

Values-Led business, 126

Van Biema, D., 57, 58

Virtues, prime: in the five models (table), 235; in Values-Based Organizations, 146, 147

Voice, in the five models (table), 234

W

Welch, J., 153

Wholeness of persons in the workplace, xv, xvi; affect or cognition and, 37, 219; and compartmentalization, 38, 133; design of research on, 32; in Evolutionary Organizations, 95, 96; interview questions probing, 32, 34, 194; qualitative results on, 37, 38; quantitative profile of, 51, 218, 220, 227; and religiousness, 73, 74; right and left brain aspects of, 220; in Socially Responsible Organizations, 132, 134; and strong emotions, 42, 45; in Values-Based Organizations, 157, 182. *See also* Emotional support by organizations

Wilber, K., 13, 26, 27, 183

Will power and spirituality, 25

Women: respondents, 198, 201, 203, 207, 209; in the workplace, 83

Word of God: as business text, 61, 62, 63, 74, 230

Work and meaning. *See* Meaning in people's work

"Working the program." *See* Alcoholics Anonymous (AA)

Wyte, D., 20

Y

YMCA (Young Men's Christian Organization), 79, 85; backlash period, 80, 82; changing business principles of, 83, 85; compared with Tom's of Maine, 77, 79, 97, 98; founding phase, 79, 80; nondenominational nature of, 97; unexpected change phase, 82, 83

"You go first" game, the, 44, 45

p. 137: Cohen, B., and Greenfield, J., pp. 118, 148.

p. 138: Cohen, B., and Greenfield, J., p. 187

Chapter Eight, epigraph and p. 144: Kingston Technology Company, "Background Information on Kingston," (Orange County, Calif.: Kingston Technology).

p. 144: Reprinted with permission of *Inc.* magazine, Goldhirsh Group, Inc., 38 Commercial Wharf, Boston, MA 02110 (http://www.inc.com). *Built on Speed* (excerpt), Edward O. Welles, October 1992. Reproduced by permission of the publisher via Copyright Clearance Center, Inc.

pp. 144–145: Reprinted from the April 5, 1993 issue of *Fortune* by special permission; copyright © 1993, Time Inc.

p. 145: Reprinted from *PC Week* September 19, 1994. Copyright © 1994 ZD, Inc.

pp. 149–150: Marcic, D., *Managing with the Wisdom of Love: Uncovering Virtue in People and Organizations* (San Francisco: Jossey-Bass Inc., Publishers, 1997), pp. 3–5.

p. 152: Shaw, R., *Trust in the Balance: Building Successful Organizations on Results, Integrity, and Concern* (San Francisco: Jossey-Bass Inc., Publishers, 1997), p. 21.

p. 153: Shaw, R., pp. 144–146.

pp. 156–157: Shaw, R., pp. xiv–xv.

p. 162: Shaw, R., p. 208.